RABBI YOSEF

AWESOME CREATION

A Study of the First Three Verses of Genesis,
with the Aid of Modern Science

gefen publishing house
JERUSALEM ◆ NEW YORK Est. 1981

Cover Design: Michal Cohen
Typesetting: Irit Nachum

ISBN: 978-965-229-868-3
3 5 7 9 8 6 4 2

Gefen Publishing House Ltd.
6 Hatzvi Street
Jerusalem 94386, Israel
972-2-538-0247
orders@gefenpublishing.com

Gefen Books
11 Edison Place
Springfield, NJ 07081
516-593-1234
orders@gefenpublishing.com

www.gefenpublishing.com

Printed in Israel

To my friend and colleague Rabbi Yosef Bitton, Shelit"a.

I have known you as an expert in Halakhic matters and in the field of Agada, and particularly for the influence you have had on so many of the youth of our community, whom you led in the ways of our Rabbis and our pious Fathers. Now, we had the merit to see you publishing an important book on a few verses of the book of Genesis, and with the help of God, your book has gained fame, and has brought many of our Jewish brothers and sisters closer to their Father in Heaven. This book explains the act of Creation according to our Tora and shows that many things are compatible with modern science. It is known that the Tora does not need any corroboration by science, as it stands on its own Truth. And still, it is so nice to see how modern science perceives that what the Tora says can contribute to scientific understanding. I have no doubt that this book will become known worldwide as the books of our late and contemporary rabbis. And I want nothing but blessing you: May it be the will of God that your springs of water [Tora] will continue flowing out from you, Amen!

23 Kislev, 5775
[Rabbi] Eliyahu Ben Hayim

In Memory of

Ephraim ben Moshe Levian, *z"l*

This book began seven years ago, when I was invited to give a lecture to a very distinguished audience. It was the anniversary of the passing of Ephraim (Abdulrahim) ben Moshe Levian, *z"l*. The hour-and-a-half-long study session took place in the offices of his sons. Following the ancient Sephardic tradition, the lecture was dedicated to their father's memory.

When I was invited to give the class, I asked them: What should we be focusing on? Talmud, the Siddur, or perhaps one of the books of the *Tanakh* (the Hebrew Bible)?

"Why don't we start from the very beginning?" suggested one of the brothers. And we did exactly that.

Personally, I always felt a strong attachment to the initial words of the Torah. From the time I took my first steps in the world of Jewish studies, I was interested in understanding the story of Creation. I always felt perplexed by the multiple questions and divergences between the Big Bang or the theory of evolution and the Biblical narrative. Now I had the opportunity to prepare and search for those answers by confronting an amicable but educated audience of about thirty men and women, who at the same time would challenge oversimplified arguments and ask the right, poignant questions.

Those lectures were given in the memory of a very special man, Ephraim ben Moshe, known for his piety, his innumerable acts of benevolence, and his love and care for our Torah. Mr. Ephraim Levian was a brilliant businessman, a world leader in several fields of gemstones in the marketplace during his lifetime, including turquoise and tanzanite. His work ethics were always unparalleled. He was known to be fair in his business dealings. He was loved by all his employees and business associates and was widely admired by his competitors. He was one of the largest benefactors of the Mashadi Jewish community, yet he stayed away from honor and never wanted to get credit or be in the spotlight.

Mr. Ephraim Levian was also well known for his acts of *chesed*. He helped young community members get started in business, and many successful community members owe their start to him. Mr. Levian and his benevolent wife Pary also helped thousands of Russian and Bukharian Jews settle in the US during the mass migration in the 1970s by distributing food, clothing, and furniture and finding them jobs.

Mr. Levian was an intellectual. He acted in the world of business, but at the same time, he possessed a deep desire to study and always felt a remarkably strong curiosity – a desire to know more. Ephraim ben Moshe was a learned man, a self-educated Jew who loved to read, studied the Torah daily, and spoke to his children about it.

Many of the ideas developed in this book were first publicly presented in those sessions, celebrated in memory of a man who inspired in his children and grandchildren the value of integrity, love for Torah, and passion for benevolence. It is thanks to the generosity of Mrs. Pary Levian, wife of Abdulrahim Ephraim Levian, *z"l*, and her sons, Larry, Eddie, and Moossa Levian, that this book is published.

CONTENTS

ACKNOWLEDGMENTS

I wrote this book with much help and inspiration from students, teachers, and friends.

While I am indebted to many, I would like to acknowledge here the help I received from my friends who read the manuscript and gave me constructive suggestions: Jorge Kaplan, Albert Aghalarian, Tony Namdar, Gabriel Etessami, and Mrs. Justina Hakimi (Hezghia), who translated twenty pages of the first draft of this book six years ago, when I was still thinking that I would write it in my native Spanish.

I am grateful to Gefen Publishing House, in particular Ilan Greenfield, Lynn Douek, and the editor, Ita Olesker, for her suggestions and for her patient work.

My gratitude to my dear parents, Jacobo and Angelica Bitton, who provided me with the foundations to study Torah and encouraged me to seek the path of its wisdom.

To my children and grandchildren Ya'aqob and Rivka, David, Keren, Tamar, and Michal, Abraham, Mijal, Orit, Shemuel, and Tehila – you are the source of light and joy in my life. The discussions we had around our Shabbat table whenever the subject of Bereshit was brought up enhanced my relationship with the text and were fundamental in the development of this work. I learned – and continue learning – so much from all of you!

To my son Ya'aqob, in particular, I owe a great deal of gratitude. He patiently reviewed the book many times, spending countless hours amidst his studies for law school and the New York Bar exam and his wedding to Rivka. He proofread the manuscripts, made his suggestions in vocabulary, grammar, syntax, and, due to his great knowledge of Torah, also in content.

My special thanks to my beloved wife, Coty, for her permanent support, encouragement, and infinite patience. *Sheli veshelakhem, shela hu*: whatever I was able to accomplish and whatever you, the readers, can learn from my book, is due to her.

Bore 'olam, the Creator of the universe, has blessed me with everything. It is with humility that I thank Him for allowing me to expound upon the wonders of His creation and the beauty of the Torah He gave us.

INTRODUCTION

As anyone who has ever read the first verses of the Torah (Jewish Scripture) knows, those few words explaining how God brought this reality to existence are fascinatingly dense, enticingly cryptic, and concern matters to which we are innately drawn: how our world came to be. The question of the origins of our existence, of the planet we call home, and of the universe we are familiar with is one that has forever engaged humans of all ages, all walks of life, and through all of history. It seems as though God tuned the human brain in a way that we are naturally driven to question the beginnings of all things we know.

No other words have promoted more scholarship, no other sentences have provoked more intelligent discourse, no other passage was met with more curiosity than the Biblical account of Genesis – the beginning of the universe.

The goal of this book is to examine the first three verses of the Torah. Particularly, the Biblical idea of creation ex nihilo (out of nothing previous) and the actions performed by the Creator to prepare planet Earth for producing and sustaining life.

I have devoted three chapters for each Biblical verse. To the novice reader, this may seem excessive. The advanced Torah scholar, however, knows well enough that a simple book could in no way be an exhaustive study of these verses. The Torah is like a deep sea, rich in treasures of wisdom that lie completely hidden, until one dares to dive into the water. And most of us, myself included, just get close to the ocean's surface, collecting some seashells from the shore. Isaac Newton said it best: "To myself I am only a child playing on the beach, while vast oceans of truth lie undiscovered before me."

Let us take the fields of cosmology and astronomy for an example. One could not realistically expect to comprehend in one single generation the entirety of what those fields try to study – however tempting that may be. Astronomers simply articulate the best explanation they are capable of coming up with, given their present knowledge and the limitations of their main tool: the telescope. Similarly, in the field of the Torah, it is always going to be possible to see more, or better. As far as Torah study is concerned, it is a perennial quest of ever-evolving understanding. In each generation, every individual who endeavors in Torah study has the potential to encounter new layers in God's infinite Book. It is true that our knowledge of Torah, our intelligence, and our cognitive abilities pale in comparison with that of the Rabbis of the Talmud. Intellectually, they were giants and we are dwarfs. We could never be able to see as far as those giants saw – except when we resolve to stand on their shoulders. Then we can perceive as much, or further, particularly when we are equipped with new tools for discovery. Modern science is one of these tools.

Consider the following. Four thousand years ago, God blessed our forefather Abraham, assuring him that his descendants will be as numerous as the grains of sand on the shore of the sea and the stars in the sky. That seemingly disproportionate Biblical comparison of *sand to stars* might have appeared puzzling to the readers and students of Torah for millennia. There are ten thousand grains in just a handful of sand; millions in just a cubic foot; trillions in a segment of a shore. But there are just one thousand or so visible stars in the darkest sky. It took a long time until telescopes were developed and men were able to pierce into deep space. Stars went from thousands to millions. Finally, in 1980, we were able to understand the precision and sophistication of God's blessing to Abraham when Carl Sagan, probably without realizing his contribution to Biblical exegesis, proclaimed that the total number of stars in the universe is larger than all the grains of sand on all the beaches of planet Earth!

Many nuggets of Torah wisdom have remained dormant for centuries, encapsulated in words and phrases so advanced that only now, in our privileged days, we begin to understand.

Following the idea developed by Rabbi Eliyahu Ben-Amozeg among others, I believe that as our comprehension of the physical reality around us expands, so does our understanding of the Torah – particularly in the area of Creation. Rabbi Ben-Amozeg explained that the new discoveries in physics and optics developed by Descartes and Newton on the nature of light allowed him to reach a better comprehension of the concept of light in the Biblical text: "As we augment our knowledge, the elucidation and solidity of the divine teachings [the Torah] increases, because what was not known to the ancients is now known to us here today."[1]

The modern scientific understanding of the Big Bang theory as it relates to the denial of the eternity of the universe, the new comprehension of the privileged placement of our planet vis-à-vis the sun, the current theories which explain that life first appeared from water, etc., are all fine tools we are fortunate to possess today. We should certainly try and use these tools to better appreciate the precision and the extreme sophistication of the Biblical story of Creation.

♦ ♦ ♦

Brilliant scientists and scholars, Jewish and non-Jewish, have written excellent theses, books, and articles harmonizing between the Biblical story of Creation and modern science. I am not one of them. Science is used in this work only to the extent it contributes to the understanding of the Biblical text, which is the main goal of this book.

Nevertheless, while this book's purpose is not necessarily to show the consonance between science and the story of Creation, it does claim that what we presently know about our physical universe is perfectly compatible with the Torah's narrative of Creation. With Jorge Luis Borges, the universe and the Bible are two books written by the same Author. We may fail to find them compatible, perhaps, because we have yet to decipher the whole meaning, or the ultimate reality, of either book. Thus, the lack of complete consonance is the want of the reader – or of the times – and not of the books or their Author.

Unlike other works which deal with Biblical homilies and interpretations, the contributions of this book derive mainly from the field of Hebrew semantics. As the reader will soon discover, if we want to understand these verses it is mandatory to revisit the meaning of the Biblical text without relying blindly on the standard translations of the Scripture. The first two

---

1   *Em laMiqra*, page 4. Written and published by Eliyahu Ben-Amozeg in Livorno, Italy, 1862.

verses, for example, have been rendered in such different ways that I felt obligated to reexamine them word by word, distinguishing between those renditions motivated by foreign theological factors (which somehow found their way into Jewish translations and exegesis) and the authentic Jewish traditions embodied in the explanations given by the Rabbis of the Talmud and by the traditional Aramaic translation.

In order to avoid reading the Torah in a way that conforms more to what we want it to say than to what it actually says, one must first read the Biblical text very carefully. Only then can one try to find ways in which new scientific information can further elucidate what the Torah says. Furthermore, such careful reading often shows that more than a few apparent conflicts between science and Torah may be attributed to a poor understanding of Biblical Hebrew and its nuances.

The reader should also know that this study of the first three verses of the Torah does not contain any esoteric material. A mystical examination of Creation, i.e., the ways the Creator brought everything into existence, and other profound mystical concepts, lie beyond the scope of this humble book. Those hidden secrets of the Torah, even when known, should not be exposed in a book. According to our Rabbis, they should be transmitted orally and in private, from a teacher to the restricted audience of one student.

This work is meant for a reader who wants to understand what the surface of this brief Biblical text is saying, when its words are examined through the eyes of the Rabbis of the Talmud and the classic commentators, especially those exegetes whose expertise was Hebrew grammar. To properly understand these verses, one must see them in the context of the entire Creation story. That is why this book will also touch upon the events of the second, third, and fourth days of Creation, exploring the question of what exactly was created on them.

♦ ♦ ♦

In the first section of this book I examine the ideas conveyed by verse 1, particularly the notion of Creation ex nihilo, i.e., the bringing of the universe to existence out of nothing previous by the will of the Almighty Creator. This is a core belief in Judaism. I discuss the extent to which we are capable of grasping the idea of Creation, an act no man has ever witnessed, and the limits of our imagination. I also explore some of the ramifications of Creation, as well as the impact the act of Creation could have had upon the age that is nowadays attributed to the cosmos and to our planet. The reader will also discover in the third chapter of this section that only when the first word, *bereshit*, is properly translated does the Torah convey the notion of Creation ex nihilo unambiguously.

Verse 2 turned out to be for me the most surprising and fascinating sentence of the story of Creation. I must admit that I only realized the meaning of this verse while writing this book, not before. Verse 2 is often overlooked or entirely skipped when paraphrasing the story of Creation.[2] For many scholars, perhaps due to the numerous and radically different ways in which it has been translated, verse 2 has been unjustly judged as an unnecessary and superfluous parenthesis between the sublime verse 1 and the renowned and illustrious verse 3.[3] After reading any standard translation, one cannot help but feel that this verse is, to say the least, confusing. "Chaos," a Greek theological term, "abyss," a mythological concept,[4] and especially "the spirit of God," an idea carrying a heavily doctrinal connotation alien to Judaism, makes very little sense to a traditional Jewish mind. In this book, I analyze this verse word by word, trying to elucidate its meaning with the help of other Biblical texts – particularly Psalm 104 – and with the invaluable words of the Rabbis, which were surprisingly not taken into consideration by most standard translations.

A different type of clarification was required for verse 3. Its words do not represent a significant problem in terms of their translation. "And God said: 'Let there be light,' and there was light" is more or less the universal consensus on the rendition of this sentence. However, few Torah readers stop to think more deeply about what light the Torah is referring to in this verse. Is it an independent physical light that God created on the first day? A symbolic, spiritual light? A metaphor? Or is it, perhaps, the light of the sun?

---

2   Aryeh Carmell and Cyril Domb, *Challenge: Torah Views on Science and Its Problems*, 2nd ed. (Jerusalem: Feldheim, 1988), p. 167.

3   Nathan Aviezer, *In the Beginning* (New York: Ktav Publishing, 1997), pp. 31–33.

4   Philip Feund, *Myths of Creation* (New York: Washington Square Press, 1965), pp. 11–12.

And an important question: How was this light described by the Rabbis of the Talmud, the heirs and spokespersons of Jewish Oral tradition?

♦ ♦ ♦

Opening and reading the Torah should be enough to satisfy our innate inquisitiveness in search for answers about the beginning; after all, its first verses contains God's own narrated version of these events. However, it is not so simple. Consisting of just 103 letters, or twenty-seven words, the first three verses of the Torah are perhaps the best-known sentences in the whole Hebrew Bible; but they may also very well be the least understood. In the matter of Creation, the Torah reveals to us much less than it conceals; it feels as though we are left with more questions than answers.

If, as you hold these pages in your hands, it is your hope to finally know for certain what exactly transpired during the creation of the universe, this may not be the book you are looking for. If, however, you wish to gain some insight into the Torah's account of these events, please read on.

VERSE ONE

"In the beginning,
God created
the heavens
and the earth."

Genesis 1:1

CHAPTER 1

THE END OF ETERNITY

The first word of the Hebrew Scripture, *bereshit* – "In the beginning" – announces that the universe had its origin in time. It says that, unlike what was commonly thought in antiquity, the universe is not eternal. Belief in the eternity of the world was not found only among the masses or in the early creation myths; for centuries, men of science also thought that the universe had existed forever. Contemporary scientists are nowadays, for the most part, inclined to accept that the universe had a beginning in time. What led scientists to embrace the notion of a beginning was the realization that the universe is expanding. As we will see in the following lines, finding the beginning was a long and unexpected discovery.

For centuries, learned men believed that the world had always existed, and therefore there was no need to find a point when everything may have begun. Around the year 500 BCE, Heraclitus of Ephesus expressed what he thought about the origins of the universe with the following words: "This cosmos, the same for all, was neither made by God nor man, but was, is, and always will be."[1]

Aristotle (384–322 BCE), the great Greek philosopher, thought that all we know about the world indicates the universe had always been the same. Aristotle watched the starry sky and sought to understand how the cosmic bodies behave. He saw that, except for a handful of planets, the celestial bodies in heaven were positioned in a predictable system of mechanical circular orbits. He perceived the motion of the heavens not as a capricious changeable mechanism, and not as one oriented in a linear direction, but as a system possessing a predictable regularity. There was no evidence of

---

1 Simon Singh, *Big Bang: The Origin of the Universe* (New York: Simon Singh, 2005), p. 79.

any kind pointing to the beginning of the universe. Quite the opposite: circularity and stability seemed to be the proof and outcome of eternity. As a result of his observations, Aristotle believed that the universe had always existed in the same way we see it now. He concluded that logically the world never had a beginning.

Make no mistake, Aristotle did believe in a deity. His god, however, was not like the God the Scripture describes: the Supreme Being Who created the heavens and the earth. For Aristotle, a divine being imbued the eternal universe with motion and order, and had eternally coexisted with the cosmos. But he wasn't its creator. From a philosophical point of view, a universe created by God would have contradicted one of the basic Aristotelian premises: Aristotle's deity was deprived of free will. For Aristotle, divinity and predictability were concepts that went hand in hand. Much like the way Aristotle perceived nature, Aristotle's deity acted through a predictable concatenation of causes and effects. God, according to the Greek philosopher, could not have suddenly changed his mind and decided to create a world. For Aristotle, change was a trait of human beings, not of gods or of nature. Creation of the universe would have implied a change in the divine mind, which could only be a function of intentionality or will, a characteristic Aristotle's theology was not ready to attribute to its deity. A stable, unchanging, and uncreated cosmos was perfectly compatible with an unchanging god. Aristotle relied on his astronomical observations to prove that the universe was eternal and that it has coexisted with the eternal-and-devoid-of-free-will deity.

These premises led Aristotle and many other major thinkers and philosophers in antiquity to conclude that the cosmos never had a beginning. The Aristotelian god had other functions and powers in the universe – that is, being primarily responsible for its permanent motion – but he did not create it. There had been no beginning and no moment of Creation.

CREATION ON THE DEFENSIVE

During the early Middle Ages, the debates between those who saw the universe as eternal and those who regarded it as created provided ample opportunity for new philosophical insights on the concept of *a beginning.* Advocating an eternal universe were the men of science of the time – Aristotelian philosophers who denied Creation. Among those who defended Biblical Creation was Maimonides (Rabbi Moshe ben Maimon, 1135–1204), a worthy champion for advancing a well-reasoned explanation of what the Scripture's concept of a beginning was all about. For Maimonides, creation of the world is the essence of the Hebrew Scripture, and whoever believes in the eternity of the world does not belong at all in the congregation of Moses and Abraham.[2] We will go back to Maimonides and his view on Creation at the end of this chapter.

Aristotle's followers then seemed to have the upper hand on the debate. Using observational evidence in the fields of astronomy and physics, they claimed that the cosmos was immutable, predictable, and eternal. Religious scholars were on the defensive. Holding on to the idea of a beginning[3] was merely a matter of faith in Biblical creation, not an argument of scientific or philosophical value. A non-eternal universe stood in defiance to the conventional common sense and popular wisdom for a very long time.

The understanding of our universe and its physical laws dramatically changed with the revolutionary astronomical discoveries of Nicolaus Copernicus (1473–1543), Galileo Galilei (1564–1642), Johannes Kepler (1571–1630), and Isaac Newton (1643–1727). Thanks to the development of new optical devices – telescopes – astronomers were able to get a closer look at our solar system, the motion of stars, and the mysterious nebulae

---

2   Early in his life, Maimonides wrote a commentary to the Mishna. In *Sanhedrin*, chapter 10, he formulated the thirteen basic Jewish beliefs. The fourth principle asserts that God is first and last, but it did not include anything related to the belief in Creation of the world. Rabbi Yosef Qafih explains that, later in his life, after writing his *Guide for the Perplexed*, Maimonides included in the fourth belief: "A fundamental principle of the Law of Moses is that the world was created anew and that God formed it and created it from absolute non-existence. That which you observe, that I repeatedly discuss the firstness of the world according to the view of the philosophers, is to demonstrate the absoluteness of the miracle of His existence as I have explained and clarified in the *Guide for the Perplexed*." See *Maimonides' Commentary on the Mishnah: Tractate Sanhedrin*, translated by Fred Rosner (New York: Sepher-Hermon Press, 1981), p. 181, n. 369. Based on this principle, Maimonides also rejected Plato's idea of a universe created from primeval matter that coexisted with God, since *only* God is first and eternal.

3   Maimonides, *More Nebukhim*, translated from Arabic to Hebrew by Professor Michael Schwarz (University of Tel Aviv, 2003), sec. 2, ch. 13.

outside our solar system. If until then the universe was thought of as the Ptolemaic (ca. 90–168) system of a circular celestial vault composed of several invisible rotating layers, this was all to change. With new observations, the Ptolemaic model was discarded: the universe was no longer a closed geocentric system, but a vast, interminable cosmos.

These new observations had an enormous impact in humanity's perception of itself. The vastness of space, and the innumerable, previously unseen stars that the telescopes were now unveiling, indicated that man – or planet Earth – was not the core of our solar system, let alone of the entire cosmos. The idea that Earth was at the center of the cosmos had originally justified the perception of a universe created by God for the sake of man.[4] The more powerful the telescopes, the more man realized his minute place in the cosmos and his astounding smallness relative to all things recently observed. Yet, even as the universe was being seen as increasingly immense, the notion of an eternal universe remained unchallenged. During the seventeenth, eighteenth, and nineteenth centuries, telescopes were still unable to produce additional evidence for either a created or an eternal universe. The status-quo prevailed, and the idea of a beginning to the universe was relegated to the realm of religion, not to the field of scientific examination.

Astronomical observations continued shaping and reshaping human ideas, and once planet Earth was displaced from the center of the cosmos, scholars found less compelling reasons to justify the existence of a Creator. Displacing God from His role as the Creator of the universe was a slow but unstoppable enterprise. Baruch Spinoza (1632–1677) took a quantum leap in that direction. By identifying God with Nature, both being eternal, Spinoza expedited the displacement of God and further strengthened the notion of an uncreated, eternal universe. Uniformitarian scientist James Hutton (1726–1797) declared, "The result, therefore, of our present enquiry is that we find no vestige of a beginning [for the universe], no prospect of

---

4   Maimonides strongly opposed the idea of an anthropocentric universe. See *Guide for the Perplexed*, sec. 3, ch. 13. Many other rabbis, including Rabbi Sa'adia Gaon, advocated the centrality of man in the cosmos. See Norman Lamm, *Faith and Doubt: Studies in Traditional Jewish Thought*, 2nd ed. (New York: Ktav Publishing, 1986), pp. 95–99.

an end."[5] As for the question of how it came into being, a self-contained, naturalistic, and eternal new trinity – Universe-God-Nature – did not seem to require any cause for its existence. As the positivist philosopher Bertrand Russell (1872–1970) succinctly put it, "The universe is just there, and that's all."[6]

Simon Singh explains: "An eternal universe seemed to strike a chord with the scientific community, because the theory had a certain elegance, simplicity, and completeness. If the universe has existed for eternity, then there was no need to explain how it was created, when it was created, why it was created, and Who created it. Scientists were particularly proud that they had developed a theory of the universe that no longer relied on invoking God."[7]

The new findings in the field of astronomy served to nurture naturalistic beliefs and intensify the challenge to the ideas held by the old Biblical religions. The further man pierced into space, the further away a God-Creator was driven.

Until 1929, when telescopes spotted the beginning.

Look Who Is Moving!

At the turn of the twentieth century, telescopes grew in size and power, making it possible to see the borders of our own galaxy, the Milky Way. It took several years, and a fascinating scientific dispute known as the Great Debate, to determine the true nature of the Milky Way. The Great Debate took place on April 26, 1920, in the Baird auditorium of the Smithsonian Museum of Natural History.

One scientific school argued that all the matter in the universe was contained within the Milky Way, whose size was calculated to be about 100,000 light-years across. The second school thought that our Milky Way was but one of many galaxies.

At the time, astronomers had been able to recognize in one of the edges of the Milky Way something that looked like a nebula. It was thought to be

5   Singh, *Big Bang*, p. 79.
6   Bertrand Russell and F. C. Copleston, "The Existence of God," in John Hick, ed., *The Existence of God*, Problems of Philosophy Series (New York: Macmillan, 1964), p. 175.
7   Singh, *Big Bang*, pp. 79–80.

just a cloud composed of gas, dust, and light. They called it "Andromeda." Observations were not accurate enough to decide with precision whether Andromeda was inside or outside our galaxy.

In 1923, in his Mount Wilson observatory and equipped with the most advanced telescope available at the time, Edwin Hubble demonstrated beyond any doubt that Andromeda was an independent galaxy. Hubble calculated that the distance between Andromeda and our planet was approximately 900,000 light-years, which meant that Andromeda was completely outside the perimeter of our – now understood to be small – Milky Way. Hubble's revelation that there was more to the universe than our own galaxy was a dramatic historic moment. With that one discovery our universe suddenly grew immeasurably bigger.

From his observatory, Hubble was able to watch and study more and more galaxies, calculating the distance between them and our planet. As he was observing new galaxies in the depths of space, Hubble became aware of another dramatic fact.

In the eternal and stationary universe of Aristotle, celestial bodies were expected to remain floating in the cosmic void (or in the fifth element, "ether"). Quasi-perfect geometrical trajectories, which we now understand are due to the dynamics of gravity, made all celestial bodies seem to have a circular, or elliptical, unchangeable course.

This was clearly not what Hubble was seeing....

Hubble found out that instead of orbiting around one another – like the moon circling the Earth and the Earth circling the sun – galaxies were moving linearly in one direction, fast, and away from the Milky Way. What could this linear motion mean in a universe where all celestial bodies move in orbits? This type of noncircular motion could mean only one thing: galaxies were not orbiting around a cosmic center, but moving away from it.[8] The universe was not static or revolving around its axis. It was expanding!

Up to that time, the notion of an expanding universe was "absolutely beyond comprehension." Through the ages, century after century, "the

8   Ibid., p. 248.

universe was regarded as fixed and immutable, and the idea that it might be changing was inconceivable."[9]

By the end of 1929, Hubble had classified forty-six galaxies. He calculated that the speed of each galaxy was proportional to its distance from earth. If one galaxy was twice as far from earth than another galaxy, then it was moving away at roughly twice the velocity. The meaning of this simple observation was the realization that, at some moment, the expanding universe with all its galaxies had developed from a very compact region. It was the first clue in the history of scientific discovery indicating that the universe was not eternal.

During the years following Hubble's observations, astronomers endowed with even more potent telescopes were able to observe with more detail the movement of galaxies, their speed, and their distance. The results supported the theory of an expanding universe. Almost twenty years after Hubble's discovery, the Ukrainian-born scientist George Gamow, using Hubble's findings, formulated a new theory. Going back in time, and running backwards the movie of the expanding universe, all the galaxies must have originated from one single entity. According to Gamow, the primeval universe must have consisted of a dense ball of fire, of super-concentrated energy, which somehow contained within it all the matter in our cosmos. Gamow also reasoned that the explosion of that ball of fire would explain the sudden beginning and the expansion of our universe. Hence, Gamow theorized the idea of a great explosion later named the "Big Bang."

In 1948, together with Ralph Alpher, Gamow formulated his Big Bang theory. This is how *Newsweek* magazine, on April 26 of that year, presented Gamow's revolutionary hypothesis to its readers: "According to this theory, all the elements were created out of a primordial fluid in a single hour and have been reshuffling themselves into the material of stars, planets, and life ever since."

---

9   Gregory L. Naber, *Spacetime and Singularities: An Introduction* (Cambridge: Cambridge University Press, 1988), pp. 126–27.

MORE EVIDENCE OF A BEGINNING

The theory that assigned a moment of beginning to the universe still needed more verification before being fully accepted by the scientific community. Gamow and Alpher predicted that as the original explosion occurred, an immeasurable blast of light-energy was launched into space. In theory, we should then be able to detect the echoes of that blast even today. If a Big Bang had ever taken place, it would have left behind a residue of its shock wave, similar to what we can expect to happen when a pebble is thrown into the water. A tossed pebble creates waves that continuously expand in the water. The waves get smaller and smaller but they never fully disappear. Similarly, the Big Bang theory predicted that the waves or echoes of a primordial cosmic explosion should still exist and they should be identifiable forever and everywhere. According to Alpher's predictions, we would be able to detect an invisible wave of light with a length of roughly one millimeter.[10]

In 1964, two investigators employed by the Bell Telephone Company in the United States, Robert Wilson and Arno Penzias, were working with one of the most advanced radio antennas of the time, originally designed to detect signals from a balloon-satellite. They realized that the antenna was picking up a minimal level of noise, a bothering interference for which they were unable to find an origin. They tried to locate the source of the noise in order to remove it completely, or at least to reduce it. This strange interference was coming from every direction toward which they pointed their antenna. Something, somehow, was incessantly emitting radio waves from all directions. At the time, the two frustrated radio-astronomers did not realize that, accidentally, they had stumbled upon one of the most important discoveries in the history of cosmology. That annoying background noise was in fact the echo of the Big Bang, which, as predicted by Gamow, had transformed itself into radio waves.[11]

Wilson and Penzias found the primordial radiation present everywhere in the cosmos: that infinite echo of the beginning of the universe. The *New York Times* wrote on May 21, 1965, "When you go out tonight and you take

---

10   Singh, *Big Bang*, p. 333.
11   Ibid., p. 429.

your hat off, you're getting a little bit of warmth from the Big Bang right on your scalp. And if you get a very good FM receiver and if you go between the stations, you will hear that sh-sh-sh sound…. Of the sound that you're listening to, about one half of one percent of that noise is coming from billions of years ago."

In 1976, astronomers and scientists embarked on a new experiment to confirm the findings of Wilson and Penzias. NASA designed a huge satellite known as COBE (Cosmic Background Explorer satellite) whose mission was to measure the CMB (cosmic microwave background radiation, i.e., the echo from the Big Bang) coming from space. The satellite was launched in 1989, and after nearly two years of orbiting, COBE detected the expected temperature variations of 30 millionths of a degree in all the far reaches of space.

The COBE experiment corroborated that a moment of beginning had taken place, leaving its fingerprints in the form of radiation and microwaves that can still be found everywhere in the vastness of the universe. Stephen Hawking stated: "It's the discovery of the century, if not of all times."[12]

THE SHORT ROMANCE BETWEEN BIG BANG AND RELIGION

George Smoot, a physicist at the University of California at Berkeley who led the analysis of COBE satellite data, famously said: "We have observed the oldest and largest structures ever seen in the early universe. These were the primordial seeds of modern-day structures such as galaxies, clusters of galaxies and so on…. Well, if you are religious, it is like seeing the face of God."[13]

Many famous naturalistic scientists of the time, Albert Einstein for example, deliberately kept away from the Big Bang model or any cosmological theory that postulated a beginning – but this was because of the consequent theological implications rather than for any scientific

---

12 Nigel Calder, *Magic Universe: A Grand Tour of Modern Science* (Oxford: Oxford University Press, 2005), p. 473.

13 Singh, *Big Bang*, pp. 462–63.

reasons.[14] They understood that "the beginning of the universe" conveys an idea too close to the notion of Creation. Arthur Eddington, an uncompromising atheist, admitted explicitly: "Philosophically, the notion of a beginning of the present order of Nature is repugnant to me. I should like to find a genuine loophole."[15]

Fred Hoyle opposed the Big Bang theory and developed his own alternative, the Steady State theory, which advocated an eternal universe. Hoyle defended his theory long after most of his colleagues had abandoned it. "Hoyle's writings make clear that he favored the Steady State theory not just on scientific grounds, but partly because he thought infinite time was more compatible with his own atheistic beliefs."[16]

In the 1940s, the Soviet communist regime rejected Hubble and Gamow's conclusions completely, despite their scientific soundness, on the grounds that their hypothesis failed to comply with the tenets of Marxist Leninist ideology (i.e., atheism). The Soviets' opinion on the Big Bang was summarized by Comrade Andrei Zhdanov: "Falsifiers of science want to revive the fairy tale of the origin of the world from nothing."[17]

The Soviets persecuted physicists who supported the Big Bang theory. Some of those scientists paid for their support of the Big Bang theory with their lives – like Matvei Bronstein, who was shot after being arrested on trumped-up charges of espionage.[18]

Stephen Hawking summarized in one sentence the reason naturalistic scientists resisted a scientific theory that posited a non-eternal universe: "So long as the universe had a beginning we could suppose it had a creator."[19]

C. J. Isham said it best: "Perhaps the best argument...that the Big Bang supports theism is the obvious unease with which it is greeted by some atheist physicists. At times this has led to scientific ideas...being advanced with a tenacity which so exceeds their intrinsic worth that one can only

---

14 Robert Jastrow, *God and the Astronomers* (New York: W. W. Norton and Company, 1992), pp. 104–7.
15 Singh, *Big Bang*, p. 281.
16 Ian G. Barbour, When Science Meets Religion: Enemies, Strangers, or Partners? (San Francisco: HarperSanFrancisco, 2000), p. 42.
17 Singh, *Big Bang*, p. 363.
18 Ibid.
19 Stephen Hawking, *A Brief History of Time* (New York: Bantam), p. 156.

suspect the operation of psychological forces lying very much deeper than the usual academic desire of a theorist to support his or her theory."[20]

Science had advocated Aristotle's idea of an eternal universe for over two thousand years. Many lay scientists could not easily accept that, as science was advancing and moving forward with new progressive conceptions, leaving behind what they regarded as the primitive ideas of religion, the latest cosmological theories were now endorsing the very first word of the Hebrew Scriptures. As aptly put by English Nobel laureate physicist George Thomson: "Probably every physicist would believe in creation if the Bible had not unfortunately said something about it many years ago and made it seem old-fashioned."[21]

Perhaps referring to the frustration of some positivist thinkers and naturalistic cosmologists in view of the new discoveries, Robert Jastrow wrote: "For the scientist who has lived by his faith in the power of reason, the story ends like a bad dream. He has scaled the mountains of ignorance; he is about to conquer the highest peak; as he pulls himself over the final rock, he is greeted by a band of theologians who have been sitting there for centuries."[22]

Some prominent world religious figures, like the Pope Pius XII, welcomed the Big Bang enthusiastically. In 1951, and while the Big Bang model was still being confronted with other cosmological theories like the Steady State theory, Pius XII delivered an address to the Pontifical Academy of Sciences entitled "The Proofs of the Existence of God in the Light of Modern Natural Science." There, he endorsed the Big Bang theory and considered it modern evidence of the existence of God.[23]

20 C. J. Isham, "Creation of the Universe as a Quantum Process," in R. J. Russell et al. (eds.), *Physics, Philosophy, and Theology: A Common Quest for Understanding* (Rome: Vatican Observatory, 1988), p. 378.
21 See Otto Struve, "Continuous Creation," *Astronomical Society of the Pacific: Leaflets*, vol. 6, leaflet 270 (1951): p. 154.
22 Jastrow, *God and the Astronomers*, p. 107.
23 Singh, *Big Bang*, p. 360.

Renewed Conflicts

One would have thought that once contemporary scientists accepted the notion of the beginning of the universe, the debate over the Biblical idea of beginning would finally be put to rest. Sooner than later, however, the brief truce between science and religion on this matter came to an abrupt end, and a new conflict replaced the old one.

Once a consensus had been reached on the question of the beginning, the estimation of the time since that beginning became the new conflict separating the two narratives. Nowadays, it is popularly believed and taught by both scientists and religious figures that Big Bang cosmology and the Biblical story of Creation stand on opposite sides, because the Hebrew Bible attributes less than six thousand years to the existence of the universe, while science estimates that the universe is fifteen billion years old.

This alleged antagonism seems to be so ingrained in people's minds that it entirely eclipses and displaces the newly discovered commonality between science and religion – i.e., a beginning to the universe. As an illustration, I will quote and briefly analyze in the following lines a few paragraphs from a lecture given by Cambridge's Professor Stephen Hawking in 1998. In this lecture, "The Origin of the Universe," Hawking begins by giving an account of the different opinions on this matter, then drawing a comparison between Biblical religions and Aristotle:[24]

> The debate about whether, and how, the universe began has been going on throughout recorded history. Basically, there were two schools of thought....

Hawking indicates his intention to present the debate on "whether, and how" the universe has had a point of beginning in time. Hawking is obviously aware that for the last twenty-five centuries scientists have assumed the eternity of the universe, in opposition to what religious traditions held.

---

24 Stephen Hawking, *Black Holes and Baby Universes and Other Essays* (New York: Bantam, 1993), p. 86.

First, he introduces the opinion of the Biblical school:

> Many early traditions, and the Jewish, Christian, and Islamic religions, held that the universe was created in the fairly recent past. For instance, Bishop Usher calculated a date of four thousand and four BC, for the creation of the universe, by adding up the ages of people in the Old Testament.

Hawking obviously knows that it was not but recently that science found solid evidence of the universe's beginning and that the Hebrew Bible and modern scientists nowadays coincide on this point. Instead of pointing to these coincidences, however, Hawking abruptly deflects from the subject of "eternity vs. beginning" to the subject of "how much time has passed since a beginning." Logically, he should have finished his presentation of the Biblical opinion by simply saying: "Many early traditions, and the Jewish, Christian and Islamic religions, held that the universe was created" (period).

It would be worthwhile to note at this time that there is no reference to the age of the universe in the Hebrew Scripture. That is why instead of referring to the Biblical text itself, which does not even talk anywhere about the date of Creation, Hawking resorts to James Usher, an Irish Anglican bishop from the seventeenth century, to present the ostensibly Biblical date of creation. Subsequently, he subtly but surely dismisses and ridicules it.

> In fact, the biblical date for the creation, is not that far off the date of the end of the last Ice Age, which is when modern humans seem first to have appeared.

Once the Biblical position is presented (or misrepresented), Hawking suddenly brings us back to the debate, correctly explaining the Aristotelian doctrine of the eternal universe:

> On the other hand, some people, such as the Greek philosopher Aristotle, did not like the idea that the universe had a beginning. They felt that would imply Divine intervention. They preferred to believe that the universe had existed, and would exist, forever.

Although Hawking's disingenuous mischaracterization of the debate may seem to us a bit extreme, it unfortunately is representative of the mainstream approach in modern academic circles, popular culture, the media, and classrooms in the public educational system in most of Western civilization. Instead of indicating how much closer observations have brought the scientific version to the Biblical version of the beginning of the universe, the emphasis is misplaced on the alleged discrepancy between both accounts on the age of the universe.

Before I examine this issue in depth (I devote the entire next chapter to a discussion of time and Creation), I will turn back to the Big Bang model.

Cosmology and Our Ability to Imagine

Ever since the notion of the beginning of the universe started being associated with the idea of Creation, it has been assumed the problem of time was the only thing remaining as an insurmountable frontier separating science from Biblical tradition. Were it not for the discrepancy in the accounting for time, it is often believed, scientists and religious scholars would have finally found a common ground on the matter of a beginning. I beg to differ. The most critical difference between Judaism's idea of Creation and the Big Bang model or any other cosmological theory is not "time since creation" but rather the recognition or rejection of human limitations to accurately formulate or even imagine the process of the origin of the universe.

For Jewish tradition, the action described by the second word of the Scripture, *bara,* stands for Creation ex nihilo. Creation ex nihilo means making something appear out of nothing previous. This concept not only runs contrary to our knowledge and experience, but it also defies the faculties of our imagination.

Our Rabbis[25] identified the process of Creation (*ma'ase bereshit*) as one of the secrets or inaccessible esoteric materials of the Torah (*sitre Torah*), a

---

25 When I mention "Rabbis" with capital R, I'm referring to the Sages, known in Hebrew as *Chazal.* They are the Rabbis of the Talmudic period, ca. 10 to 500 CE. They were the authors and protagonists of the Mishna, the Gemara, and the Midrash. These Rabbis represent the classic Jewish normative tradition, which includes Jewish Law, Jewish doctrines, and Biblical exegesis.

type of information to which simple humans have no access on their own.[26]

To better understand and illustrate the approach Jewish tradition has taken on the issue of how much we can possibly know about cosmology – the field of science that examines the origin of the universe – let us first recall the basics of the Big Bang theory.

By observing the heavens with the newest telescopes, astronomers noticed that galaxies were moving away from each other. Once the expansion of the universe was demonstrated, they reasoned that going back in time one should be able to reach some sort of a "point zero": "[The] Big Bang theory rests on the observation that the universe is expanding. Take this idea and run it backward, and you must conclude the universe was smaller, denser, and hotter in the distant past. The further you rewind the cosmological movie, the smaller, denser, and hotter the universe gets."[27]

Cosmologists play the movie of the expanding universe backwards, retracing the motion of the outward moving galaxies. Modern scientists would contend that the young primeval universe was the size of the dot you find at the end of this sentence; that dot contained all existing matter and energy.[28] The movie of the history of the cosmos would begin from that presumed point of beginning and would be played forward. Although there are many different theories and variations, the mainstream Big Bang model says roughly this: In the beginning, the primeval universe was extremely dense, filled with incredibly high energy, temperature, and pressure. Then it began to rapidly expand, undergoing many different phases (inflation, baryogenesis, nucleosynthesis, etc.), which caused its exponential growth

---

26 In a similar (but not identical) fashion, Colin McGinn explains, for example, that monkeys do not have the ability to attain knowledge of electrons. They may be able to understand the basics about electricity, like touching the electric fence is bad, but they will never be able to understand an electron the way we do. They are *cognitively closed* to it. See Colin McGinn, "Can We Solve the Mind-Body Problem?" *Mind* 98, no. 391 (July 1989): 349–66. I am grateful to Mr. Gabriel Etessami for referring me to McGinn's work.

27 Adam Frank, *Astronomy Magazine*, September 2006, p. 36.

28 Interestingly, as scientists progress in their investigations of the universe's origins, they seem to attribute a progressively smaller size to that primeval concentration of energy. From a Jewish perspective, science is indeed advancing toward the rabbinical idea, further developed by *chakhme haKabbala*, of creation יש מאין, or "something out of nothingness."

and subsequent explosion. Eventually it cooled off, forming our present universe, which is since then in a state of expansion. This is, roughly, how scientists describe the process of gestation of our cosmos.

Obviously, all theories about the size, nature, composition, dynamics, and development of the young universe, and the process that brought it from its inception until it became the universe we observe today, are entirely based on the information at hand and on the physical laws we know and hold true today. Scientists go millions and billions of years back in time, formulating calculations and theories about what might have happened at this primitive state of the universe,[29] taking for granted that the physical laws that ruled the universe then have always been so – constant, immutable, and eternal. Consider, for example, the timeline given to the universe's development. The reason scientists attribute between thirteen and fifteen billon years to our universe is because of the size, composition, and, particularly, the speed of the universe's expansion they see today. But how much can one really claim to know about the origins of the universe?

Do We Know What We Don't Know?

Although the mainstream scientific community and media industry is generally hesitant to acknowledge any limits in investigating the origins of the cosmos, there are some notable exceptions. An example is the work of scientific journalist Dennis Overbye, who questions how much of the big picture we really get when we talk about the universe considering our space and time limitations.[30] This might be regarded as an excellent introduction to the Jewish idea of the boundaries of inquiry in the field of cosmology.

In one of his columns, Overbye analyzes a paper by Lawrence M. Krauss and Robert J. Scherrer, published in the *Journal of General Relativity and Gravitation*.[31] These two scientists asserted that, if the universe keeps

---

29 Cf. Steven Weinberg, *The First Three Minutes: A Modern View of the Origin of the Universe* (New York: Basic Books, 1993).

30 Dennis Overbye, "The Universe, Expanding Beyond All Understanding," *New York Times*, June 5, 2007.

31 Lawrence M. Krauss and Robert J. Scherrer, "The Return of a Static Universe and the End of Cosmology," *Journal of General Relativity and Gravitation* 39, no. 10 (October 2007): pp. 1545–50.

expanding, in one hundred billion years or so most galaxies will pass over the universe horizon. In other words, galaxies will cross outside the scope of our telescopes' sight, and we will be left with only a few galaxies to observe. In the future, "unable to see any galaxies flying away, those astronomers will not know the universe is expanding and will think instead that they are back in the static island-universe of Einstein." They concluded, "With such limited information at sight…those observers…will be fundamentally incapable of determining the true nature of the universe."

Overbye then reflects on the information we possess today – not one hundred billion years from now – and our own present limitations. How could we possibly know whether what we see today is in fact the whole picture?

There is a kind of horizon to the universe beyond which we cannot see anything. Overbye quotes Krauss as saying: "There may be fundamentally important things that determine the universe that we can't see…. You can have the right physics, but the evidence at hand could lead to the wrong conclusion." Many of cosmology's and physics' theories today are based on observing the facts at our disposal, and just like Krauss and Scherrer's view of what the situation will be in one hundred billion years, the facts within the reach of our observations today may very well be lacking.

And then, there are time limitations. Observation of the cosmos through any form of telescope began a mere few centuries ago. Observations of the cosmos through more advanced and reliable technology started being conducted a only few decades ago. These observations are used to produce theories about what must have happened across billions and billions of years. Reflecting on the apparently unworried way scientists elaborate theories over billions of years, Overbye reasons that if we really wish to understand how things evolve in the cosmos we need to closely follow these matters for a very long time. These phenomena will become undetectable "…unless astronomers want to follow the course of the occasional star that gets thrown out of the galaxy and is caught up in the dark cosmic current." But it would have to be followed for ten billion years, Overbye explains, "an experiment the National Science foundation would be unlikely to finance."

We have been following the galaxies not for a million years, and not even for a hundred thousand years (which in astronomical terms is still insignificant), but only for less than a century. What can we possibly know really?

Overbye humbly concludes: "The lesson, in the meantime, is that we don't know what we don't know, and we never will – a lesson that extends beyond astronomy."

MAIMONIDES VS. COSMOLOGY

More than eight hundred years ago, Maimonides, commenting on the debate of creation vs. eternity of the world, expressed his skepticism regarding the field of cosmology, i.e., the investigation of the origins of the universe. Maimonides thought that it would be impossible to bring conclusive evidence for the creation of the world from our present reality. He did not attribute our cognitive boundaries to the galaxies slipping beyond our sight, or the short time we have been examining a moving star, as Overbye did.[32] In his famous philosophical work, *More Nebukhim* (Guide for the Perplexed), Maimonides asserted that what makes it impossible to formulate a cosmological theory reenacting in any way the universe's origins and formation is *precisely* our knowledge and awareness of the physical reality we know, and from which we cannot separate. Maimonides, accordingly, denied the essence and believability of *any* cosmological theory. For Maimonides:

> Cosmology pertains to another realm of reality. Physical sciences focus on the structured order, interpreting natural phenomena in terms of causality. Cosmology focuses on the process of becoming, prior to being structured into law (and integrated with other systems into a general organization). To explore the question of cosmology on the basis of present physical condition is to premise the inquiry by negating cosmology altogether.... Maimonides regarded the efforts to deduce cosmology from physics as trying to infer embryology from the physiology of a mature specimen. Aristotelian cosmology

---

32 See also Lawrence M. Krauss and Robert J. Scherrer,, "The End of Cosmology? An Accelerating Universe Wipes Out Traces of Its Own Origins," *Scientific American*, February 25, 2008.

is deceptive. Its methodology consists in extrapolating ideas derived from the structured physical phenomena and applying them to prestructured phenomena, in which case there is no cosmology.[33]

According to Maimonides, we *do* know what we are *not* capable of knowing. We face an insuperable epistemological problem regarding the possibility of understanding God's creative act. We have no way of knowing what the laws or conditions of Creation were.

It is when we fall prey to a sense of pretentious anthropocentrism that we bring ourselves to think that a human mind could eventually figure out God's mind.[34] In the Torah, this preposterous contention was attributed to Balaam, the pagan prophet who claimed having access to "the mind of the Most High."[35]

A MODERN PARABLE: PLANET X SCIENTISTS' IMAGINATION

Maimonides illustrates the idea of the limits of human imagination with a fantastic parable.[36] A child who had been abandoned on a deserted island at birth and had never seen a woman could not figure out on his own how he was born. He would never be able to envision or even accept the

---

33 José Faur, *Homo Mysticus: A Guide to Maimonides's Guide for the Perplexed* (Syracuse, NY: Syracuse University Press, 1999), pp. 116–17.
34 This idea is developed in the book of Job, chapter 38, where the secrets of Creation are shown to be as inaccessible as the "mind of God." See next chapter.
35 See Numbers 24:16. The following statement by Stephen Hawking provides a good illustration of such presumptuousness: "If we do discover a complete theory...then we shall all, philosophers, scientists, and just ordinary people, be able to take part in the discussion of the question of why it is that we and the universe exist. If we find the answer to that, it would be the ultimate triumph of human reason – for then we would know the mind of God" (*Black Holes and Baby Universes*, pp. 133–35). For Maimonides, "to presume that human reason can partake in the divine reason is the supreme expression of arrogance.... To the Hebrew ethos there could be no greater affront than pretending to know the mind of God" (Faur, *Homo Mysticus*, pp. 121, 124). Max Tegmark, a cosmologist at MIT, has a more optimistic approach to scientific arrogance: "Human arrogance – [is] a necessary but unfortunate condition for scientific progress" (quoted by Dennis Overbye, "The Universe, Expanding").
36 *More Nebukhim* 2:21.

idea that humans are conceived as they in fact are. All he can go by are facts he is familiar with; and, from that perspective, he could not possibly know, deduce, or imagine the processes of conception, pregnancy, or birth. To better understand Maimonides's brilliant illustration, I present an adaptation of his parable, making it a little friendlier to the modern reader.

It so happened that on one sunny morning, a group of robot-like intelligent aliens from Planet X had a one-time opportunity to pay a visit to planet Earth. Upon seeing the human species for the first time, they decided it would be wise to borrow one of them and examine this newly discovered life-form. They thus abducted Adam, a three-year-old boy who was playing with a yellow plastic tractor in his backyard. The aliens took Adam to their spaceship and began to study this fascinating specimen. For two months, they kept Adam in a specially adapted environment, with oxygen, water, and food. The aliens observed and analyzed Adam very carefully and learned from him the basics of human physiology. After sixty days, they returned Adam home, safe and sound.

Back on Planet X, the aliens formulated their theories about the human species. They had learned that humans eat through their mouths, breath oxygen through their noses, and need space to move. They also saw that Adam grew taller from day to day, although at a very slow pace, half-an-inch in sixty days. The aliens then formulated their first scientific theory regarding Adam's expansion: by simply projecting Adam's growth-pace – half an inch every two months – they determined that Adam would grow six inches every year. In ten years, they concluded, Adam would be five feet taller. Twenty years from now, Adam would have grown ten feet taller; and so on, as his body would continue to expand.

The scientists of Planet X were also eager to figure out how Adam was born. The formula they developed to explain Adam's first days of life was a quite simple inductive formula: since Adam was always expanding upward, all they had to do to figure out how Adam was born was to play Adam's body-expansion movie backward. They plugged into the equation Adam's actual height and the speed of his growth, and they concluded that at the initial stage of his life – say, when Adam was a week old – he must have been approximately a quarter of an inch tall. Then, they tried to understand Adam's physiology in such extreme circumstances. Some scientists proposed that Adam probably ate through his mouth 0.001 ounces of food and drank approximately 0.001 ounces of water per day. Planet X's scientists had quite a hard time trying to figure out how Adam's organs could have been operating within such density. They estimated that, under those extreme circumstances, all the laws of human biology they had now learned about Adam would not make sense!

Rewinding the movie of Adam's evolution further back, they theorized that there must have been a "time-zero," a moment of beginning, when Adam was as large as the dot you see at the end of this sentence. Some Planet X scientists tried to devise alternative theories to explain Adam's origins, hypothesizing that Adam's body went through a series of periods of expansion, inflation, biosynthesis, etc. They declared that Adam's first seconds of life represented a *singularity*, which could only be explained by quantum physics (there was no word for "miracle" in Planet X's scientific jargon).

Throughout all their studies, investigations, and speculations about Adam's origin, scientists of Planet X never even got close to fathoming what we know to have been the real circumstances surrounding Adam's birth. The reason for their failure is very simple. No matter how smart and savvy these scientists might be, and how hard they might try, no scientist could ever deduce from Adam's physiology the process of Adam's conception. Why? Because these scientists were never privy to a very simple, yet crucial, fact that would dramatically modify their conclusions. They never saw or knew about Adam's mother. Having seen only Adam, they did not know of the existence of the human female gender. Without that significant piece of information, all they had learned about Adam's physiology would actually *prevent* them from imagining the possibility of life inside another human's womb. The process of pregnancy *contradicts* everything they learned from observing Adam's eating and breathing. The thought of Adam living inside somebody else's body, without space, without food, and without air, would never have crossed their minds.

As with Adam's birth, Maimonides maintained that Creation was the gestational period of our universe, the embryology of the cosmos. Formulating a cosmological theory would be inevitably an illusory inductive process, a projection of our present dimension, and would imply the negation of the singularity and uniqueness of the universe's gestation and birth. "Indeed, a scientifically based theory of cosmology is an oxymoron. To prove a theory of cosmology one would have to presuppose that the present state of the universe is analogous to its initial stages, in which case, cosmology will be indistinguishable from physics and not a topic on its own."[37]

From the point of view of Jewish tradition, therefore, the commonalities between the Big Bang model and the first act of Creation described in the Scripture (Gen. 1:1) are restricted to the idea of there being a beginning, that which is conveyed by the very first word of the Torah: "in the beginning." The matter of how the existence of the universe came about is considered a singularity, an untraceable act or series of acts irremediably out of the reach of human knowledge and imagination.

What can be known about the creation of the universe, then?

The area of *ma'ase bereshit,* the Biblical account of Creation and the rabbinical tradition found in centuries of Biblical exegesis, represents a healthy balance. Given that the Creator also authored a Torah, we forever hover somewhere in between two extremes: thinking we can know everything, and thinking we should not bother to try ever investigating anything. It is "the middle point between the skeptic view that nothing can be known about the origins of the world and the naive theorization of cosmology,"[38] that everything could be known on the basis of inference.

With humility, and sensitive to our limitations, we will start exploring further the significance of the First Verse of the Torah.

Summary

For centuries, scientists and philosophers thought that the universe was eternal, and rejected the idea postulated by the Torah's first word: *bereshit,* "in the beginning." While the eternity of the universe was viewed as a well-founded scientific principle, there was no evidence to support the notion of a starting point to the cosmos. In 1930, when Hubble discovered the universe's expansion, this idea began to change. Many theories were

---

37 *Homo Mysticus,* pp. 117–18.
38 Ibid., p. 118.

formulated to explain the new findings, until scientists finally conceded that the universe must have had a beginning in time.[39] After centuries of conflicts between science and religion, the idea conveyed by the first word of the Hebrew Bible was, finally, corroborated by scientific discoveries.

At its inception, the Big Bang model was considered – and by some *denounced* – as a religion-oriented theory, the closest Bible and science had ever come in the matter of the origins of the universe. Moreover, a universe with a beginning in time was regarded as a created universe. Many scientists, unhappy with the new coincidences, pointed out that far from being friendly to a religious perspective, the new cosmological theories completely contradict the Biblical story of Creation. Why? Because the Hebrew Bible, they argue, dates the creation of the universe at less than six thousand years ago.

Before we analyze the Jewish viewpoint in the matter of timing, we should bear in mind that, from a Jewish perspective, the Big Bang theory – or any theory that traces the origin of the universe – could never be taken blindly as a serious account of what "truly happened" in the process of Creation. The exclusion of the act of Creation in regards to the universe's origin would parallel the exclusion of pregnancy from the understanding of human birth. The Rabbis considered Creation – *ma'ase bereshit* – a realm whose details lie beyond the reach of our minds and outside the grasp of our imaginations. Creation occurred within a dimension which is categorically different from our physical dimension.

Some modern scientists, in their own way, have arrived at similar conclusions regarding our limitations in describing or even identifying the origins of the universe.

John Mather, the founder of the COBE project, admitted: "The origins of the early expanding phase of the universe were so extreme that they may

---

39 Stephen Hawking and other naturalistic scientists would still endeavor to demonstrate that although the Big Bang theory is correct, it does not imply a beginning. As Isham so eloquently pointed out, one should look for the psychological forces behind that scientific crusade. See *A Brief History of Time: The Updated and Expanded, Tenth Anniversary Edition* (New York: Bantam, 1998).

have erased traces of earlier events,[40] which in turn involved unknowable laws of physics…. Perhaps one day we will have imagined the right theory and we will think it is so beautiful that it must be true. Of course, it is just as likely that the real truth is so complicated or obscure that we cannot discover it or recognize it even if we encounter it directly."[41]

---

40 The irremediable destruction of evidence as an expected consequence of the Big Bang is an interesting argument utilized by Robert Jastrow in his book *God and the Astronomers* to justify his skepticism on the examination of the universe's origin.

41 John C. Mather and John Boslough, *The Very First Light: The True Inside Story of the Scientific Journey Back to the Dawn of the Universe* (New York: Basic Books, 2008), p. 294.

CHAPTER 2

THE CREATION OF TIME

As we have seen in the previous chapter, it is nowadays assumed that the Biblical story of Creation should not be taken seriously because the universe was in fact born billions, and not just thousands, of years ago – as the Torah ostensibly declares. Second probably to the debate of "Intelligent Design vs. Evolution," the age of the universe is often seen as one of the main points which compel us to see science and Judaism as opposing each other. A modern man or woman, Jew or gentile, who accepts Creation and simultaneously values and embraces modern knowledge, feels irremediably caught up in a dilemma: the choice between fifteen billion or six thousand years.[1]

In an attempt to find a solution to this conflict, some scholars have engaged in discussions about the literal or the symbolic nature of the six days of Creation. They have construed the length of the Creation days to fit

---

1   Although the date of Creation was never considered one of the principles (*'iqarim*) of Jewish faith, Judaism affirms that the world was created 5773 years ago. The Rabbis of the Talmud disagreed on the definite date of Creation, particularly the identification of the month in which Creation occurred, a consideration that was left inconclusive: Rabbi Joshua believed that the world was created in the month of Nisan and Rabbi Eli'ezer in the month of Tishri. Atypically, in this matter, Jewish practice validated the two opposite opinions without trying to exclude either of them. For the prayers of Rosh HaShana (New Year), for example, the Rabbis considered that the world was created in Tishri, but for Birkat haChama (the blessing for the sun), that it was created in Nisan. It seems as if the Rabbis did not feel it was necessary, philosophically or otherwise, to solve this conflict. Anyone wishing to draw a comparison between science and Judaism in the matter of timing should carefully examine this case. For a magnificent discussion of the two opinions see *The Conciliator*, question 79 (New York: Hermon Press, 1972), pp. 126–29. *The Conciliator* was originally written in Spanish by Rabbi Menashe (Mannasseh) ben Israel (1604–1657), published first in Frankfurt in 1632. It was translated into English by E. H. Lindo in 1841 and republished many times.

the scientific time estimations, arguing, for example, that one Biblical day equals one million years, and so forth. While I will not venture to judge the overall value of these allegorical or literal approaches to the Scripture, I believe this type of conciliatory effort is unnecessary.

Cosmology (or cosmogony) and Creation are based on opposite assumptions. Whereas the idea of Creation ex nihilo implies the divine application of laws and forces beyond our understanding and ability to fathom, cosmology assumes as a basic premise that the universe has always been the way it is. Therefore, if our departure point is the premise that the beginning of our cosmos lies within our investigative grasp, the natural consonance between our world and the idea of Creation disappears, and we are left with countless conflicts. The age of the universe is but one of these inconsistencies. However, when the point of departure to understand our universe is the Scriptural story of Creation, the present cosmos and its physical laws are comprehensible and entirely compatible with the modern principles of science, including the age scientists attribute to the world.

In order to demonstrate this critical point, I will first show that according to the Biblical text and rabbinic tradition, all creations were fashioned with a mature form – a form that, in our present reality, would have taken billions of years to develop.

Concerning the age of the cosmos as suggested by the vastness of space, we will show that the expansion of the universe – something that Jewish tradition explicitly reports as having been the essence of the creation of the heavens – not only affects our perception of the universe's age, but might in itself have caused the creation of time.

Additionally, the process of Creation and transformation that took place during the six days materialized within a singular reality, alien to our present reality. In the dimension of Creation, time did not behave as in our physical realm. This time irregularity necessarily affected our perception of the age of the cosmos, making the universe appear older than what it might actually be.

In short, hopefully by the end of this chapter we will come to understand that the main controversy between science and Judaism regarding the origin of our cosmos is not the age of the universe, but whether the world was created or not. Once Creation is assumed, Torah and science are beautifully congruent. Like two books written by the same Author.

MATURE CREATION

Our first task will be to look for statements in the Scripture and in the Rabbis' words providing any information as to the state of the creatures, living beings, and geological structures after they were created. Since the question of the age of the world never preoccupied our Rabbis, we should not expect to find almost anything that was said directly on this matter. We will have to be content with just a few hints of information incidentally scattered throughout the Scripture and rabbinical tradition. Nonetheless, it is my hope that even with those few clues and indirect allusions, we may arrive at a more educated understanding of the debate on the age of the universe.

The Biblical text is almost silent about the appearance of all creatures in the aftermath of their creation. This is not unusual. Hebrew tradition admonishes us to emphasize substance over appearance, and the Torah, as a general rule, is never abundant in graphic details. Nevertheless, at least one element has been depicted in the story of Creation with priceless detail. I'm referring to the trees.

Before we proceed with the trees, there is something about the process of Creation that needs to be clarified. The Torah suggests that there were two distinct stages to the creation of the world: (1) Creation ex nihilo (*beri-a*) and (2) formation (*'asia*). The initial act of Creation, by which the whole universe was made, is depicted in the first verse of the Torah (Genesis 1:1) using the term *bara*, "[God] created." In Biblical Hebrew, the verb "to create" (*libro*) is utilized within a restricted semantic field. It refers to bringing something to exist out of nothing previous: an action that the Torah attributes exclusively to God[2] and never to a human agent.

---

2   Rabbi David Qimchi, *Sefer haShorashim*, page 94: וכל לשון בריאה הוא התחדש הדבר
וצאתו מאין ליש, "Whenever *beri-a* is used, [it indicates the creation of] the thing that went from 'nothing' to 'something.'" A second verb, "to make" (*'asa*), indicates "improvement" – the reorganization of a structure into a more complex structure. In certain cases it also means "completion." This verb is widely used in the Scripture to describe God's activity during the six days. "In six days God 'made' the heavens

However, Creation ex nihilo was not the end of the Creation process. During the six days that followed the initial act of Creation and until the establishment of the Shabbat, God kept re-creating and transforming those first elements into life and the structures that would sustain it. Virtually all the creative activities reported in the first chapter of Genesis do not pertain to the category of "Creation ex nihilo,"[3] but to the formation of elements or systems deriving from the original Creation ex nihilo. For example, God created the earth ex nihilo, but he created the plants and trees from the earth, not ex nihilo (Genesis 1:12).

Maimonides distinguished between the first act of Creation and the other creative acts using the example of seeds that are sown by a farmer: "The strewing is done simultaneously, at a single moment. The growth and development unfolds successively: each cosmic seed grows and unfolds separately, according to its own timing and makeup."[4]

Back to our subject, let us now see what the Biblical text had to say about the trees. The Torah gave us one small but revealing characteristic about them, which served the Rabbis in developing a general theory concerning all of Creation: both the initial stage – when the basic ingredients of the universe were created out of nothing – as well as the second stage – the development of those initial ingredients into more complex structures to finally allow for the sustenance of life. In the following lines, we investigate whether God created the first trees as saplings or as full-sized, mature trees.

Genesis 1:11
God said: "The earth shall send forth vegetation. Seed-bearing plants and fruit trees that produce their own kinds of fruits with seeds shall be on the earth." And it happened.

---

and the earth" (Genesis 2:2). A third verb, "to form" (*yatzar*) is sometimes used to indicate a creation from something previous or a transformation. For example, "And God Almighty formed [*yatzar*] Adam's body from the earth" (Genesis 2:7). We will analyze these verbs more deeply in the following chapters.

3   The verb *libro*, "create," is seldom used throughout the story of Creation. Other than in the opening statement, it appears only twice: one time in 1:21 and the second time in 1:27 for the creation of humans, or – more precisely – man's soul.

4   See Faur, *Homo Mysticus*, p. 116.

In this verse, we see God's instructions to the earth regarding bringing forth all kinds of vegetation. As we said, God did not create the plants or trees from nothing, but out of the already created elements, which appear to be somehow "in" or "within" the earth. As expected, we are given no other details about the process by which those elements became living trees. The trees, we are told, will consist of diverse species and will be intelligently designed to perpetuate themselves through the fruits they produce. Those fruits will contain the seeds to guarantee a next generation of trees. Plants and trees are the first form of life to be created, and the Torah emphasizes that they were designed carrying within them their own means for reproduction and perpetuation.

In the following verse, the earth performs God's command. Now, the Torah briefly describes the newly created trees.

> Genesis 1:12
> The earth sent forth vegetation, plants bearing their own kinds
> of seeds and trees producing fruits containing their own kind
> of seeds.[5]

Although the Scripture rarely focuses on this type of technical facts, in this verse we find a pair of revealing words: 'ose peri – which we have translated following rabbinic tradition and most English translations as "producing fruit" (or fruits). The Biblical text thus asserts that, at the moment of their creation, the fruit trees were already bearing fruit ('etz peri, 'ose peri). This means that the trees were not created as roots, shrubs, or saplings, but as fully formed trees with their fruits already grown, i.e., at the peak of their maturity. The fruit-bearing trees are the only example about whose appearance the Torah is explicit. As shown, trees were created in their fruit-bearing maturity. Although it is but one example, the Rabbis asserted that *all* creations were fashioned by God at their fully developed state.

---

5   Aryeh Kaplan, *The Living Torah: A New Translation Based on Traditional Jewish Sources* (New York: Moznaim, 1981). King James and most other English translations used the words "yielding" or "bearing" instead of "producing" fruits ("and trees yielding fruit"). Still, all English translations I checked rendered this expression as implying that the trees were *actually* bearing or yielding fruits.

Unlike phenomena we would classify as natural – like birth, death, and growth – Creation was a singularity: a divine event and a one-time occurrence. It had unique effects and side-effects that could not – and should not – be perceived and analyzed in terms of current post-Creation parameters. In our present world, everything that exists was born. As such, all things and creatures naturally evolved from an incipient stage, throughout a predictable period of time, into their mature state. The word we use to define the length of time a thing or a living being has existed since its birth is "age." Age is the time that elapses from the moment someone or something is born until it reaches its present condition. To comprehend the uniqueness of Creation, it is essential to bear in mind that you would never think that a twenty-year-old-looking man has been around in the world just for five years or so. Except for the world of fiction, in the real world the age of an individual starts at the moment of his birth. No one is born with a mature body. Living creatures naturally come to this world as newborns. However, as we will soon see, this may not apply to what God creates from nothing (ex nihilo).

THE FIRST TREE

Biblical Creation, we learn, was completely different from natural birth. God created things in a state of maturity. Over seventeen hundred years ago, the Rabbis of the Talmud formulated this interesting statement: *kol ma'ase bereshit beqomatan ubetzibionam nibra-u.*[6] At the time of their creation, "all creatures were created in their height and [evolved] beauty." This is how Rabbi Menashe ben Israel translated and explained the above mentioned midrash, parenthesis included, in his book *The Conciliator*: "On their creation all things appeared in perfection, as it is said in the Gemara of Rosh HaShana *beqomatan ubetzibionam* ['in their height and beauty'] and according to this, the trees were brought forth loaded with their fruits."[7]

---

6   כל מעשי בראשית בקומתן ובצביונם נבראו. See Talmud Babli, *Rosh HaShana* 11a. Maimonides was very appreciative of this particular midrash. See *More Nebukhim* 2:30. Maimonides explained that the unusual word *tzibionam* had the same meaning as in צבי לכל הארצות, i.e., the most perfect land (Israel). See the following note.

7   See ben Israel, *Conciliator*, question 79, p. 127. In the original Spanish version, Rabbi Menashe ben Israel translates *tzibionam* as "*hermosura*," which in ancient Spanish

Rabbi Menashe ben Israel reaffirms that according to the Rabbis *everything* created during the six days was fashioned by God Almighty at its mature and optimal design. The first chicken was not created as an egg or as a chick, but as a mature fowl – and so on. Put in a slightly different way, once God conjures things out of nothing, it would be the same for Him to create them at their newborn stage or at their fully formed stage of development. In terms of Creation, the distance from zero to one is far greater than the distance from one to one million. Transitioning from zero to one is the same kind of – impossible – event as is the transition from zero to one million, directly. Therefore, why would God create His world in a state other than a mature state?

Now, we begin to understand that if God created the world already evolved, in a mature state, it is not just *possible* but rather *necessary* that science would attribute to the world an older age than the world has. Let us travel back in time to the day God created trees. We are now examining the first tree, five minutes after its creation. Following the tradition conveyed by the Rabbis, this tree would *look* like a mature tree. Tall, beautiful and loaded with fruits. Should we cut the tree, we could find, say, fifty rings. If we evaluate this particular tree from the perspective of our present physical reality and the facts we have at hand, we would necessarily conclude that the tree was born fifty years ago. The inevitable disparity between the scientific and the Biblical perspective on the age of the tree, five minutes or fifty years, is a unique side-effect of the act of Creation!

If Creation happened the way the Torah and rabbinic tradition describe it, then, inevitably, two different ages would simultaneously coexist in every created thing: (1) A chronological age of a creature or a thing, estimated since the time of its inception from Creation (five minutes), and (2) an internal age (fifty years) – i.e., the virtual or theoretical age of the tree, estimated as the time it would have taken the tree to evolve from inception to its present state, had it not been *created*.

Let me illustrate this idea with yet another example.

---

stands not only for beauty but also for plenitude ("the noble proportion between all the parts of the whole, and the qualities that make something excellent in its type"). That is how the word "beauty" should be understood in this context: plenitude and completion.

How would a modern-day geologist estimate the age of a mountain? If we were to ask a geologist to determine today the estimated age of Mount Everest, he would obviously compute all expected geological movements that must have taken place to naturally erect the mountain from the ground up. When the geologist says: "Mount Everest is sixty million years old" he is calculating the time needed for the mountain to be formed by a natural, slow, and lengthy process. Is the geologist mistaken? Yes, and no.

From the point of view of Creation, by estimating that Mount Everest is sixty million years old the geologist is correctly assessing the internal age of the mountain at the moment it was created. By saying that all creatures were created in their height or evolved state, Jewish tradition concedes that Mount Everest was created with its actual height, not as an incipient sea of lava-stone. And, certainly, if not for Creation, it should have taken sixty million years for Mount Everest to reach its present height.

The old age that science attributes to the world is not a contradiction to the Biblical story of Creation, but is rather the necessary result of examining Creation without considering the uniqueness of an act of Creation. Again, it is only when we look at Creation from the perspective of science (and assuming all premises assumed by scientists) that science contradicts religion. However, when we look at science's findings from the point of view of Biblical Creation, the conflicts disappear.

The Curious Case of Mr. Adam

The easiest way to explain the concept of mature creation, and my favorite example, is the case of Adam – the first human. Have you ever wondered how Adam looked when he was created? Was Adam fashioned by God as a crawling baby or as a mature adult? The Torah says nothing about it and there are no references in the Biblical text that can allow us to estimate his exact age at the time of his Creation.[8] Rabbinic tradition, nevertheless,

---

8   Perhaps the only direct indication of Adam's maturity is when he talked for the first time. Babies are not born as linguistic creatures, so we should deduce that Adam could not have been a newborn baby at this point. However, the first time he talks is in Genesis 2:23. Without rabbinic tradition, we would not have known from the Biblical text alone how much time passed from the moment God created Adam (1:27) until the moment Adam talked (2:23).

holds that Adam was not created as a baby or a child. In line with all other creations, they said, he was fashioned as a grown man with a fully developed body. The Rabbis asserted that God made Adam with a body of a twenty-year-old young man. In the words of Menashe ben Israel: "Adam and Eve were created of a perfect stature, like that of persons twenty years of age."[9]

Now, is it that Adam *looked* twenty years old, or that he indeed *was* twenty years old when created? The answer would be: both. Yet another paradox generated by the side-effects of Creation ex nihilo.

Imagine you are a biologist sent on a special mission through a time-tunnel, back to the very first day of Adam's life. Your objective is to determine how old Adam is. You arrive at your destination five minutes after Adam was made. Your mission is to analyze Adam's body and establish his age. You must estimate this young man's age based on what you have in front of you. As a diligent and well-trained scientist, you would most probably begin by measuring his height, the size of his bones, skull, etc., and you would use whatever other modern techniques available in order to determine his age. Finally, you will probably conclude that this young man must be between eighteen and twenty-two years of age. From a strictly empirical point of view you are absolutely on point. Adam (or his body) appears – or is – twenty years old. However, if you would simply ask Adam: "How old are you?" and assuming Adam would have had any kind of awareness about time[10] and knowledge of his own inception, he would have probably said: "I was created one hundred breaths ago," or something to that effect, indicating that his life began only a few minutes ago...

If you were to examine Adam's body, based on all the information at hand, you could have never guessed Adam was five minutes old. Other than by Adam's own testimony – being that he was the only creature with a consciousness of time – there would not be any way to know his real or

---

9   Ben Israel, *Conciliator*, question 79, p. 128.

10   A midrash tells that at some point after the summer solstice Adam realized sunlight was available for increasingly shorter periods of time every day and feared this may signal the end of the world. This means that for our Rabbis, it was a given that Adam possessed a notion of the passing of time *independent* of sunlight! (Otherwise, how could he ever realize the days were getting shorter?) See Talmud Babli, *'Aboda Zara* 8a.

chronological age. What is more, there were no visible Creation-marks on Adam's body or in any of God's direct creations.

Let us develop this last point a little further. The Rabbis affirmed that the God of Israel does not leave traces or evidences of His Presence or actions. When the Red Sea returned to its normal state after the Hebrew slaves crossed through it to freedom, the Torah says, "And the sea came back in the morning to its course" (Ex. 14:27). The Rabbis analyzed a verse in Psalms that elaborates on this event. The verse affirms that God's Presence or His intervention in our world does not leave any visible evidence. It says, "Your path is in the sea, Your trails in many waters, yet your footprints cannot be known" (Psalms 77:20). God Almighty does not leave fingerprints of His miracles. "Only a mythological deity leaves traces of its presence. The God of Israel even when performing the most astounding miracles leaves no evidence of His presence. Referring to the splitting of the sea, the Rabbis taught that the sea returned to its original condition bearing no marks of God's intervention. The same is true of all other miracles. Concerning this fundamental principle, the psalmist sang: 'Your path is in the sea, Your trails in many waters, yet Your footprints cannot be known.'"[11]

According to Jewish tradition, then, the original creatures fashioned *directly* by God must have looked more or less like their own offspring. Without any special indications on their bodies announcing they were fashioned out of nothingness by God, all created beings leave scientists no choice but to use standard methods for figuring out their origins. Thus, scientists come up with one-size-fits-all yardsticks, with which they evaluate the age of structures and creatures. These methods are applied to all beings, and the results are nothing but what you would expect. The bigger and more elaborate the structure, the older the age that will be attributed to it. Five minutes after the creation of Mount Everest, for example, the mountain has the appearance of a sixty-million-year-old mountain. Same as the first tree or the first chicken, the mountains, stones, stars, and galaxies would not

---

11   Faur, *Homo Mysticus*, pp. 13–14. Incidentally, this is the basis for Maimonides's argument about the impossibility of demonstrating Creation. Since the Creator leaves no traces or marks of His intervention in this world, Creation cannot possibly be proven or demonstrated. After all, since God leaves no fingerprints, there is no *evidence* in this world to prove Creation or to prove non-Creation.

bear any evidence of being created a short time ago. On the contrary, they will have the appearance of being *billions* of years of age.

When viewed in light of our midrash, the difference between Torah and science on the age of the world is exactly what we should expect to find if Creation had happened the way Jewish tradition states it happened. There will always exist two conflicting estimations of how old a geological structure or a celestial body is. Not because God wants to confuse us or test us, but because of the way Creation took place; there will be, necessarily, two discrepant ways of measuring how old things or creatures are. As we have explained in the previous chapter, if Planet X's scientists ignore (or disregard) the existence of a female human gender, their theories about Adam's birth, age, and growth will necessarily conflict with what the facts of Adam's birth are.

A TIME FACTORY

The creation of *shamayim* – heavens – is reported in a way that allows for an alternative explanation of how scientists arrive at their conclusions on the age of the universe. The creation of heavens is one of the best examples of mature creation. Perhaps, from all of God's creative activity, the way in which space at large was created is most responsible for causing the universe to appear (or to be) older than the time attributed by Jewish tradition.

What the first verse of the Torah describes – the creation of the entire universe, out of no preexistent matter – is absolutely impenetrable and beyond our understanding. The initial Creative act was the most comprehensive and sizable act of Creation, which produced all the existent matter, space, energy, and time. Although the nature and scope of this initial act of Creation in itself is and will remain unknowable and unimaginable, we may trace and see its effects in the movement of the heavens, i.e., the universe's expansion, which is still emitting an echo or microwave-length radiation, and can be detected on any TV screen or radio transmitter.

It was precisely because of the expansion of the universe that scientists were able to figure out that the cosmos had a beginning. Because they observed the expansion of the universe, cosmologists also asserted that the initial act of Creation must have consisted of an indescribable explosion which produced the original mega-blast and the ensuing endless cosmic expansion. What else but an explosion could have caused a continuous expansion and leave a microwave echo?

THE BIG BANG OF THE PROPHETS

The initial act of Creation (Gen. 1:1) brought into existence (1) the heavens, and (2) the earth. The Torah dedicates the rest of the story to planet Earth, but it says nothing else about heavens. Beyond stating that the cosmos was created by God, no additional information is provided. As we will see in the next section, heavens are left aside and – starting with the second verse of Genesis – the Biblical story continues exclusively with planet Earth and its transformation into the habitat of life.

With so little detail revealed by the Biblical text on its face, the Rabbis took a close interest in the particular order in which the events of the verse 1:1 are described. Looking at the second part of the first verse ("the heavens and the earth") they asked whether we should understand from the specific order of the terms that heavens were created before the earth or simultaneously with the earth.[12] In other words, the Rabbis wondered if the first verse of the Torah sees the creation of heavens and the creation of earth as one and the same act, or as two separate acts or creations. Based on the fourth verse of the second chapter of Genesis, the Rabbis observed that the order of the terms is interchangeable throughout, and concluded that heavens and earth were created simultaneously.[13] In conformity with the opening verse of the Torah, other classic Biblical expressions dealing with Creation would generally include both entities, heavens and earth, within one single creative act: "[God,] Maker of the heavens and the earth" ("'Ose shamayim va-aretz..." or "Qone shamayim va-aretz...").

Nonetheless, a number of times, the making of heavens and earth was accounted for separately, with the Biblical text using one word for the creation of the earth and a different term for the creation of heaven. We

---

12 Bet Hillel and Bet Shammai argued on this point. See Talmud Babli, *Chagiga* 12. The Midrash refers to this matter as one of the questions that Alexander the Great asked the Sages of Israel. The Rabbis actually answered Alexander that the heavens were created first. See *Torah Shelemah* 38:228.

13 *Torah Shelemah* 38:230.

should not be surprised. It is not uncommon for the Tanakh[14] to elaborate on and further develop some seminal ideas previously expressed in the Torah. Furthering the maxim that the best commentary on the Scripture should be found in the Scripture itself, King David in his Psalms and the Prophets of Israel in their books have referred to the creation of the heavens[15] in ways that could prove very enlightening to us. Using ideas and words that were *not* borrowed from the original narrative in Genesis, these Biblical passages broaden our understanding of the initial act of Creation.

For example, in Psalm 33, the making of heavens is retold poetically, with some notably significant differences. Many acts of Creation and formation are narrated in the Torah as being made by God's speech. For instance, the creation of light follows from God's utterance *yehi OR*[16] ("Let there be light"). No speech is mentioned, however, when God performs the very first act of Creation. The Torah simply states that *in the beginning, God created.* But while the first verse of the Torah does not mention God's actual speech in the creating of heavens and earth,[17] Psalms does state that heavens, too, were forged through God's word: "By the word of God the heavens were made; and all their army [of heaven, namely, the stars] by the breath of His mouth."[18]

There is yet another significant difference in the way that other texts in the Tanakh refer to the making of the heavens. In the Torah, Creation is depicted with one of the following three terms: *bara, qana,* or *'asa.* Nevertheless, King David and the prophets of Israel alluded to the creation of heavens using, consistently, a word – a verb – entirely different from those the Torah uses. They coined a rather surprising term, which is not

---

14 *Tanakh* (תנ״ך) is the Hebrew acronym for *Torah, Nebi-im* (the Prophets), and *Ketubim* (Writings). In this book I use the term Torah in its narrow sense referring to the Pentateuch, the five books of the law, and I use the word *Tanakh* – as opposed to Torah – to include the other two sections, or the entirety of the twenty-four-book Hebrew Bible.

15 For purposes of our subject – how the singularity of Creation affected the scientifically popular estimation of the age of the universe – we will refer now to those Biblical texts referring specifically to the creation of the heavens and not of the earth.

16 I write the Hebrew word אור as *OR* with capital letters just to differentiate it from the English particle "or."

17 See next chapter.

18 Psalms 33:6. This expression is, of course, a metaphor.

semantically connected with the original expression "created" (*bara*). It is a term which I find remarkably in tune with our modern understanding of the universe's expansion. To depict the creation of heavens, the Prophets routinely used the verb *na-ta*, which means "stretching" or "extending." This term is used in different contexts. It might describe the extending of one's hand (as with Moses' hand[19] or, metaphorically, with God's arm[20]) and is also normally used in the contexts of the spreading-out of a curtain or the pitching of a tent. Again, and to better appreciate the exquisite choice of words by the Prophets of Israel, let us bear in mind that no such verb, or any similar verb, was used in the context of Genesis or anywhere else in the Torah to describe the creation of heavens.[21]

Several times in the Tanakh we come across explicit references to the "stretching" of the heavens. The expression *no-te shamayim* ("[He Who] stretches out the heavens") is used more than ten times in the Tanakh.[22] Job, for example, describes God as He "Who by Himself *stretches out* heavens" (9:8).

For some reason, this expression is found repeatedly in the book of the prophet Isaiah, where a number of verses state that God Almighty "stretches" (like in Job, the verb is used in a present-continuous tense) the heavens. "It is I Who made the earth, and created man upon it. I *stretched out the heavens* with My hands and I ordained their entire host" (Isaiah 45:12).

One particular verse in Isaiah could prove most informative: "Thus says God, HaShem, Creator of the heavens and [He Who] stretches them out" (Isaiah 42:5). In this verse, the prophet notably used the two complementary ideas in one single sentence: God is the *bore*, the Creator of heavens, and He also is the One Who stretches out heavens. The interaction between *creating* and *stretching* can be understood as referring to two distinct

---

19 Ex. 14:26–27, among other places.
20 Ibid. 6:6.
21 Following the Biblical word used in Genesis for the extension of the sky, *raqia'*, we would have expected the prophets to use the verb רקע – instead of נטה. Ironically, רקע is consistently employed outside the story of Creation to describe the extension of the earth or land above the water (רוקע הארץ על המים) and not the extension of the sky.
22 See also Isaiah 40:22, 44:24, 48:13, 51:13, Jeremiah 10:12, 51:15, Zechariah 12:1.

actions – creation of heavens and, later on, stretching of heavens – or as one single action: He created the heavens *by* stretching them.[23] This last interpretation could be supported by the fact that the Rabbis incorporated the idea of "stretching the heavens," leaving out the original expression "created" heavens, used in the first Biblical verse, in the traditional prayer *'Alenu leshabeach* – considered to be one of the most ancient texts in Jewish liturgy for High Holidays – and adopted in our days as the invocation with which Jews end every prayer service: "We prostrate ourselves before He Who is King, the King of kings, the Holy One, blessed is He; He Who *stretches out* heavens and *bases* the earth."[24]

A few things are important to note about the phraseology employed by the prophets and the Rabbis. First, one could easily sense a stark contrast between the wording used to describe God's creating of the earth and the wording used to describe God's creating of the heavens. With regard to the earth, allusions to God "basing the earth" suggest it is a static entity, solidly *based* by its Creator as firm ground. On the other hand, with heavens, the words used connote dynamism: the heavens are being spread out and expanded – by definition, those verbs are undefined processes that could very well continue indefinitely.[25] Secondly, we should also notice that the wording used by the Rabbis stands in the present form, *no-te*, not in the past, *na-ta*. As it were, God is continuously expanding the heavens; this stands in syntagmatic opposition to the perpetually solid structure with which God endows earth.

---

23 In Biblical Hebrew, the second parallel verb is usually understood as the semantic expansion of the first: כפל ענין במלים שונות.

24 The authorship of *'Alenu leshabeach* is traditionally attributed to Joshua bin Nun. Later works, like the famous *Agadelkha* poem by Rabbi Abraham Eben 'Ezra (1089–1164), also refer to the creation of the heavens with the verb נטה ("The heavens standing high above – He *stretched out* with an utterance, and the land – He based her on empty space").

25 Psalms 33:9 also used a similar expression to convey the stationary nature of earth: *vaya'amod* – "[the earth] stood firm."

Cherry–Picking Words

The Biblical term "stretching" – the rendition of *no-te* by virtually every classic English translation[26] – is not inappropriate to depict what we today know about the universe's expansion. Some modern astrophysicists could not be more in agreement with the term *stretching* heavens. They explain that the scientific idea of the expansion of the universe should not be understood literally as the universe reaching out into out-of-universe-empty-space, but rather as the universe stretching itself and *producing* new space.

In Psalms 104, the beautiful Biblical Psalm that poetically recounts with great detail the six days of Creation, the king and most famous poet of Israel described the stretching of the Heavens in a precise and beautiful imagery: "*No-te shamayim kayri'a*" (104:2). As if it were, God Almighty "covers Himself with light, and He *stretches out heavens like a curtain*." Interestingly, while other ancient civilizations imagined heavens as a transparent but fixed and solid vault (hence the word "firmament," from the Latin *firmus*, which means "firm"), the prophets of Israel and King David compared the heavens (the universe at large) with a curtain that God "stretches out"; i.e., continuously stretches.

King David's motif, comparing heavens with an unfolding curtain,[27] is an exquisitely accurate metaphor. To describe an idea similar to the one coined by King David and the prophets of Israel, modern astrophysicists have toyed with several slightly different motifs – like the "ultimate plastic" imagery (which in my opinion pales in comparison with the "unfolding curtain"). Remarkably, they ended up using the same verb for the expansion of the universe as King David has employed: "stretching."

One example:

> To appreciate Hubble's evidence for cosmic expansion, consider first an imaginary pocket toy, similar to the types that appeared in advertisements in old comic books. The ad

---

26 See for example, Psalms 104:2 (King James' translation as well as many other translations).

27 This motif was later on used by Isaiah (42:5), as was already mentioned.

might read "Ultimate Plastic™: Imagine holding a universe in the palm of your hand." The toy comes as a cube the size of a sugar lump, with handles at each corner for you and for some friends to stretch apart. Pull on the handles and the cube grows in size. Keep pulling and you can make the cube as big as a room. Inside the plastic the makers have sprinkled tiny models of galaxies that you can see spreading apart from one another as the cube expands. The model galaxies are made of a hard material so that they do not expand when the cube is stretched – only the space between them does. This was Hubble's mental image of a chunk of the expanding universe.[28]

Saying that the universe is expanding would only make sense if the universe were extending into empty space. However, modern understanding of astrophysics posits that space only exists between two physical entities. Space is being created as the array of physical entities stretches out and away from one another. Hence, scientists would insist that the idiom *stretching* of the universe is far more accurate than the more common term *expanding*, because there is no space beyond the universe-space.

The following priceless lines made me think that, sometimes, you must be a prophet of Israel to know what are the most precise words to use, twenty-eight centuries in advance:

If the universe is infinitely big, then the answer is simply that it isn't expanding into anything; instead, what is happening is that every region of the universe, every distance between every pair of galaxies, is being "stretched".... "Expanding" isn't really the best word to describe what is happening to the universe, although that is the word that is often used – a word choice which I think leads to a lot of unnecessary confusion regarding what is already a difficult topic! A more accurate word for what the universe is doing might be "stretching"...as time goes on, the space between the galaxies "stretches," sort of like what

28 Paul J. Steinhardt and Neil Turok, *Endless Universe: Beyond the Big Bang* (New York: Doubleday, 2007), p. 29.

happens when you take a sheet of rubber and pull at it on both ends.[29]

STRETCHING HEAVENS, STRETCHING TIME

The expansion of the universe is what led cosmologists to attribute to the universe its old appearance: fifteen billion years. They assumed the universe grew from nothing, linearly, and uniformly at a steady pace known as the Hubble constant (or Hubble parameter) – approximately 72 kilometers every second. But, as we know in modern days, there is an intrinsic relation between time and space. The following illustration will help us understand one basic aspect of this relationship.

Assume that there are two galaxies, Galaxy A and Galaxy B, standing apart one thousand light-years from each other. When we say that something is a certain number of light-years away, we mean to say that if light were to traverse that distance, it would take light that number of years to arrive at its destination. Given that light travels at approximately 186,000 miles per second, and given that there are 31,557,600,000 seconds in one thousand years – being one thousand light-years away is equivalent to being 5,869,713,600,000,000 (or $5.87 * 10^{15}$) miles away. If I were to stand on Galaxy A and point a light toward Galaxy B, the light would only be seen at Galaxy B one thousand years later.

Now, if I were to grab Galaxy A, standing at 5,869,713,600,000,000 miles away from Galaxy B, and move it further away from galaxy B, I would be in fact *creating* space, and – simultaneously – I would be generating the perception of the time that normally would have been necessary for these two galaxies to be at the distance they are right now. Any added distance between the two galaxies that is due to this stretching is newly created space, and the perception of newly added time. Now, if I were to move it faster than the speed of light, then I would have created space, *and also time!* In other words, let us say that – after pointing the light toward Galaxy B – I moved Galaxy A another thousand light-years away from Galaxy B,

---

29 Dave Rothstein, astronomy department of Cornell University, "Curious about Astronomy? Ask an astronomer":
http://curious.astro.cornell.edu/question.php?number=274.

and this process took me only five hundred light-years. In this five hundred years, light only traveled five hundred light-years. The distance between both galaxies is now two thousand light-years. It will take light another fifteen hundred years to make up for merely one thousand light-years of created space. This, in physics, would mean that time was, actually, created.

Depending on the acceleration at the first stages of the creation of the universe, when by God's word the initial act of Creation detonated[30] the universe's expansion, extra time must have been automatically engendered with it. The creation and/or expansion of the universe might not have created just an *illusion* of time or *virtual* time, but it might have created *actual* time. As a by-product of the expansion of the universe, billions of years-of-time must have been directly or indirectly brought into being. Space-expansion is perhaps the best way to see the production of time as an inevitable effect of the act of Creation.

From a Biblical perspective, the "stretching" of heavens, done by God at an undisclosed speed (or perhaps, outside the dimension of time) resulted in the subsequent creation of time, leading thus to a perception of an older universe. If that was so, the differences in the universe's estimated age between the scientific and the biblical account are entirely what we should expect to find.

UNSTABLE TIME

The very interesting midrash we are now about to analyze might contribute to a better understanding of the differences between science and religion on the age of the universe. A rabbinic source from the Talmud intimates an additional way in which the creative processes were very particular. During the six days of Creation, *time* is what may have behaved somehow differently than it does today.

After the initial act of Creation ex nihilo (Gen. 1:1) some (or all) structures and creatures were formed through a step-by-step mechanism,

---

30 On the dramatic effects of the voice of God in nature – but limited to planet Earth – see Psalms 29, *Mizmor leDavid*, which mentions seven times the effects of the *qol*, voice of God, on earth, triggering cataclysms, etc. On the effects of the universe's expansion on the distinction between day and night on planet Earth, or Olber's paradox, see section 3, chapter 7.

much like the gradual processes that affected (and affects) the age and development of things in our present reality. However, the timing of these actions was very different from what we would observe today. Obviously, a scientist who examines a structure constructed of many layers will assume that these layers signify a very lengthy process.

The midrash concedes, on the one hand, that the formation of things and beings developed in many separate steps – something that modern geologists continuously try to demonstrate. On the other hand, the midrash also suggests that these steps might have happened in an accelerated manner. Therefore, even those creations that were fashioned with an internal age already imbedded in them (as we explained above) might have undergone a gradual but accelerated process of formation. Hence, all Creative processes, and not only the first act of Creation ex nihilo, were exceptional.

The six days of Creation are considered as a whole a *unique* category in terms of timing and dating. Pointedly, the Hebrew calendar – the official Jewish account of time – does not count the years from the first day of Creation. Our calendar begins, rather, from the seventh day: *Shabbat Bereshit*. Adam – the first human – was created on the sixth day of Creation, which the Rabbis regarded[31] as the thirtieth day of Elul.[32] Rosh HaShana, the actual first day of the Jewish year, falls on the first of Tishri, at the end of the process of Creation (Shabbat day). As we will see later on, it is only once the six days' creative processes were completed that time was stabilized and began to flow as we know it today. The first day of the Jewish calendar, is the day *after* the creation process was over. The six days of Creation were left by the Rabbis outside the realm of normal time, as if they pertained to a different time-dimension.

Accelerated Creation

The midrash we are referring to is found in the Talmud Babli, tractate *Sanhedrin* 38b. The author is a Rabbi from Israel (second century CE) who

---

31 Notice that, although today in our fixed calendars Elul is always *chaser* (twenty-nine days), before our present calendar Elul could also have had thirty days. See Rambam, *Qiddush haChodesh* 3:9.

32 As we explained before, there is a second opinion that maintains the world was created on the 25th of Adar.

relates an unusual hour-by-hour account of the occurrences involving the birth of Adam and Eve and the most famous events of their lives.

> Rabbi Yochanan bar Chanina said: That day had twelve hours. In the first hour, the dust was gathered; second hour, the unformed body [of Adam] was created; third, his limbs were formed; fourth, a soul was insufflated into him; fifth, he stood on his feet; sixth, he called names to the animals; seventh, he was joined by Eve; eighth, two went to bed and four got out of bed;[33] ninth, he was commanded not to eat from the tree; tenth, he transgressed [by eating from the tree]; eleventh, he was judged; twelfth, he was sent away [from *Gan Eden*].

All of the above mentioned events, says Rabbi Yochanan bar Chanina, took place during daytime of the sixth day, from morning (*boqer*) to evening (*'ereb*).

The Torah devotes almost three chapters to describe the formation of Adam and Eve, their union, the birth of their children, the sin of the forbidden fruit, and their expulsion from the Garden of Eden, etc. What should normally have taken several years to occur, for our midrash happened within a matter of hours.[34] The eighth hour certainly provides the most verifiable example of this time anomaly. The midrash affirms that Eve conceived and gave birth to Cain and Abel, who were not even twins, in the lapse of one hour. How could two full pregnancies happen during one single hour?

---

33 A euphemism for the birth of their two sons: Cain and Abel.

34 This rabbinic tradition, approximately 1,800 years old, might be better understood today thanks to the present advances in astrophysics. We now know that events that would normally take months or years to happen, might occur in a matter of mere hours – relative to an outside observer, within a different time frame. One of the best known examples is the phenomenon of a black hole (see Martin Rees, *Just Six Numbers: The Deep Forces That Shape the Universe* [New York: Basic Books, 2001], pp. 40–41). Jorge Luis Borges (1899–1986) formulated a similar idea in his beautiful fiction "The Secret Miracle," where time continues to flow for the protagonist while it stops for the rest of the world. Jorge Luis Borges, *Labyrinths: Selected Stories and Other Writings*, edited by Donald A. Yates and James E. Irby (New York: New Directions, 2007), pp. 88–94.

Let us remember that Biblical and rabbinic traditions, being non-mythical institutions, are extremely conscientious of *time* and hold a very cogent sense of history. There is no other source in rabbinic literature that relates events which necessitate many years as occurring within mere hours. As far as I know, this temporal oddity is unique to our midrash. It is important to note that regarding the reputation of this midrash,[35] Maimonides viewed it as very esteemed one, and hinted that this midrash was conveying a belief shared by all Rabbis, not only by its author, Rabbi Yochanan ben Chanina.[36]

Anticipating what is known today as fluctuating or relative time, our midrash seems to be saying that during the sixth day of Creation time was flowing at a pace different than the pace we experience in today's physical universe. That is, those events described in it, pregnancy and birth, for example, did not occur at the pace we would expect today.

If the Rabbis understood that time behaved in a unique way during the six days of Creation, it would be acceptable for them to speak of lengthy processes as though they had happened in a mere hour. I would redefine those time periods that our midrash describes and consider them not as "hours" but as "Creation-hours" (perhaps windows of creative-activity in which time, because of its irregularity, is an *inconsequential* factor). In conformity with our modern view of time, the Rabbis might have perceived time as a purely relative phenomenon. The concept of time used in the Creation story may be seen as a reference of the progress of God's creative

---

35 Not all midrashim are considered of the same value or repute. Some of them expressed a particular view, not necessarily shared by all rabbis. In his *Guide for the Perplexed*, Maimonides very often points out which midrashim should be seen as expressing an idea conforming with the majority of the rabbis and which midrashim were not. In section 2, chapter 30, the chapter where he deals with Creation, Maimonides, for example, rejects the midrash which says that God was building worlds and then destroying them (בונה עולמות ומחריבם), or the midrash that says that time existed before Creation (סדר זמנים). He considered these two midrashim as the private opinion of the authors, which he dismissed, and not as an accepted normative Jewish opinion.

36 See Maimonides in *More Nebukhim* 2:30, where he greatly praises this midrash and mentions that all the events described in chapters 2 and 3 of Genesis happened during the sixth day. It is worth pointing out that this midrash is not based on a textual interpretation (*derasha*) of the verses or its words. Rather, it is probably a development of an ancient oral tradition.

activity, more than as the measurement of ordinary change. Since Einstein's Theory of Relativity, scientists have begun to perceive time as an abstraction we use to organize sequential events, rather than a physical phenomenon that can be measured in absolute terms. "Nobody ever measures some absolute phenomenon called time; what one measures is the rate of some physical change in the universe. It could be the fall of sand in an egg timer, the movement of the hands on a clock face, or the dripping of a tap. There are countless changing phenomena that could be used to define the passage of time."[37]

Needless to say, if time did behave in an unstable or irregular way during the process of Creation, making the progress of "natural" events during the six days to be different than ours, the debate between science and religion concerning the age of the universe is based entirely on wrong premises – an apples-to-bananas debate which should not distract our attention from the important coincidences. For example, when the Torah describes the formation of the sky in the second day, we could assume that the processes of formation of our atmosphere might have happened during one Creation-hour (or day) but at a different speed, same as with pregnancy and birth in the above-mentioned midrash. Thus, events which in normal circumstances might have taken years or even centuries to happen, might well have happened within those unique Creation-hours – as if the creative operation was one of accelerated Creation.

The idea of accelerated Creation, as one particular property of the six days of Creation, will allow us to avoid the debate over the length of the six days and, once again, would render the controversy over the age of the world virtually pointless. Indeed, why would we not assume that God built this world at high speed? The alternative, that the Almighty Creator may have taken unnecessary millions of present-day years to build a mountain, would be the more absurd hypothesis.

Significantly, according to rabbinic tradition, the sixth day of Creation was no different than the other five days of Creation. We could safely assume that although our midrash focuses on the events of the sixth day – probably due to a natural heightened interest in the creation of our

---

37   John D. Barrow, *The Origin of the Universe* (New York: Basic Books, 1997), p. 94.

first ancestor – the Rabbis saw the six days of Creation as a unique but homogenous category (which means that what is true regarding time during the sixth day is also true about the other five days). Commenting on the primeval state of Creation during the six days, Rabbi Menashe ben Israel quotes two rabbinical commentaries explaining that, during the entire span of the six days, every creation and creature was functioning in an unnatural, non-independent state of existence: "Rabbi Isaac 'Arama and don Isaac Abarbanel say that although the Lord God gave existence to every thing in the six days, yet until the seventh, which He blessed, they did not commence acting naturally or by themselves, which then they did, and attained the end for which they were created."[38]

According to Maimonides, during the process of the six days of Creation, time was still unstable and not operational. "Time is a magnitude pertaining to the present realm of things. Its application to the initial stages of the universe is a fallacious extrapolation of our imagination."[39] The universe began to operate "normally" only after the sixth day.

The six days of Creation were seen, indeed, as the embryological phase of the cosmos – one may say, an entirely different dimension.

Six Days of Gradual Transformations

There is yet another lesson we can learn from this midrash that will be extremely important for the rest of this book. Along with hinting that the creation and formation process might have occurred within an undefined time frame, our midrash also suggests that God's creative activity might have taken place as a step-by-step process. As we shall see later on, the

---

38 Ben Israel, *Conciliator*, question 15, p. 25. Incidentally, Rabbi Menashe quotes Nachmanides and Abarbanel on the length of the Six Days of Creation, for whom these were not regular twenty-four hour days: "They maintain that saying it was created in six days, was to signify in days of one thousand years each...." There are other opinions that view these days as days of twenty-four hours.

39 See Faur, *Homo Mysticus*, p. 116. Maimonides also maintained in *More Nebukhim* 2:30 that plants, for example, were created but did not continue to grow, "neither did they produce their species until the sixth day, when natural germination commenced and all things began to act conformably to their nature, procreating their kinds." Quoted by ben Israel, *Conciliator*, question 3, p. 9.

whole of the narrative of Genesis suggests that our universe gained its present form through distinct and gradual steps.

A procedure involving many steps may lead someone to assume that the process was a lengthy one. However, one should take into account that time – as we saw above – may have been functioning differently than it does today.

Our midrash describes in detail the formation of man, from the moment the dust was gathered until he was able to stand up on his feet. The fashioning of the first man is depicted as an operation that consisted of five acts or Creation-hours. "In the first hour, the dust was gathered; second hour, the unformed body was created; third, his limbs were formed; fourth, a soul was insufflated into him; fifth, he stood on his feet."

For this midrash, Creation was not a one-time operation by which things appeared suddenly in the planet, but a gradual process consisting of several acts, most of which were *not* explicitly recorded in the Biblical text. God created Adam as an intelligent being, endowed with a divine soul, and with an earth-made body that appeared to be twenty years old. Our midrash clarifies that the formation of Adam's body from the dust, the fine-tuned fashioning of his body, and the integration of his living soul to his body, were all done in separated steps.

Graduality, or step-by-step processes, was likely the standard *modus operandi* of God in creating the world. Incidentally, this is the pattern of God's interventions (or miracles) in the Scripture as well. When God divided the Red Sea, allowing the Jews to escape from their Egyptian masters to freedom, He did not split the sea instantaneously in one swift act, as occurs in acts of magic and mythology. The waters were divided gradually and progressively throughout the entire night.[40] In the story of Creation, nonetheless, the Torah never says explicitly that God operated in one way or another, whether things and creatures were brought into existence by an instantaneous act or in a progressive way. This is why our midrash is so enlightening, as it opens a door for the latter possibility.

Concerning what we have called the internal age of God's creations, the gradual fashion in which things were formed can have radical consequences.

---

40 Exodus 14:21.

If before we said that Mount Everest would appear to be sixty million years old, its age being an illusory side-effect of mature creation, then when considering the possibility of a progressive creation, Mount Everest, in a sense, *is* and not just *appears* to be sixty million years old.

Let me explain.

As we have already seen, most scientists follow the uniformitarian school of thought. They believe that the laws of the physical world have been *uniformly* constant always and will be so forever. Discounting the possibility of Creation, they look at the present world and simply project this reality backward in a uniform way. So, how would a uniformitarian scientist date, say, Mount Everest? He would affirm that mountains did not materialize overnight but were rather formed over the course of millions of years at the rate of a few millimeters per year. After all, the process of crust formation has a well-developed theory. Demonstrably, heat and pressure coming from within the earth constantly produce changes and movements under the Earth's crust (these movements are known as plate tectonics). As a gigantic spherical puzzle, the Earth's crust is made of plates – separated pieces of solid matter that fit onto each other. The plates are not still. They move constantly, affecting very slowly the geological structures of our planet through volcanism and erosion. All these factors that are still observed in our planet, the geologist will reason, must have been fully responsible for mountains' formation from point zero. By a rate of a few inches per year, this geologist would infer that it must have taken Mount Everest approximately sixty million years to grow up to its present 29,000 feet.

Obviously, the premise of uniformitarian scientists – that the universe has had the same physical rules eternally, and that no Creator has ever brought the universe to existence or ever interfered with the physical rules – is not compatible with Hebrew tradition. However, our midrash seems to conform with at least one of the premises of uniformitarian theory. Creation may have occurred not in a swift single event, but as an evolving or gradual process of growth where things were brought to existence layer by layer. In other words, in the same way the Creator did not bring Adam to existence in one single act, but in a process involving five distinct steps, the Creator made the full-size mountain emerge not at once on the ground instantaneously, as if it fell from heaven to earth. Rather, He might have set in motion the volcanic and geological movements needed for a step-by-step progressive formation of the mountain. If Creation happened as a step-by-step process rather than an instantaneous act, then in a real sense, those sixty million years attributed to Mount Everest indeed *are* Mount Everest's age, not just as a virtual illusion, but factually, as one of the inherent and very real qualities of Mount Everest's body and structure.

Another midrash in *Bereshit Rabba* seems to support the idea of a progressive and gradual – rather than instantaneous – process of Creation. This second midrash discusses an unusual word expressed in the book of Job. The book of Job (Iyob) tells of an encounter (according to one Talmudic opinion, a fictional one)[41] between a human being – Job – and God.[42] At the climax of this extraordinary experience, God reveals Himself to Job from within a storm, challenging him to articulate any of the secrets of Creation. With this clear showcase of the limits of the human mind, God dissuades Job (and the reader) from expecting to understand the mind of God in His administration of justice – the main subject of Job's inquiry. Job is unable to grasp even matters within reach of his physical reality. God confronts Job with a series of questions showing him clearly that a man could never be able to comprehend how heavens and earth were formed. Left with no answers, the poignant questions achieved the desired impact, and Job humbly accepts the limitations of his mind, renouncing his pretension to decipher God's administration of justice.

Back to Creation, when Job is asked if he has any notion about the formation of our planet, the question God asks is: "[Where were you] when the earth melted into a mass and its clods stuck together [*betzeqet 'afar lamutzaq*]?" This expression, *betzeqet 'afar lemutzaq,* found nowhere else in the Scripture, inspired the Rabbis to elaborate the following insight: our planet did not appear all at once, fully formed, but rather God fashioned it "clod by clod" – layer by layer. The *Be-ur,* a contemporary commentary

---

41 Talmud Babli, *Baba Batra* 15a: "Job [as a historical figure] never existed, but was rather [meant to be read as] a parable."
42 This might be one of the reasons why some Sages affirmed that the book of Job was written by Moshe Rabbenu, the only human being according to Jewish tradition who experienced this kind of encounter.

on *Bereshit Rabba*, links this midrash with another rabbinic source[43] that reaffirms the rabbinic tradition that God built our planet "layer after layer." Hence, the *Be-ur* says, "This would make our planet look older than it really is." Indeed, the process of forming our planet clod-by-clod is what, according to the *Be-ur*, "brought the nonbelievers to attribute millions of years between layer and layer."[44]

PROGRESSIVELY, BUT FAST

Creatures, geological structures, and planets all present evidence of a gradual process of formation, and of having reached their actual state through a series of distinct steps and stages. A uniformitarian scientist would be in agreement with our midrash by recognizing that the formation of things was a gradual process. However, the midrash also suggested that time and/ or speed may have been functioning differently than what we experience today. As we have learned from our midrash, during the six days of creation, the flowing of time was somehow different than what we experience in our present reality. The creation process might have happened at any speed. Instead of taking millions of present-day years for the mountain to emerge, the entire cataclysmic process might have happened in merely one of those Creation-hours suggested by our midrash.

And, after all, how fast is too fast for God? Let's remember that in our present reality the highest possible speed is roughly 186,000 miles per second. Hypothetically, even if Creation occurred *just* at the speed of light, it would certainly explain away the differences between the Biblical timing and the scientific timing for the origins of the universe. All known geological processes reported in the first chapter of Genesis – the formation of the atmosphere, continental drifts, appearance of vegetation, all those mega-events – might have taken place at the speed of light, the frontier of reachable speed known to us.

Allow me to analogize what I am envisioning in my mind with a filming technique called "time-lapse photography." In time-lapse photography, an

---

43 Rashi, Talmud Babli, *Yoma* 54b.
44 *Midrash Bereshit Rabba haMebo-ar* (R. Abraham Shteinberger, ed. [Jerusalem: Makhon haMidrash haMebo-ar, 5740 (1980)], p. 13, see footnotes).

artistic photographer captures very slow processes, whose gradual changes would be imperceptible to the naked eye, and presents them in brief video documentaries. For instance, the photographer may want to apply this method to capture the majestic blossoming and opening of a rose. A flower naturally opens very slowly, and our eyes can't perceive the minute changes while they are taking place. Time-lapse photography allows one to see the flower opening in all its majesty in a matter of seconds. How do they do it? A camera is placed in front of the flower, and a picture is taken every five minutes or so. Then, a short movie is composed compiling all the pictures and running the movie forward. The effect is that you see in a matter of seconds a process that took place during hours or days. This visual effect is nothing short of magnificent and it allows us to appreciate the beauty of a blossoming flower in all of its splendor.

To visualize what I mean by *accelerated* and *progressive* Creation, simply imagine a time-lapse movie of Mount Everest, emerging from underground lava up, reaching its grandiose stature of 29,000 feet, and all of it happening in a matter of seconds. In the dimension of Creation, the birth of Cain and Abel; the formation of the atmosphere, the erosion processes, continental drifts, the birth of the earth's mountains, etc., all might have occurred step-by-step at an incredibly fast pace. As with time-lapse photography, when the right technique is being employed, a movie of an event which normally would take hours might only take a couple of seconds. A person who is asked "How long would you expect a movie about the blossoming of a rose to be?" may very well answer, "Probably a couple of hours long." However, the movie may be less than a minute long when shown in time-lapse photography.

Obviously, if Creation happened in the way I'm describing it, if super-speed was applied during the Creation process, the step-by-step accelerated process will necessarily be translated by a geologist who examines it into millions or billions of years. Similarly, anyone who has ever owned an analog watch knows that to have the hour-indicator hand move from "1" to "3," one could wait two hours for the watch's hand to move alone, aided by its internal mechanism, or one could simply manually fast-forward the watch two hours in a mere second. In either case the hand will have moved two hours. With no other information available, an observer, unaware of anyone's intervention, will assuredly assert that the analog watch must have run for 7,200 seconds for the hand to move from "1" to "3," while in reality it was moved by an external force – one's hand – from "1" to "3" in just one second.

The notion of a progressive and accelerated Creation might definitely explain the time differences between science and the Biblical narrative. A clock's hand could move from "1" to "3" in two hours, or in one second – if manually brought to that position. Mount Everest could grow to 29,000 feet in sixty million years, or in one mere "creation-hour" – if this occurred during the first six days of Creation.

Indeed, the midrash's assertion that speed and/or time were exceptional during the first six days of creation is very reasonable when considered in light of the particular forces that might have been applied during that singular and unrepeatable period, when God created and formed out of nothing the world we know today.

And finally, knowing that the time issue is indeed a non-issue, we should feel at liberty – or almost compelled – to make use of scientific data that will help us visualize the progress of the Biblical Creation story without being restrained by time considerations.

Since on the one hand, we now understand why scientists may arrive at different conclusions about the time it took for those processes to occur, in a sense, these time differences are entirely expected. On the other hand, the way scientists explain how those processes themselves have unfolded may be quite enlightening for understanding the Biblical account of the events of the six days of Creation. I feel, therefore, that there is no harm in benefitting from that wisdom. The reader should simply refer back to this section to understand why what scientists conclude about the *length* of those processes is rather inconsequential.

SUMMARY

Creation was a singularity. An untraceable singularity with laws belonging to a different physical reality or dimension. A reality which conflicts with the established natural laws of our present physical existence (as embryology is to physiology). When trying to reconstruct Creation, based on our post-Creation knowledge and information, one would find himself imagining and extrapolating a reflection of one's own reality into an unknowable dimension. The matter of the age of the universe is a very good example of this type of projection and the paradoxical conclusions one might find at the end of that road.

Rabbinical tradition, preserved in the Midrash, mentions that God created the first things and creatures in a state of maturity. An external observer investigating Creation would not be able to avoid perceiving planet Earth and the universe at large as very old structures. The phenomenon we described as mature creation generates the inevitable coexistence of two conflicting calculations of age: that of science and the other attributed to the Biblical account. When the universe, however, is appraised assuming a mature Creation, these conflicts disappear.

The act of Creation also implies the ensuing creation of time. Coinciding with our modern knowledge about the universe's expansion, the creation of heavens was recorded by the prophets of Israel as the *stretching* of heavens. That expansion, especially at the first steps, must have consequently created enormous amounts of time – billions of years – which might give the universe the appearance of an older age. Whether this stretching took God six thousand years, one day, some "Creation-hours," or just an imperceptible instant, or no time at all, the resulting heavens – once stretched – would intrinsically possess within them the fifteen billion years calculated by some modern scientists.

The last section of this chapter examined a midrash positing that, during the six days of Creation, events did not evolve at a standard present time or time did not flow at its present pace. According to this midrash, there were "Creation-hours" with seemingly irregular time frames. Finally, this rabbinic source suggested that we might conceive of Creation as a series of processes. These processes are to be seen as step-by-step operations, which may however have taken place at super-fast speed, just like with the time-lapse photography technique.

When Creation is our point of departure, we realize that, in terms of the universe's age, science is finding exactly what it is supposed to find: an old and mature universe. All things considered, the present cosmos and its physical laws become comprehensible and entirely compatible with the principles of Creation. While Creation, by its ineffable own nature, cannot be proven, there are no elements in our world that contradict the foundations of Creation.[45]

This idea is beautifully formulated by Arno Penzias when describing the new findings in physics on the beginning of the universe:

> The best data we have are exactly what I would have predicted, had I had nothing to go on but the five books of Moses, the Psalms and the Bible. As a whole the creation of the universe is supported by all the observable data astronomy has produced so far.... Astronomy leads us to a unique event, a universe which was created out of nothing, one with the very delicate balance needed to provide exactly the conditions required to permit life, and one which has an underlying [one might say "supernatural"] plan.[46]

---

45 The same cannot be said, for example, about Near Eastern myths of creation and pagan mythology.

46 Nobel laureate Arno Penzias in *Cosmos, Bios, Theos: Scientists Reflect on Science, God, and the Origins of the Universe, Life, and Homo Sapiens* [Paperback], edited by Henry Margenau and Roy Varghese (Chicago: Open Court, 1992), Bracketed comment appears in original.

CHAPTER 3

TRANSLATING CREATION

Now that we have exposed some of the theoretical debates on Creation and some of the tensions between the Biblical story of Creation and modern science, we might proceed to explore what the Torah has said about Creation in its first verse. Soon we will realize that even without considering all the potential issues raised by contemporary scientific knowledge, understanding what the Torah said about Creation – at the simplest level – is no easy task.

To begin with, the very first verse of the Scripture could be understood and translated in two substantially different ways. Sometimes, differences in interpretation between one rendition and others are not fundamental, and the basic meaning of the verse or the meaning of the original Hebrew words is not really affected. Taking, as an example, the first verse of the Torah, whether one were to translate *bereshit* as "In the beginning" or "At the beginning," or whether *et hashamayim ve-et ha-aretz* would be "heavens and earth" or "the heavens and the earth," is – in the large scale of things – of little consequence.

On the other hand, there are some key words whose translation might very radically alter the overall meaning of the text. In the first verse of the Torah, Genesis 1:1, the inclusion or exclusion of one small word – a preposition – might have crucial implications for the way one understands the story of Creation altogether.

We find two approaches to the rendition of the first verse. And they convey two conflicting perspectives on the order and even on the nature of Creation. The first verse could be translated as:

(1) "In the beginning, God created heavens and earth,"
or,
(2) "In the beginning, when God created heavens and earth...."

The first translation, which is the traditional one, views this verse as describing an actual act of Creation. It recounts what we call the First Act of Creation, that is, bringing into existence the entire universe out of nothing.

According to the second translation, our verse does not report necessarily an act of Creation. The entire sentence could be understood just as a temporal clause, introducing the creation of light – an alternative *first* act of creation – which is reported in verse 1:3. According to this rendition, the making of heavens and earth might not have been reported at all in the Torah. One is left to wonder if they were at all created or if they had eternally existed.

In this chapter we will analyze in detail how the varying ways Rabbis and scholars read and comprehended the first verse lead to opposite conceptions of what transpired in the Biblical story of Creation. We will soon realize that the interpretation of the first verse by and large depends on how we understand the opening word of the Torah: the Hebrew word *bereshit*. The majority of this chapter is devoted to examining this word.

What Was Created First?

In the previous chapters, we have analyzed the notion of a *beginning* and we have become, hopefully, a bit more aware of the uncertainties involved in the concept of Creation. We are now conscious of some of the limitations of the human mind in this area, and of why it is impossible to fully comprehend what precisely occurred at the moment of Creation. With this state of mind it is now time to ask ourselves: What is the Torah saying that God created in the first place?

It is important to note that no particular *details* of whatever happened during Creation – as opposed to the identity of the Creator, which is a fundamental tenet of Judaism – were ever considered an unquestionable credo in Jewish tradition. In fact, rabbinical sources were not in full agreement as to what the exact order of Creation was. Identifying what God brought first into existence was a matter open to debate among the Sages of the Midrash.

Two Rabbis of the second century (ca. 150 CE), Rabbi Yehuda and Rabbi Nechemia, argued about the initial act of Creation. Rabbi Yehuda maintained that first God created *light*. He said: "Light was the first creation.

Like a King who wished to build a palace, and the [construction] site was dark. What did the King do? He lit candles and torches to see how to build the foundations of the palace. In the same way, the Almighty first created light."[1] Rabbi Nechemia disagreed. According to him, heavens and earth – the entire universe – were created first, and the creation of light took place in a second stage: "Like a King Who built a palace and *then* installed all its lights."

As is the case with many classic Talmudic discussions, the two opinions were not based on different sources but on different interpretations of the same verse. Both Rabbi Nechemia and Rabbi Yehuda based their views on their respective readings of the first sentence of the Torah: "In the beginning God created heavens and earth." The Rabbis' debate on the order of Creation sheds light – and ultimately depends – on the way they interpreted this pivotal verse.

In order to opine that light was created first, Rabbi Yehuda would have to read the opening verse as *not* describing any act of creation. If it did talk of something being created, then light would no longer be the *first* thing God brought into existence. Hence, the first verse should be understood, according to Rabbi Yehuda, as: "In the beginning, *as* God was creating heavens and earth…." This Biblical sentence would then be setting the stage for the third verse, which deals with the creation of light, which Rabbi Yehuda held was the first thing God created out of nothing.

Rabbi Yehuda's reading can be justified fairly simply. In the first verse of the Torah, God does not speak. The verse does *not* say: "In the beginning God said, 'Let the heavens and earth be' – and it was so." Most other acts of Creation reported in the Biblical text were performed by God's speech. Creative acts are for the most part introduced by the words *vayomer Elohim*, "and God said." When God fashioned the first living creatures He commanded the waters to bring living organisms into existence ("And God said, '…*yishretzu hamayim sheretz nefesh chaya*'"; Gen. 1:20). God creates with His speech.[2] And we don't find God *saying* anything in the first verse

---

1   See *Torah Shelemah* 33:205.
2   The idea of God's speech as God's creative tool is beautifully expressed in the prayer ברוך שאמר והיה העולם (Blessed is He Who spoke and the world came into existence).

of the Torah. Are we to understand that the absence of the phrase "And God said" and the absence of any kind of speech by God, mean that the opening verse of the Torah is not describing an act of Creation?

This was Rabbi Yehuda's position. And, consequently, he sees the first verse as nothing more than an introduction to what he believes was the real initial act of Creation: the creation of light. When God creates light, the Torah indeed employs – for the first time – the phrase "And God said..." ("And God said, 'Let there be light,' and there was light"; Gen. 1:3).

For Rabbi Yehuda, therefore, the first Biblical verse just plays the role of a *temporal clause* for the two following verses. Verse 1:1 and verse 1:2 describe an empty and dark world stage, where the first creation – light – would make its luminous impact.

Rabbi Yehuda would read the first three verses in more or less the following way:

> (1) "In the beginning, when God began creating heavens and earth..."
> (2) "the earth was empty, and it was dark over the surface of the abyss, etc. ..."
> (3) "[Then] God said: 'Let there be light!' And there was light."

As will become evident, Rabbi Yehuda's approach gives rise to some sensitive questions about the seminal idea of Creation ex nihilo. If light was indeed the first creation, were heavens and earth still uncreated as of that moment? Or, perhaps, heavens and earth were never created and had existed eternally, as Aristotle taught? We might infer from Rabbi Yehuda's words – in his allegory that compared God with a King building a palace – that there was some preexistent reality ("a dark construction site...") which had to be adapted and rebuilt.

Challenging the opinion of Rabbi Yehuda, we have that of Rabbi Nechemia – who would read verse 1:1 as: "In the beginning, God created heavens and earth [period]." This reading clearly expresses that heavens and earth were created first. Obviously, *before* light. Rabbi Nechemia understands that the absence of the expression "And God said..." does not affect the plain sense of the verse. That the Torah is not explicit in telling us the first act of creation was done through God's speech does not mean it wasn't through His speech.[3] Rather, by omitting such a term the Torah might be saying that God created heavens and earth in a way that was entirely different from the rest of the Creation process. It would have been such an indescribable singularity that the Torah preferred to omit any term telling us anything about the "how" of that event (even a term as innocuous as one telling us that God created through speech). What is beyond doubt is that for Rabbi Nechemia, the actual *act* of creation is clearly and explicitly conveyed in this verse, even if not by any reference to speech, but by the second Biblical word: *bara*, "[God] created."

In Talmudic literature these kinds of disputes are abundant. The next generations of scholars will often revisit earlier debates. Many times, the Rabbis of the following generation don't feel the need to choose between the two or more opinions. Sometimes, as in our case, they do. Seemingly, both sides in this debate had valid textual cues that support their reading. Approximately a century after this debate, the Rabbis added a new element to the argument, which eventually would help to tilt the scales of this debate to Rabbi Nechemia's side.[4]

THE RABBIS' CONCLUSION

In the Mishna – the most authoritative text of rabbinic literature – the tractate of *Pirqe Abot* records an observation by the Rabbis that is very illuminating when read to the backdrop of our debate. The Rabbis noted that in the Torah, God uses ten separate utterances to create the world. Had God wanted, they reasoned, He could have created the world through one sole utterance. God could have simply said: "Let the universe come

---

3   We have previously explained that such would be the idea expressed by Psalms 33, "By the word of God heavens were made."

4   Parenthetically, in the area of Jewish thought, settling – officially – for one school of thought over the other does not mean the permanent exclusion of the rejected idea. Rabbinic Judaism is very open to multiple ideas and interpretations of Biblical stories, and virtually no opinion is ever definitely excluded. This is not the case – for obvious practical reasons – in the realm of Halakha (Jewish Law), where the adoption of a unified, concrete application of the law is often held to the exclusion of all other approaches. In the realm of Haggada, i.e., all non-legal Biblical interpretations, one opinion does not exclude the opposing view. Therefore, the official resolution of a controversy in the realm of Haggada should be understood as "the prevalent" or "the majority's opinion."

into existence," and thus create all what the universe contains. The Rabbis questioned then: Why did God create the world using more than just one expression? Why would God Almighty decide to perform *ten* creative acts instead of just *one*?

The Rabbis explained that the Creator used nine extra statements to create the world, so that we learn from it a lesson in effort, dedication, and care: "God created the world with so much dedication that, instead of merely making it with a single utterance, He used ten entire sentences to create it. This is why the wicked deserve such great punishment. They are destroying a world for which God invested so much more love than what was needed, and which He holds so very precious."[5]

Just like an artisan would dedicate extra effort and additional work to express his love and dedication for the recipient of his art, God Almighty conveyed His love for His creatures by creating this world with ten statements, rather than with one. The punishment for those who destroy this world is ten times severer, and the reward for the righteous – those who care to maintain and preserve this precious world – ten times dearer, because God Almighty invested a tenfold effort in His creative work.

But the Rabbis of the Mishna left one point unclear. That is, what are those ten sentences of Creation, the ten distinct acts or speeches by which – according to their opinion – God created the world? For our discussion on the understanding of the first verse, the answer to this question will prove to be absolutely critical.

Finding ten expressions of Creation would seem to be an easy task. Apparently we just need to locate within the story of Creation the ten instances where the Torah said *vayomer Elohim* ("and God said..."). For example: "And God said: 'Let there be light...'"; "And God said: 'Let there be a sky'"; "And God said: 'Let there be luminaries...,'" etc. But surprisingly, in the Biblical story of Creation, the expression *vayomer Elohim* appears only *nine* times![6]

---

5   Translation from *Torah Anthology, Meʾam Loʾez Commentary of Pirqe Abot* (5:1), by Rabbi Yaʾaqob Kholi, translated from the original Ladino by Aryeh Kaplan, *zʾl* (New York: Moznaim, 1977).

6   In Genesis ch. 1, on the first, second, fourth, and fifth days, the Torah uses for each

In the Talmudic tractate of *Rosh HaShana*, the Rabbis analyzed the statement of the Mishna brought above and discussed *what* the tenth statement may have been.[7] The Rabbis concluded that the first verse of the Torah, "In the beginning God created heavens and earth," should be in itself counted as the first of these ten *expressions* of Creation.[8] In other words, according to the Talmud – which records this opinion and then, notably, offers no challenge to it – the first verse should definitely be seen as the description[9] of an act of Creation, even though divine speech is nowhere explicit in that sentence.

For the Talmud, then, the first verse should not be considered a temporal clause for the creation of light, as suggested by Rabbi Yehuda. On the contrary. The Rabbis validated Rabbi Nechemia's opinion, for whom heavens and earth were created first. The creation of light took place only as a second event.

Following the conclusion of the Rabbis of the Talmud, the first verse has been traditionally understood and translated accordingly:

> "In the beginning, God created heavens and earth [period],"
> and not,
> "In the beginning, *when* God created heavens and earth…."

Additionally, and following unambiguously Rabbi Nechemia's opinion, Maimonides considered that the belief in the Creation ex nihilo of the universe is implied in the fourth principle of the Jewish faith.[10] The fourth principle asserts that *only* God is eternal and excludes, therefore, the idea of any preexistent matter.

But the debate over the translation of the first verse, was not over…

---

day only once the expression "and God said." On the third and sixth days we have two times each day "and God said" and once more in Genesis 2:18.

7   I presented the most basic understanding of the "ten statements of Creation." *Torah Shelemah*, Gen. 9:40, explains that there are five different opinions as to what these ten statements were.

8   Talmud Babli, *Rosh HaShana* 32a. See also *Me'am Lo'ez*, note 7.

9   As we observed in the last chapter, Psalms 33 says: "The heavens were made by the word of God Almighty," and that verse alludes to the first verse of the Torah.

10 See chapter 1, note 2.

Rashi and the "Construct Chain"

"In the beginning, God created heavens and earth,"

or

"In the beginning *of* God's creating heavens and earth...”?

Almost one thousand years after the argument between Rabbi Yehuda and Rabbi Nechemia had taken place, Rashi (Rabbi Shelomo Itzchaqi, 1040–1105), the most famous Biblical commentator, resuscitated the old debate. To better comprehend Rashi's opinion, we need to explore the complexities of the first iconic word of the Torah: *bereshit*, "in the beginning." Although made up of merely six letters, the first Hebrew word of the Torah is not a simple term. It is, perhaps, one of the most sophisticated and complex words in the whole Hebrew Scripture. It is not self-evident what the word *bereshit* really means. This complex Hebrew word is written within an unusual context. Literally translated, *bereshit* means: "In the beginning *of*... God created..." and it leaves the reader wondering: "In the beginning of... *what*?"

Rashi noticed this anomaly and proposed an interpretation that would tentatively resolve the problem. This is the thrust of Rashi's rationale in his commentary to verse 1:1:

1. The first word of the Torah, *bereshit*, does not mean "In the beginning" but according to the basic Hebrew grammatical rules it means "In the beginning *of*...."
2. Consequently, the second word of the Torah, *bara* ("created"), should not be taken literally. It must be interpreted and reread[11] as the participle form *bero* ("to create" or "creating").

---

11 To understand Rashi's commentary and what seems to be an arbitrary alternative reading, the reader should know that the Torah text consists only of consonants; its vocalization depends on the Masoretic tradition, which indicates what the official vocalization of each term is. In other words, the absence of vowels allows, in theory, for several "readings." However, most rabbis would agree that a reading that departs from the Masoretic tradition has only an exegetical value (called *derasha*) which should not replace the literal reading and translation.

3. These two words – *bereshit* and *bero* – should now be considered as one single *semantic unit*, what in grammar is called a "construct chain" (in Hebrew, *semikhut*), and therefore we should read these words as saying: "In the beginning *of* [God's] *creating*...."

4. The first verse is not saying that heavens and earth were created first; consequently, light was the first creation.

Similar to Rabbi Yehuda, Rashi also saw the first verse as a temporal clause setting the stage for the creation of light. Following Rashi's view, the first three verses should be translated in this way:

(1) "In the beginning of God's creating heavens and earth,"
(2) "When the earth was astonishingly empty, with darkness upon the surface of the deep, etc."
(3) "God said: 'Let there be light!' And there was light."[12]

We may now ask ourselves, what brought Rashi to revive this interpretation, after it had been seemingly rejected by the Rabbis of the Talmud?

Conspicuously, Rashi did not mention explicitly Rabbi Yehuda as the source of his opinion.[13] This could be, perhaps, because Rabbi Yehuda's view was rejected by the Rabbis. In any case, Rashi's insight seems to come from an entirely different angle than Rabbi Yehuda's. Rashi elaborates on the unusual form and context of the first Biblical word, *bereshit*, a grammatical inconsistency, as we explained, that begs for an interpretation. Rashi questions the traditionally accepted understanding of *bereshit* as "In the beginning, ..." (with a comma, as it will be explained later), arguing that if the Scripture would have wanted to indicate "In the beginning," the most appropriate word to use would have been *barishona* (at first) and not *bereshit*.[14]

---

12 This is the way Artscroll translates the fist three verses of the Torah. (See *The Chumash*, Artscroll ed. [Brooklyn, NY: Mesorah Publications, 1998].)

13 *Torah Shelemah* 33:205 suggests that the grammatical form of the word *bereshit* is also what brought Rabbi Yehuda to his conclusion about the order of Creation. He sees this point as the connection between Rabbi Yehuda and Rashi.

14 The expression *barishona*, meaning "In the beginning," appears more than twenty times in the Hebrew Bible. See, for example, II Samuel 20:18.

In order to understand Rashi's question and his proposed answer, we need to become familiar with a basic grammatical structure of Hebrew language: the "construct chain."

THE CONSTRUCT CHAIN (*SEMIKHUT*)

At the grammatical level, *bereshit* is a term composed by (1) the Hebrew preposition *be* which means "in, on, or at," followed by (2) the word *reshit*, which is the construct state (explained below) of the noun *rosh*, "head, principal, or beginning."[15]

The Hebrew construct chain (*semikhut*), similar to the English "genitive case," consists in the connection of two words – normally two nouns – forming one semantic unit.

Let us see a classic example of a construct chain. How would you properly say in English "the children of Yosef"?

In English, to build the genitive you must (1) remove the definite article "the" (children of Yosef). Then, you (2) eliminate the preposition "of" (children Yosef), and you (3) add the suffix "*'s*" after the second noun (children Yosef*'s*). Finally, (4) you reverse the order of the terms: "the children of Yosef" will become "Yosef's children."

In Hebrew, to build the construct chain you (1) eliminate the definite article *ha-* ("the"), and (2) the preposition *shel* ("of"). You don't need a suffix,[16] and you don't need to reverse the order of the nouns, but (3) you will have to modify the first noun. Hence, *habanim shel Yosef* ("the children of Yosef") will become *bene Yosef*. The noun *banim* was modified to *bene*.

Once modified, the first word of the construct chain (in English called the "construct state") is known as the *nismakh*. Unlike English, where you will use the same universal pattern – i.e., adding the suffix "*'s*" to the first noun – the Hebrew version of it, the *nismakh*, varies from word to word to convey the construct state.[17] There is no fixed rule as to how you change

---

15 See *Da'at Miqra*, p. 3, note 19.

16 In most cases, the construct chain will also include the hyphen or *maqaf*, e.g., bene-Yisrael.

17 Some suffixes are expressed in the construct state systematically in the same way. For example, the plural -*im* will be modified to *e* (i.e., the vowel *tzere* complemented by a silent letter *yod*). So, *yeladim* will become *yalde*; *sefarim* will become *sifre*, etc.

the first word and convert it into its construct state. The second term in the construct chain (in our example of *bene Yosef*, this would be the word *Yosef*) is called in Hebrew *somekh*, and it always remains unaffected.

Example: The Hebrew word *habayit* means "the house." To use it in the construct state, the word *bayit* is modified to *bet*. To say *habayit shel* ("the house of") *hakeneset* ("the congregation") you should use the construct chain. Removing the definite article *ha*, then removing the preposition *shel* and modifying the first word, *habayit shel hakeneset* will become *bet-hakeneset* ("the congregation's house" = the synagogue).

One last point before we go back to our word *bereshit*. Obviously, at times you may find the word *bayit* (a house) or *habayit* (the house) in isolation or followed by an adjective, as in *habayit halaban* (the white house) or *bayit gadol* (a big house). However, you should expect to *never* find the word *bet* – "the house of..." – in isolation, without being followed by the next word (the absolute or *somekh*)![18] Similarly, in the English language the possessive case always will be followed by another word, usually a noun. To say "the book of John" you will say: "John's book." You might use the noun "John" or the noun "book" in isolation, but you will never use the word "John's" in isolation or followed by a verb.

Now we might be ready to understand Rashi's problem with the word *bereshit*. The word *bereshit* is written in the form that grammarians call the construct state. There are two indications of it being a construct form: First, the word *reshit* is the construct state form of the term *rosh* (beginning).[19] Second, it says **b**e*reshit* and not **b**a*reshit*. In Hebrew, the prefix *ba* is composed of two words: *be* ("in") and *ha* ("the," the definite article) – *be* + *ha* = *ba*. The term **b**a*reshit* would include the definite article *ha* ("the") integrated into the preposition *be*. However, as we have explained, in the

---

18 Very graphically, Hebrew grammar calls or describes the first word of the construct chain as *nismakh*, which means: a word that completely "relies on" the second word. And the second word, which literally "bears" the first word, is a *somekh* (the supporter). In other words, a *nismakh* without its support – a *somekh* – will collapse, by not having any word to rest upon.

19 There are plenty of verses in the Tanakh where *reshit* ("beginning") appears as a construct state of *rosh* ("head" or "beginning"). See, for example, Exodus 23:19, 43:26, etc. The word *reshit* (*bereshit*, *mereshit*) in the construct state form followed by a noun appears forty times in the Tanakh.

construct chain the definite article *ha* is eliminated. The absence of *ba* indicates that this word is in the construct state. Therefore, as Rashi pointed out then, the word *bereshit* means "In the beginning of...."

Literally and linearly, the first verse says:

> *Bereshit / bara / Elohim / et hashamayim / ve-et ha-aretz.*
> "In the beginning of.../ created / God / the heavens / and the earth."

Now, we can finally appreciate Rashi's implicit question: In the beginning of...*what*?

Noticing this irregularity, Rashi writes: "[The anomaly of] this text certainly begs for an interpretation." To solve the problem Rashi opts to recreate a virtual construct chain, suggesting that the word *bereshit* be read followed by an "absolute" (the second word of the construct chain). And to make up for the absent "absolute" (*somekh*), Rashi resorted to interpreting the second Biblical word, *bara* – originally a verb in the past tense – rereading it as the participle: "creating." Why? Because a verb in the past tense cannot be used in a construct chain. You cannot say in English "John's *wrote*..." But you could definitely use a participle and say: "John's *writing*" or "God's *creating*." The verb *bara* ("created"), reinterpreted by Rashi as a participle *bero* ("creating"),[20] plays now a new role – it is the absolute, the second term of the construct chain – allowing us to acknowledge the first word as a construct state.

Therefore, Rashi's rewriting of the initial Biblical verse reads:

> "In the beginning of God's creating heavens and earth...."

Although an infrequent combination – in both Hebrew and English – it is still within the acceptable boundaries of Hebrew and English grammar.

Albeit not explicitly and perhaps involuntarily, Rashi brings us back to the discussion between Rabbi Nechemia and Rabbi Yehuda. His interpretation modifies the traditional reading of the first verse. As Rashi himself argues, the first two verses are now prefacing the creation of light.

---

20 This type of interpretation of the Biblical text is not uncommon. What is indeed unusual is to use this interpretation to render the words in the vernacular.

BEYOND RASHI'S COMMENTARY

Apart from Rashi, other commentators also addressed the problem of the construct state of the word *bereshit*.[21] But unlike Rashi, they found alternative solutions, which did not contradict Rabbi Nechemia's view, that heavens and earth were created first.

One example is the commentary of Ramban, Moshe Nachmanides (1194–1270). Instead of interpreting the verb *bara* as the participle *bero* and reading it as an absolute, he proposed that the reader should add a virtual noun after *bereshit*: an unwritten word that would follow the preposition "of," serving as the absolute we were missing for the construct chain. Anticipating a post-Newtonian conception of physics, Nachmanides proposed the concept "time" as the hidden absolute. Accordingly, *bereshit* would be understood by Nachmanides as:

> "In the beginning of [time], God created the heavens and the earth."[22]

---

21 Not all Biblical commentators agreed that the word *bereshit* is written in a construct state form. No less than Radaq, Rabbi David Qimchi, one of the most illustrious Spanish grammarians of the twelfth century, affirmed in his book *Sefer haShorashim* that the word *reshit* should not be seen as the construct state form of *rosh*, but as a normal independent noun ("beginning"). As a proof for his thesis he refers the reader to a verse in Isaiah 46:10, *Maggid mereshit acharit*, "From the beginning, foretell the end," in which we find the word *reshit* ("beginning") in the role of a standard noun. Rabbi Eliyahu Ashkenazi haMedaqdeq, in his glosses to Radaq's *Sefer haShorashim*, asserts that *reshit* might be considered indeed a normal noun, but the composed word *bereshit* should still be considered a construct state form. Not because of the word *reshit* but because of the vowel under the letter *bet*. If *reshit* were used in a normal way, the letter *bet* should have been written with a *patach* (**ba**reshit), which signals the definitive article. Instead, the Masoretic tradition has the letter *bet* with a *sheva* (**be**reshit), and as we explained, the absence of the definite article is a sign of a *semikhut*. In Hebrew, the noun in isolation and the same noun in the construct state form would have the preposition vocalized differently. For example, the word *sefer* (book) when in a construct state will say: *besefer*, for example, **be***sefer milchamot HaShem*: "in the book of God's battles" (Num. 21:14). When used in isolation, *basefer*, for example: *ketob zot zikaron* **ba***sefer*, "write this as a memorial on the book" (Ex. 17:14).

22 See Nachmanides's commentary in Genesis 1:4. "From the *appearance* of heaven and earth from nothingness to existence, which is mentioned in the first verse, time came into existence. And although our time is [measured] by minutes and hours, established by light and darkness, existence included time." Before Nachmanides, Maimonides also said that time was part of God's creation. See *More Nebukhim* 2:30.

Rashi too contemplated the possibility of conceiving a virtual absolute after the words "In the beginning of..." He proposed that *hakol* ("everything") might be the absent absolute, reading then the first verse as:

"In the beginning of [everything], God created the heavens and the earth."

However, Rashi himself dismissed this hypothesis in favor of his final explanation.

What is worthy of attention is that, in spite of Rashi's arguments, and even though Rashi is considered the father of Biblical commentaries, virtually *all* translators of the Bible – Jewish and non-Jewish alike – have kept with the traditional reading and interpretation of this verse as expressing the initial act of Creation, i.e., the creation of the whole universe, not an introduction to the creation of light. The consensus has been to depart from Rashi's interpretation and to consider *bereshit* the first verse as an independent sentence, not as the temporal clause for the creation of light.

"For some 2,200 years – since the Septuagint version of the Torah...all official translations of the Bible have rendered *bereshit bara Elohim*... In the beginning God created..."[23] That includes no less than Targum Onkelos, the first official rabbinic translation,[24] which also renders *bereshit* as Rabbi Nechemia did: *"beqadmin"* – "In the beginning, God created heavens and earth."

In our days, however, a few contemporary translations of the Torah have diverged from the traditional rendition of the first verse. One translation, for instance, did so simply because its express and declared purpose is to present Rashi's reading of the Torah, rather than the Hebrew Scripture itself.[25] Another modern popular English translation also deviated from

---

23 Harry Orlinsky, *Notes on the New Translation of the Torah* (Philadelphia: Jewish Publication Society, 1962), p. 49.

24 Although the Septuagint is an earlier translation, and according to our tradition it was executed by 70 (or 72) esteemed rabbis, the Jews never considered it a "reliable" Jewish translation, because the rabbis themselves admitted that they felt forced to make certain changes in the translation to avoid offending the sensitivities of the Greek monarch, and other considerations.

25 Loyal to its declared intention (preface, page xiv), the ArtScroll translation of the Pentateuch (*The Chumash*, Brooklyn, NY: Mesorah Publications, 1998) does not

the traditional rendition, because of some considerations of a nature other than semantic, which were factored into the publishers' decision of how to translate the Torah.[26]

I suppose that, over the centuries, translators might have understood that rendering this verse as per Rashi's interpretation would suggest, unintentionally,[27] that God's first creation was light. This is problematic as it suggests a creation unlike the traditional Jewish idea of Creation. Positing light as the first creation might lead one to think that heavens and earth had always been there. Aristotle himself would have been proud of that translation.

---

translate the Torah following necessarily Hebrew grammar, but Rashi's exegesis. All previous traditional Jewish translations viewed Rashi's comment as an interpretation, not as the literal explanation of the first verse. As far as I know, this is the first *traditional* Jewish translation to bring the Scripture closer to the idea of a preexistent cosmos.

26 I'm referring to JPS's translation of Gen.1:1, "When God began to create heaven and earth" (*The Jewish Bible: The Holy Scriptures – The New JPS Translation According to the Traditional Hebrew Text*, 1st ed. (Philadelphia: Jewish Publication Society, 1985), which deviates from Hebrew semantics to conform with Biblical criticism's and Assyriologists' theories. JPS *forced* the word "When" at the very beginning of their Bible to fit the idea that all near Eastern *creation myths* should begin with the proposition "when," following the style of the Sumerian epic *Enuma Elish*, ostensibly the origin of all near Eastern creation myths. According to JPS, the Hebrew Bible as well must have followed the footsteps of those texts, and therefore it is not but logic to impose the preposition "when" at its very beginning – asserting thus, from the first word, their belief in the pagan origin of the Biblical text (see Orlinsky, *Notes*, p. 4). In the first JPS edition in 1917 the first verse was rendered in the traditional way.

27 As we said, ArtScroll radically changed the way traditional Jews have for centuries translated the first *pasuq*. The explicit intention of this reputable publication was undoubtedly to assert the importance of the Oral Torah and the Written Torah's dependence on it. I still believe that a translation based on exegesis rather than in Hebrew semantics is an unnecessary overstatement, which in many instances – and ours is a perfect example – could be detrimental to the original text and involuntarily oppose traditional Jewish principles (i.e., creation ex nihilo). A Jewish translation should follow, first, Hebrew semantics and Hebrew syntax rules (טעמי מקרא). Interpretations should be left as a parallel dimension – a commentary – not integrated into the rendition. By not doing so, one restricts the infinitely rich realm of Biblical exegesis to just one particular view. The art of a Jewish translator consists in finding a word in the vernacular that captures the nuances of the Hebrew term, making sense, as much as possible, of its *many* rabbinic interpretations.

Aptly explained by Levenson: "The traditional Jewish...doctrine of creation ex nihilo can be found in this chapter only if one translates its first verse as: 'In the beginning, God created the heaven and the earth' and understands it to refer to some comprehensive creative act on the first day."[28]

T<small>A</small>'<small>AMIM</small>: B<small>EYOND</small> C<small>ANTILLATION</small>

I believe there is also a very solid grammatical reason to explain why, although written in a construct state form, we should not expect the word *bereshit* to be connected to the next word, as in a construct chain. Rather, *bereshit* should be viewed as an exceptional case of a construct state in isolation – or perhaps as an exceptional *reflexive* construct chain. We explain.

When reading the original Hebrew Biblical text, one will notice that on – or under – each and virtually every word of the Scripture there are "signs" that are not consonants or vowels. They are called the *ta'amim* (plural of *ta'am*), or Masoretic accents.[29] Although it is beyond the scope of these pages to exhaustively explain all the important functions of the *ta'amim*, we must know that these twenty-six signs are absolutely indispensable in order to comprehend the syntax of the Biblical text.[30] The *ta'amim* are the Hebrew punctuation marks, which serve to indicate the end of a verse, the division of the Biblical sentences into half sentences, and the length and composition of smaller semantic units or clauses.

The twenty-six signs of *ta'amim* are divided into two categories:[31] Kings (*melakhim*), and Servants (*mesharetim*) or Assistants to the Kings. Each segment in a Biblical verse is typically composed of one or two of the Servants *ta'amim* and one or two of the Kings type. The Servants' role is to introduce the Kings, to indicate a connection between that word and the following word. The Kings type will always mark a pause in the verse, the

---

28 Jon D. Levenson, *Creation and the Persistence of Evil: The Jewish Drama of Divine Omnipotence* (Princeton, NJ: Princeton University Press, 1998), p. 5.

29 The *ta'amim*, or טעמי מקרא, are sometimes referred to as cantillation marks. They should not be confused with musical notes. The intonation given by each of the *ta'amim* indicates the different roles each *word* plays in the sentence.

30 The main role of the *ta'amim* is to signal which syllable should be accentuated.

31 The Ashkenazi tradition counts three categories: Emperors, Kings and Ministers. The logic behind both traditions is virtually the same.

end of the semantic unit; it will signal unambiguously that the word having a Kings sign is disconnected from the next word.

Some examples of the King-type *ta'amim* are: (1) *Sof-pasuq*. This *ta'am* indicates the end of a verse, a period. It is the most decisive pause in the array of *ta'amim*. (2) *Atnach*. It signals a pause and the thematic halving of a verse. (3) *Tarcha*. It conveys a brief pause, similar to a comma in English.

Now, the word *bereshit* has a *tarcha* mark underneath it, which is a typical *ta'am* of the Kings type. As we explained, the *tarcha* signals a pause, similar to a comma in English. Now, if the word *bereshit* ("In the beginning") comes with a comma, it precludes any semantic connection with the following word (*bara*, "created"). To refresh our memories, by its morphological structure *bereshit* might be viewed as the first term of a construct chain. However, it is impossible to have a construct chain with a King-type *ta'am* separating between the two terms of the construct chain! You cannot have in English a genitive case with a comma in between the two words (as in "Yosef's, children" or "John's, book").

A normal construct-state word would require a Servant-type *ta'am* underneath it, or a hyphen (*maqaf*) in order to point out to the reader that the two (or more) terms of this construct chain are to be read as one continuous semantic unit.[32] The fact that the *ta'am* underneath the word *bereshit* is a *tarcha* is a clear indication of a called-for pause between the first word *bereshit*, and the next one *bara*. We are obligated to read the first Biblical word in isolation, which then eliminates the need – or the possibility – to reread or reinterpret the second word *bara* as *bero*, simply because no construct chain can be built without the necessary connection between a word and the following word.

Because of the *ta'amim*, a reading based upon the construct-chain theory ("In the beginning of God's *creating*...") cannot be considered to be the literal meaning of the word *bereshit*. Rather, it has to be classified under the rubric of non-literal interpretation (in Hebrew, *derasha*).

---

32 As is the case, for example with the second and the third words of the Torah: *bara Elohim*, "God created." Both terms are connected by two *ta'amim*: *shofar holekh* (Servant) under the word "created" and *zaqef qaton* (King) under the word "God."

A Reflexive Construct State?

Once the theory of a construct chain is discarded, we might realize that *bereshit* is a strange – and as far as I know unique – case, with just one of the ingredients of a construct chain. How should we understand, then, the very first word of the Scripture, vocalized as if to be a construct state, but punctuated to stand in isolation?

I would like to offer a possible explanation.

What if this unique combination of a construct-state word ("In the beginning of...") and a comma (*tarcha*) is signaling that the construct state should not be looking to connect with the following word, but rather to connect with, or reflect unto, itself? What if in this case the *construct state* and the *absolute* term were actually the same word? Accordingly, the word *bereshit*, "In the beginning of...," would be reflecting back on itself as a superlative. One would then read *bereshit* as "In the beginning of *beginnings.*" In other words: "In the most absolute beginning."[33] Granted, this syntactical combination would be, as far as I know, unique and unparalleled. But let us not forget that the subject matter dealt with is also unique. The first Biblical term, I believe, might be seen as a *sui generis* word expressing, in an exceptional way, the exceptional idea of the "absolute" beginning. The departure from nothingness. The beginning of time, space, energy, and matter. The initial point of Creation and existence generated by God. An idea which lies beyond human comprehension. It is a construct state to which no second term can be attached, because there is no second term yet. I believe this explanation would be compatible with the traditional translation, and it would also settle Rashi's dilemma.

Summary

We will now present a summary of the main ideas of the first verse of the Torah, when understood as expressing the initial act of Creation.

---

33 Perhaps there is a similar example in Biblical Hebrew. The word "Lords," plural of "Lord," is written *alef-dalet-nun-yod* and a *patach* (a short "a") under the letter *nun*. The most common name of God, *adnut*, is written with exactly the same consonants and vowels, except for the *patach* which is replaced by the *qamatz*, a longer but closed "a." The meaning of this name of God cannot be "Lords" but "Lord of Lords."

The first verse announces the most important and sizable act of Creation. As we will later explain, *the first* is also *the only* act of Creation ex nihilo to take place in the Biblical story of Creation.

Let us now examine it briefly, word by word.

Bereshit: In the Beginning

In the first chapter of this section we compared science's new findings on the origin of the universe with the Biblical story of Creation. We showed how modern science accepts the notion of a non-eternal universe. However, the Biblical principle of creation is not just about the universe having a starting point, but also about the universe having been created by God out of nothing. The fact that the universe was not self-created but was brought to its existence by God makes the studying, understanding, and identifying of the processes of the universe's gestation impossible. When God clarifies to Job that a simple mortal would not be able to fathom God's ways in administrating justice, God illustrates man's intellectual limitations by pointing to the process of Creation: "Where were you when I laid the earth's foundation? Tell me, if you understand.... Who marked off its dimensions? Surely you know! Who stretched a measuring line across it? On what were its foundations set, or who laid its cornerstone" (Job 38:4–6).

The initial act of Creation, by which the whole universe was brought into being, is depicted with a key verb: *bara* (created). In Biblical Hebrew, the verb "to create" (*libro*) is used very meticulously and in limited circumstances. As we will see later on, it refers to bringing something into existence out of nothing previous. The Torah attributes this action exclusively to God and never to a human subject. Creation ex nihilo is a process which no man has ever witnessed and which lies beyond the grasp of human comprehension. This is why the Rabbis regarded cosmology's endeavors – that is, the examination of the origin of the universe – as a journey that will result in mere projections of human imagination and, unsurprisingly, will bring one even further away from what the Biblical story of Creation says truly transpired.

Creation ex nihilo, however, was not the end of the Creation process but just its beginning. There was a second creative step, which following the terminology utilized by the Torah we could call *'asia* or "formation."

There were two distinct stages: (1) Creation ex nihilo (or *beri-a*), and (2) formation (or *'asia*). During the six days that followed the initial act of Creation and until the establishment of the Shabbat, God kept re-creating and transforming planet Earth[34] into a habitat capable of sustaining life, and transforming some previously created elements into life itself. Most creative activities reported in the first chapter of Genesis do not pertain to the category "Creation ex nihilo" but rather to the formation of structures and systems vital to the existence of life, using, modifying, and applying the original elements created ex nihilo; and, as well, to the creation of life. From its second verse and on, the sole focus of the Torah is planet Earth, and there is no Creation ex nihilo anymore. The first verse of the Torah, therefore, reports the creation of the whole universe and it represents the beginning and the end of Creation ex nihilo. Hence its cardinal importance.

Bara: **Created**

In the second chapter of this book we showed that the Biblical Creation story, when read through the eyes of rabbinic tradition, is completely compatible with science's modern discoveries. The main remaining differences are due to: (1) cosmology's conception that the universe appeared through spontaneous generation and evolved through uniform, unchanging, and eternal physical laws; and (2) a poor understanding of the Biblical text.

At this point, I want to add another insight to illustrate this last statement. One of the many questions we should ask ourselves when examining the critical importance of the first verse is related once again to the age of the universe. This time, we are not referring to the age of the universe from the point of view of science as opposed to the age given by the Torah. We want to find out, rather, strictly from the point of view of the Torah: How old is our universe? In other words, when we say "5773 years from the creation of the world," what are we counting from? Is it the verse Genesis 1:1, which describes the beginning of Creation, or is it verse 1:5, when the Torah announces the end of Day One? Or is it the creation of the sun in verse 1:16? Or perhaps it is the creation of Adam?

---

34 I will explain in the following chapter that heavens were not modified any further.

We have already suggested that the six days of Creation might well be considered altogether outside the framework of normal time. Thus, we proposed that they should not be accounted for as normal days, either because of the peculiar flowing of time or because of the nature of the Creation process. Regardless of whether one considers the six days to be within the counting of the 5773 years or outside of that count, there is another more fundamental point to consider. The initial act of Creation, the one we have been referring to – the act in which God brought heavens and earth to being from nothing, the act reported by the second word of the Torah – happened *before* the first day!

Allow me to explain this last point. When did the first day begin? Should we view the initial act of Creation as what initiated the events of the first day? From the textual point of view, the answer is yes. Verse 1:1 is written within the paragraph which deals with the first day (1:1–5). There is no textual indication of a pause between verse number 1 (or 1 and 2) and the other verses of the first day.[35] However, conceptually, a "day" – being as it is a unit of time – needs some referent. A Biblical day is explicitly defined by light. The appearance of light is first reported in verse 1:3. In verses 1:4 and 1:5, light and darkness are separated and the subsequent separation between day and night is established, by which we arrive to the inauguration of Day One (light-darkness = day-night = Day One). If Day One is established by the transition between light and darkness – morning and evening – then its beginning cannot be conceived before light is operative, that is, in verse 1:3! Therefore, heavens and earth were clearly created *prior to* the creation of light, i.e., before Day One began!

If that is so – if the initial creation of earth and the rest of the universe occurred *before* the first day began – then nothing restrains us from assuming that the first act of Creation took place in an *undefined* past, outside the time frame of the six days of Creation, thus rendering the debate on the age of the universe irrelevant.

---

35 The Biblical text is divided by *parashiyot*, i.e., Biblical paragraphs. Each of the days of Creation is enclosed within one *parasha*. The first two verses are integrated within the first day of Creation.

Elohim: **God Almighty**

Elohim, God, is obviously the most important word and the central message of this verse. It affirms that no one else but God created the universe. *When* and *how* the universe was created is of relative importance; the cardinal point of Judaism is that the world was created by God, and is not eternal or self-generated. In the Sephardic tradition God is referred to as *Bore 'Olam* – Creator of the World. From the Biblical point of view, this is the most basic understanding of God.

In tune with this idea, I would like to share with the reader a very bright interpretation of the first word, *bereshit*, by the Italian commentator Rabbi Moshe Chefetz (1663–1711). In his book *Melekhet Machashebet*, Rabbi Chefetz suggests an unconventional interpretation of the word *bereshit* as a construct state in isolation. Unlike the traditional reading of it as a *time* clause for the first verse, Rabbi Chefetz proposed to read it as an axiomatic introduction to the whole Torah. In his view, the first and main purpose of the Hebrew Scripture is to tell its readers that the world has a Supreme Creator: the God of Israel, Who revealed Himself to the people of Israel at Sinai. It is He, the Creator, Who is the Supreme Ruler and the One we need to seek to find our existential mission (of which the Torah is a recipe of sorts). Rabbi Chefetz would interpret the word *bereshit* not as commonly rendered, "In the beginning" (signifying some reference to temporal linearity to the history that follows), but rather as a conceptual *premise*: a word that sets forth to the reader what the book at hand is all about. Accordingly, for Rabbi Chefetz the word *bereshit* should be understood as: "To begin with…."

Following this interpretation the first verse will be saying roughly this: "[The reader of this book should know that] *bereshit* [to begin with]: God is the Creator of heavens and earth."[36]

---

36 This reading, however, is a *derasha*, a creative interpretation. It has not and would likely not be used for an actual translation of the word *bereshit*, not even by Rabbi Chefetz himself.

Et haShamayim ve-et ha-Aretz: **Heavens and Earth**

The final words of our verse say that in this initial act God created the heavens and the earth. If *shamayim* includes everything in the universe except earth, as we have explained, then the idiom *et hashamayim ve-et ha-aretz*, "the heavens and the earth," includes everything – except *life*. And although life itself will be created at a later stage, all the ingredients necessary for the molecular structures of living organisms seem to be part of the creation of heavens and earth. The seeds of life, the basic chemical elements required for biochemical functions – carbon, hydrogen, nitrogen – were probably created within the water and within the earth, as we see from verses 1:20 and 1:24, where God commands water and earth to "bring forth" life from within them.

In the next section, which analyzes the second verse of the Torah, we will witness the state of planet Earth upon its creation and the tools the Creator used to transform it into the habitat of life.

VERSE TWO

"But the earth was desolate and uninhabited, and darkness was over the face of the primitive seas, and a divine wind was blowing over the face of the water."

Genesis 1:2

CHAPTER 4

EARTH'S INVENTORY

While the first verse of Genesis announced the creation of "heavens and earth" by God Almighty, the second verse describes the conditions of planet Earth immediately after its creation and prior to its readiness for harboring life.

> But the earth was desolate and uninhabited, and darkness was over the face of the primitive seas, and a divine wind was blowing over the face of the water.

Genesis 1:2 represents the answer to a simple question: What was the state of the earth upon its initial creation? The first part of the verse focuses mainly on what planet Earth did *not* have. It reports the elements our planet lacked with words and images understandable by those already aware of planet Earth's potential. In its second part, the verse mentions two critical components with which planet Earth was initially endowed. Eventually, these two elements would be used by the Creator to modify earth and produce a living planet. If we are serious about getting a clear picture of the newborn planet, and appreciating how precise is the account given by the Torah on its evolution and adaptation, then we should put an effort into comprehending the particular significance of each and every term of this verse.

The second verse of the Torah is not so easy to understand. It has been explained and translated in such a variety of ways that it is necessary to revisit it word by word. Its strategic placement among the first verses of the Torah makes it all the more important that we understand this verse properly. The elements mentioned in it will be systemically used by the Creator as the story of Creation unfolds. At times this is said very explicitly by the verses; other times it becomes apparent only after a more careful reading. Moreover, a right translation of the second verse will prove critical in light of the theological implications affecting the sensitive issues of creation ex nihilo, anthropomorphism, monotheism, and other basic principles of the Jewish creed.

To achieve our first goal, in this chapter we will focus on finding the *peshat*, the plain conventional meaning of each term, leaving aside allegoric and esoteric interpretations.

The following sources will aid us in our task:

Midrash: The classic Jewish commentators of the Torah were the Rabbis of the Mishna and the Talmud (first to fifth centuries CE). The Midrash (plural *midrashim*) was also composed by them and often included in the Talmud. The Rabbis did not always reach a consensus on the meaning of a Biblical term. Nevertheless, even in such cases, one can easily discern between the minority and majority opinions. I will obviously follow the latter. Another crucial issue we need to examine is if the Rabbis' commentary on a word is meant to be an explanation of that word's *peshat* (the conventional meaning) or a *derasha* (an exegetical exposition of the Hebrew word).

The Targum Onkelos: The Aramaic translation of the Torah, ca. 100 CE, is probably the most important tool at our disposal in the field of Biblical semantics. It was considered the first *official* Jewish translation of the Bible, fully endorsed by the Rabbis of the Mishna.[1] The Targum reflects the lore, exegesis, and formal views of the Jews in rabbinical times. The Targum was considered by the Rabbis part of the oral Torah, the authoritative explanation of the Pentateuch. The Rabbis made it mandatory for every

---

1   The Septuagint (third century BCE), although written by the Jewish Sages of that time, was composed to please the Greek monarch Talmai (Ptolomei), and in many instances the Rabbis deliberately, and sensibly, deviated from the traditional understanding of the Biblical term, adapting the text to Greek culture. They were especially careful not to offend Greek sensitivities. See Talmud Yerushalmi, *Megilla* 1:9; see also ben Israel, *Conciliator*, p. 24, and his observation on the Rabbis' translation of Genesis 2:2: "God ended His creative activity on the sixth day" instead of the original "seventh day." Obviously, the Septuagint does not represent the Jewish tradition but a diplomatic effort necessary in those circumstances.

member of the Jewish people to read the Targum every week as the indispensable companion to the weekly Torah portion.[2]

Word context: An additional and simple way to search for the meaning of a Biblical word is by finding the same term used elsewhere in the Torah or Tanakh. If a term is found in a certain context, the reader may safely assume that term is the most appropriate for that context. Therefore, one can allow the context of a term in one passage to shed light on the meaning of that same term in a different passage. Hopefully, using this technique of finding the same term in a second context – in some cases utilizing Biblical parallelisms or oppositions between the words – should illuminate and elucidate the meaning of an obscure term in our text as well.

The classic commentaries: Finally, the classic commentaries of the Torah, Rashi, Eben 'Ezra, Radaq, Maimonides, and others, who have elucidated the traditional understanding of the Torah based on the above sources, will also guide our task. Once again, for the purpose of this book, I will choose those commentaries and translations that convey the conventional meaning of a word, and which are based primarily on linguistic considerations rather than on exegetical or creative interpretations.

VEHA–ARETZ: "BUT THE EARTH"

An intelligent reading of the Torah demands that we notice not just what the Torah says but also what the Torah is silent about. On that note, an attentive reader will immediately realize an inconsistency between the first and second verses of the Torah. "Heavens," whose creation was acknowledged in the first verse, were omitted from our verse: they are eloquently ignored. In the second verse, the Torah focuses its attention exclusively on planet Earth, while heavens literally disappear from the biblical scene. Radaq[3] explains that the Torah would no longer refer to heavens – which in

---

2   *Berakhot* 8a–b. The Targum is called by the Rabbis תרגום דידן, "our Targum," which means the translation "officially approved by the Rabbis of the Talmud."

3   Rabbi David Qimchi (1160–1235), also known by the Hebrew acronym RaDaQ (רד"ק), was a Biblical commentator, philosopher, and grammarian. Born in Narbonne, Provence, he was the son of Rabbi Joseph Qimchi, a Biblical commentator and grammarian as well. He explains in Genesis 1:2: כי השמים נבראו בשלמותם, "The heavens, all of it, were created in their state of completion...unlike earth that was created incomplete, *tohu vabohu.*"

the context of verse 1 means the whole of the universe except for earth – because through the initial act of Creation, the heavens were finished. The Creator would not modify or improve *these* heavens any further. The formation of the sun, the moon, and the stars on the fourth day will indeed take place in extraterrestrial space. But whatever transformation they are to be subjected to is for the sake of planet Earth (*leha-ir 'al ha-aretz*). These processes belong to the context of earth (the visual "sky"), not to that of heavens.[4]

Rabbi Morris J. Raphall (1798–1868), who coauthored the first Jewish English translation of the book of Genesis with Rabbi David Aron de Sola,[5] found the above idea clearly expressed at the very beginning of verse 2. Raphall does not translate our verse in the traditional way: "*And* the earth was...." Rather, he rendered the first word differently: "*But* the earth was...." Rabbi Raphall, a Ph.D. in Semitic languages, explained in his brief commentary to the Torah that the reason for this variable is due to the *ta'amim*: "The tonic accent *rabia*, which is above this word, indicates that the *vav* prefixed to it is not conjunctive; it must be therefore rendered *but* not *and*." Following the tradition of the great Hebrew grammarians, Raphall understood that the *ta'amim* affect the semantic field of a word.[6]

Following Radaq and Raphall, we should interpret these two verses in the following way:

> In the beginning, God created the heavens and the earth. *Except that earth unlike heavens was still incomplete* [desolate/uninhabited]...

---

4 This concept will be further clarified in the next section of this book.

5 Rabbi David Aron de Sola, I. L. Lindenthal, and Rabbi Morris Raphall, *The Sacred Scriptures in Hebrew and English* (London: Samuel Bagsters and Sons, 1844). The section of Genesis was translated and commented on by Rabbi Raphall.

6 I have examined, superficially, this rule and I've found that in Biblical stories, as opposed to lists, reports, and names, the rule that the *vav* and *rabia'* at the beginning of a sentence conveys a contrast serves to elucidate difficult texts and, very often, helps us understand the rationale of rabbinical exegesis. See, for example, Numbers 22:19 – the story of Balaam and his willingness to accept the mission requested by Balaq is revealed by the rule established by Rabbi Raphall. See also Rabbi Aryeh Kaplan's translation there.

The heavens – roughly 200 billion galaxies, what was called in the language of the Rabbis of the Talmud *tzeba hashamayim*, or "the army of heavens"[7] – had been completed and finalized during that first act of Creation reported in verse 1. Planet Earth at this point is still a work in progress.

Radaq's insight, saying that the Torah leaves the heavens unattended for good, corroborates one of the premises of our present work: that the Torah has no interest or intent in describing the cosmology of the universe-at-large or explaining the physics of the initial act of Creation – i.e., the Big-Bang kind of event. "The heavens are God's heavens; it is earth which [He] gave for man," said the psalmist.[8] The Torah does not seem to consider it necessary to provide the reader with additional information about what went on outside the immediate vicinity of earth. The Torah was written for human beings and intends to provide human beings with context for understanding who we are, what we are, and what our place in God's Creation is. It is *our* planet and its adaptation for life that will take, from now on, the center of the Biblical stage.

HAYETA: "WAS"

As we said previously, the second verse of the Torah is concerned with reporting what was the status of planet Earth in the aftermath of the initial act of Creation described in Genesis 1:1 – not with reporting any new act of creation. This can be inferred, formally, by the tense used for the verb describing the status of the earth: the phrase "the earth was" (*veha-aretz hayeta*) is written in the past-perfect tense (something which, in the past when the events are unfolding, was *already* a reality). This verb form seems to confirm our hypothesis, now from a linguistic viewpoint, that the creation of heavens and earth was separate from, and actually preceded, the events of Day One. The Torah is reporting the *status* of things at a certain point in the past (namely, right after the initial act of Creation), hence setting the stage for more developments and events that start to unfold in verse 3 and further on.

---

7   See Radaq, Gen. 1:2; Talmud Babli, *Berakhot* 35b.
8   Psalms 115:16.

In Hebrew, both simple past (like *bara*, verse 1:1) and present-perfect would be expressed with the same verbal form: *akhal*. However, as pointed out by Rabbi Shmuel David Luzzato (1800–1865),[9] some forms of past-perfect can indeed be expressed in Hebrew by placing the subject before the verb. Here, "*veha-aretz hayeta…*," first the subject and then the verb, should be read as "and the earth was *at that time…*" – namely, at the time it was created. Genesis 1:1 and 1:2, in that sense, are disconnected from the beginning of Day One (Gen. 1:3). The usage of this past-perfect tense "denote[s] an event that took place before the main storyline got underway."[10]

TOHU VABOHU…

Soon into the narrative of Genesis, the Torah provides us with a list (an inventory of sorts) of the elements the earth was equipped with at the moment of its creation, and before it became the hospitable place with which we are familiar. The text describes the present state of the planet, and its readiness or unreadiness for its ultimate goal: sustaining living creatures. The first words the Torah uses to describe our planet are "*tohu vabohu*."

What is *tohu vabohu*? Judging by the diversity of renditions they were given and their profuse exegesis, it seems that these two Hebrew words have perplexed Biblical commentators and translators for centuries. Allow me to begin the analysis of these words by showing how non-Jewish translators and commentators understood *tohu vabohu*.

Most non-Jewish translations have rendered *tohu vabohu* as "chaos," "formless," "disordered," "wasted," "confusion," just to mention a few examples.

These translations convey the idea that at the very beginning, our planet was in a state of a *primeval chaos and disorder*. This is a notion eerily similar to what the Greeks thought the beginning of the world looked like. "Chaos, in early Greek cosmology, is the primeval emptiness of the universe before

---

9   See his מאמר ביסודי הדקדוק, a treatise on Hebrew grammar (Vienna, 1865). If you wish to say in Hebrew "the boy ate" and "the boy has eaten" you would use the same verbal form: הילד אכל. But to say "The boy ate an apple; and the boy had already eaten cake" the Torah would use ויאכל הילד תפוח; והילד אכל עגה.

10 See C. John Collins, *Genesis 1–4: A Linguistic, Literary, and Theological Commentary* (Phillipsburg, NJ: P & R Publishing, 2005), p. 43.

things came into being. In later cosmologies, chaos generally designated the original state of things, however conceived."[11] It seems that these uncommon words *tohu vabohu* allowed opportunistic translators to insert a Greek idea, the concept of primeval chaos, into the Torah.

The following text illustrates what most non-Jewish commentaries would say about *tohu vabohu*:

> The earth was without form and void – The original term Tohu and Bohu, which we translate "without form and void," are of uncertain etymology; but in this place, and wherever else they are used, they convey the idea of confusion and disorder. From these terms it is probable that the ancient Syrians and Egyptians borrowed their gods, Theuth and Bau, and the Greeks their Chaos.[12] God seems at first to have created the elementary principles of all things; and this formed the grand mass of matter, which in this state must be without arrangement, or any distinction of parts: a vast collection of indescribably confused materials, of nameless entities strangely mixed.[13]

Ironically, the alleged Biblical "chaos" – a fabrication of the translators – is uncritically used to show the exchange of mythological ideas like primeval chaos between the Hebrew Bible and ancient cosmogonic myths, particularly, the *striking* parallels between Genesis and the Babylonian myth of creation, *enuma elish*.[14]

The idea of primeval chaos, however, runs against the Jewish view of Creation ex nihilo. A chaotic planet is a perfect Platonic scenario, in which God creates the universe not at a mature and functional state, but just as "matter without form"; that is, matter in a state of chaos. As we are about to see, while the Greeks described a chaotic primeval world, and the god of the Greeks was an arranger of the matter initially created in a pandemonium, the Torah describes a planet that was orderly but not yet ready for life. The

---

11 *Encyclopedia Britannica* (Macropedia), 15th ed., s.v. "chaos."
12 What happened, obviously, is exactly the opposite: *tohu vabohu* was translated as "wasted and unformed," having in mind the Greek Primeval Chaos.
13 Adam Clarke (1762–1832) in his commentary to the Bible, Genesis 1:2.
14 H. Gunkel, Genesis, HKAT I.1, Göttingen, 1910.

creation of light, the weather system, the atmosphere, dry land, etc., are not meant to overcome primeval chaos, but rather to allow the existence of living organisms.

Most classic Jewish commentaries – and the Biblical text itself – confirm that *tohu vabohu* convey an idea different from "primordial chaos."

The Targum Onkelos, written more than 1,900 years ago, defined *tohu vabohu* as "desolate and empty" (*tzadya vereqanya*). The Aramaic word *tsada* or *tsadi* means desolate, unpopulated.[15] The second Aramaic word, *reqanya,* like the Hebrew *req,* means "empty." For the Targum, no primitive chaos is implied in the words *tohu vabohu.* The earth being desolate and empty implies absolutely nothing that could be associated with "a vast collection of indescribably confused materials, of nameless entities strangely mixed." According to the Targum Onkelos, *tohu vabohu* is not referring to the chemical or physical *disorder* of the planet. What the text is saying, simply, is that planet Earth – created to eventually blossom with life – is still lifeless at this early stage. In other words, life was not included within earth's original package. At this moment, planet Earth is formed as a planet, but is still deserted and desolate, unready to host life.

A second translation to Aramaic, traditionally known as Targum Yehonatan Ben 'Uziel, expands on Targum Onkelos' rendition and provides us with some more detail on the intended meaning of the original pair of words. Targum Yehonatan writes that the earth was: "desolate *of people* and empty *of animals.*" Not chaos, but biological desolation and lifelessness. Neither humans nor animals inhabited planet Earth at its inception.

Further analysis of these words elsewhere in the Bible reveal time and again that *tohu vabohu* express "desolation" and "solitude," rather than "chaos," "lack of form," "waste," or "confusion." In the book of Isaiah (45:18), the term *tohu* defines a desolate and unsettled land. In one particular passage, the prophet describes God as the Supreme Creator of the universe. At one point the text states: "[God] did not create this world to be *tohu* [desolate] but *lashebet yetzarah* [to be settled, He created it]."[16]

---

15 Marcus Jastrow, *Dictionary of Targumim, the Talmud Babli and Yerushalmi, and the Midrashic Literature* (1926), p. 1262.

16 The word *tohu*, which is actually more frequent in the Hebrew Scripture than *bohu*, appears once again in the Torah in a Biblical poem *Shirat Ha-azinu*: ובתהו ילל ישמן,

The syntagmatic opposition of *tohu* with *lashebet* ("settled") leaves no doubt about the meaning of the first word. *Tohu* means unsettled.

As if conveying the modern literary concept of a flashback (also known by its technical term "analepsis"), our Rabbis understood that the first verses of the second chapter of Genesis are really expounding upon, and in greater detail, the same events which had been narrated in the first chapter. Verse 4 of the second chapter (2:4) "These are the accounts of the heavens and the earth when they were created, on the day that God made earth and heavens," parallels Genesis 1:1. Verse 2:5 paraphrases the content of verse 1:2, reporting the absence of life in our planet: "And no plant of the field was yet in the earth, and no herb of the field had yet sprung up; for HaShem God had not caused it to rain upon the earth: and man did not yet exist, who could work the land." To me, it is as if this verse could be seen in its entirety as the explanation of the words *tohu vabohu* – the absolute lifelessness that reigned on earth when it was created. No plants, no rain, nor animals or humans. These two words, *tohu vabohu*, are paraphrased by one entire verse, Genesis 2:5.

Unlike the standard renditions "wasted," "formless," and "void," the notion of "deserted and desolate" indicates the biological or demographic condition of our planet. *Tohu vabohu*, if said about planet Mars, would be the language chosen by a biologist who explores the presence of life on the red planet, and not the terms conveyed by a chemist or a physicist, who is likely more interested in Mars' mineralogy, chaotic landscape, or unstable climate.

In conclusion, *tohu vabohu* does not mean that the planet was created in a state of chaos and confusion, but that no life was found in it. *Tohu vabohu* means to say that earth was *still* "uninhabited" and "desolate."[17] Both words convey the idea of complete lifelessness. Pointedly summed up by Radaq: "And the earth, in the beginning of its creation, was not finished but *tohu vabohu*, that is, desolate from every living creature on it, because [the earth]

"[a land] in desolation, a howling wilderness" (Deut. 32:10). The parallelism is *eretz midbar*, a "deserted" or a "desolated" land. This expresses the same meaning the Targumim conveyed in our verse: a lifeless place or an unpopulated area.

17 I prefer these terms to the term "emptiness," which might be a little more ambiguous.

was completely covered by water."[18] As Radaq pointed out, at the stage of Genesis 1:2, planet Earth still needs to undergo a process of dramatic adaptation during the following six days, before finally being ready for hosting living creatures (*nefesh chaya*). Earth's ultimate potential will be achieved only when the planet is equipped to host intelligent life, which will effectively happen only at the end of the sixth day, which culminates the process of Creation altogether.

On this note, we might ask ourselves: Why was planet Earth created *tohu vabohu* – lifeless? Why didn't God create instead a planet thriving with life from its inception? The Torah wished to convey that life was not "naturally" generated by the elements that God created during the initial act of Creation. God did not create a self-sufficient and will-deprived mechanism known as "Nature," which would eventually engender and sustain life *spontaneously*. Life would be designed, crafted, gradually produced, and supported by the Creator's will: "The substance of all things, and their properties, and the laws that regulate and determine their activities, were created by God out of His free will. He could have created the Universe in a different way; and, consequently, He could change them [these laws], if he wishes so. There is no necessary inherent order in the cosmos. The concept of Nature as a self-contained system is profane to Judaism."[19]

The next two terms we are about to explore, "darkness" and *tehom*, or "deep waters," will expand on the meaning of *tohu vabohu* – our planet's lifelessness. With fascinating textual dynamics, the second pair of words will subtly modify the first pair of words. *Tohu vabohu* will be redefined from "uninhabit-*ed*" to "uninhabit-*able*," and from "desolate" to "inhospitable."

VECHOSHEKH: "AND DARKNESS..."

"Darkness" – *choshekh* – was one of the elements planet Earth contained at the time of its creation.

The term *choshekh*, darkness, is normally understood as absence of light. Both in Genesis 1:4 ("And God saw that light was good; and God

---

18 Radaq, Gen. 1:2.
19 José Faur, *The Naked Crowd: The Jewish Alternative to Cunning Humanity*, 1st ed. (Pompano Beach, FL: Derusha Publishing, 2009), p. 105.

separated light from darkness") and in Genesis 1:5 ("And God called the light Day, and the darkness He called Night"), darkness is presented in clear syntagmatic opposition to light. In the context of verses 1:4 and 1:5, all Jewish Biblical commentaries agree that darkness simply means absence-of-light. However, there is no consensus among the Rabbis about the nature of the darkness presented earlier, in our verse Genesis 1:2.[20]

Rabbi Sa'adia Gaon (882–942)[21] and a few other commentators maintained that "darkness" in verse 1:2 should also be understood as absence of light. For them, the darkness of Genesis 1:2 is the same darkness as that in Genesis 1:4, which God distinguished from "light" and then named "night" (Gen. 1:4). In Rabbi Sa'adia Gaon's opinion, the difference between the formation of darkness and the formation of light is that the Torah did not narrate the creation of darkness as being a discrete act of Creation – as opposed to what it did with light.

Most Biblical commentaries and midrashim disagree with this position. Darkness in Genesis 1:2 could not be referring to absence of light, because light had not yet been created. In Plato's famous metaphor of the dark cave, those who have lived forever in darkness cannot perceive darkness as such, unless they first grasp what light is. Similarly, Biblical commentators reasoned darkness as absence of light would not make sense before light is created.

The Rabbis explain that although the Torah uses the word "darkness" in verse 1:2, the Biblical text is referring to something of an entirely different nature than darkness in verses 1:4 and 1:5.

Before I continue with the elucidation of the concept of darkness in Genesis 1:2, allow me to explain a very important principle, often ignored in Biblical exegesis,[22] which is absolutely critical for the understanding of

---

20 This was actually one of the questions Alexander the Great asked the Rabbis of the Negeb: whether light preceded darkness or darkness preceded light. See Talmud Babli, *Tamid* 32a. The Rabbis opted for a diplomatic answer.

21 Rabbi Sa'adia Gaon was born in Egypt in 882 and died in Baghdad in 942. He was a prominent rabbi, philosopher, and Biblical commentator during the Geonic period. He is considered the founder of Judeo-Arabic literature. He was known for his works on Hebrew linguistics and Jewish philosophy.

22 Especially for those defined as Biblical literalists, homonyms represent a heavy

the debate about darkness, and in general, to realize the intricacy of the story of Creation.

In his work *More Nebukhim* (*Guide for the Perplexed*), Maimonides wrote extensively about the wide usage of homonyms[23] in the Hebrew Scripture. Homonyms are two words that, having the same pronunciation, convey different meanings. Maimonides states in the introduction to his book that the first reason he wrote the *More Nebukhim* is to explain this puzzling phenomenon, and clarify Biblical homonyms[24] according to their different contexts. Homonyms are common throughout the Tanakh, and they are exceedingly prevalent in the Creation story.

A few examples:

1. In Genesis 1:1 the term "heavens" (*shamayim*) – standing in opposition to earth – clearly means "everything in the universe aside from earth." However, in Genesis 1:8, the same word "heavens" means "sky" – a newly created entity, the earth's atmosphere – the locale of the clouds.

2. In Genesis 1:1, "earth" (*eretz*) means planet Earth, whereas in Genesis 1:10 "earth" means dry land or continental land. In Genesis 11:1 "earth" means: men, humankind, civilization. Within the same semantic field, sometimes *eretz* means ground or dirt,[25] sometimes a piece of land, a property,[26] and most of the times in the Hebrew Bible it means: a land, a location, a country, or the Land of Israel.

3. In Genesis 1:1, the term *Elohim* means God Almighty, and in the very next verse, as we will later explain, it might also mean "powerful." Elsewhere, *elohim* also means judges or a judicial court, prophets, angels, powerful men, and gods or idols.

stumbling block on the way to apply the same meaning into numerous different contexts.

23 Maimonides calls them שמות משותפים.

24 *More Nebukhim* (Schwarz, p. 9). See note 8 where Professor Schwarz explains the differences between homonyms and other instances in which the semantic field of a word is expanded beyond its conventional meaning.

25 Probably Gen. 2:5 and in many more occasions.

26 Gen. 23:15.

4. The term *yom* ("day") is probably the most polysemic term of the Creation story. In Genesis 1:5 the word *yom* appears twice. The first time it means "daytime," in opposition to "nighttime." The second time, it clearly indicates the continuum of day-night: a whole day. In Genesis 2:4 *yom* – "day" – does not mean one day, daylight, or a solar day, but rather signifies an indefinite period of time, consisting of a series of many days (or at least six days). In a different context it means "night"! As noted by Rabbi Menashe ben Israel, in Numbers 8:17, "On the *day* that I smote the firstborns," the word "day" actually means "midnight."[27]

The esoteric character of the story of creation (*maʾase bereshit*) – and why we need tradition to achieve any understanding of it whatsoever – might be attributed to the profusion of homonyms rather than to the obscurity of its terms.

Back to darkness. Given the abundance of homonyms in the Creation narrative,[28] it should not be in any way surprising that most commentators view darkness in verse 1:2 as of a different essence than darkness in verses 1:4 and 1:5.

There is an additional reason why the Rabbis thought that darkness in Genesis 1:2 should not be understood as the mere absence of light. The prophet Isaiah said that God "created" darkness: [God is] "the Producer of light, and the Creator of darkness" (Isaiah 45:7). This implies that darkness was created, much like light was created (or formed) at a second independent step, and not as part of the initial act of Creation reported in verse 1:1. Furthermore, the order in which these two Creations are presented in Isaiah, first light and then darkness, should lead us to understand that

---

27 "...[F]or the plague of smiting the firstborn occurred at night, therefore it [*yom*] cannot correctly be there translated day. Rabbi Samuel of Urbino cites many other passages in his [book of] synonyms, where it [the word *yom*] will admit no other interpretation" (Ben Israel, *Conciliator*, p. 26). Samuel or Solomon de Urbino was the author of *Ohel Moʾed*, a concise lexicon of Hebrew synonyms (Venice, 1548).

28 Accordingly, the challenge of Genesis chapter 1 lies in finding the meaning of every word according to the different contexts. Probably Maimonides was hinting to this at the very end of *More Nebukhim* 2:29.

the darkness of verses 1:4–5 is not merely the inherent state of a reality before light, but an independent creation posterior to light. The Rabbis did not find it sensible that mere absence of light, before light was brought into existence, would be technically called by the verse in Isaiah a "creation,"[29] or that the terms of this verse could be reversed, referring to pre-light darkness.

Now, if the darkness of verse 1:2 is not merely the absence of light, because light had not yet been created, what then was the nature of this darkness? (For practical reasons and to explain these last opinions, we will hereafter refer to the darkness of 1:2 as "primeval darkness").

Two main schools defined primeval darkness:

1. Maimonides construed verse 1:2 as listing the four primeval forms of matter: Earth, Water, Air, and Fire. Earth in his view is signified by *tehom*, the bottom or surface of the planet. Water, *mayim*, is explicitly mentioned at the end of the verse. Air is the *ruach* ("wind"). And Fire is...*choshekh* ("darkness")! Maimonides understood the term darkness not as an obscure but rather as an *invisible* element.[30] Anticipating modern science – or post-modern science – Maimonides identified darkness as the primeval fire (*esh yesodit*), an invisible fire, or, as explained by Rabbi Menachem Kasher in *Torah Shelemah*, an invisible form of energy.[31]

---

29 See *Torah Shelemah*, Gen. 54:294.

30 *More Nebukhim* 2:30.

31 Maimonides's opinion on the nature or substance of primordial darkness, and Rabbi Menachem Kasher's (1895–1983) interpretation of it is fascinating. In Rabbi Kasher's monumental book *Torah Shelemah*, published in New York in 1949 – an encyclopedic work that quotes virtually all Midrashic and Kabbalistic sources on each Biblical verse, with his interpretations and commentaries – he quotes Maimonides's explanation of "darkness," adding that, in his opinion, the nature of this primeval dark fire was finally revealed in modern times. He then identifies darkness with radioactivity: "In the year 5651 (1891) 'radios' was discovered. [An energy] which is treasured in the element called Uranium...and it can illumine by itself without reflecting a light...." Rabbi Kasher also hinted that *choshekh* or *esh yesodit* could be identified with *chomer ha-electry* (electricity), which was also "discovered by a celestial event"... probably hinting to Benjamin Franklin's famous kite experiment; see *Torah Shelemah* 55:294. As we

2. Most Rabbis identified primeval darkness with a dense substance, which would potentially impede light but is not necessarily related to light.[32] The vast majority of commentators said that it must have consisted of a substance similar to a thick fog – *edim 'abim memiyim* ("[dark] watery vapors") – and they compared primeval darkness with the ninth plague, also called *choshekh*, which God Almighty brought upon Egypt before the exodus took place.[33] There the Torah reports that due to this darkness "no one could recognize his brother, and no one stood up in Egypt, for three days."[34] Nachmanides reasoned that had the darkness in Egypt been merely the absence of light – like a major eclipse or any other natural phenomenon preventing sunlight – the Egyptians could have used candles, torches, or fire to illuminate their residences and continue their lives, as they did during normal nighttime. But this darkness that descended upon Egypt, we are told, literally *paralyzed* Egypt for three consecutive days. Nachmanides then concluded that the ninth plague was not merely the absence of light. The land of Egypt was enveloped by a dark substance, which, besides impeding light to come through, also "extinguished fire, similar to what happens in deep caves or high in the mountains...."[35]

---

said, this dark fire should be understood as invisible energy. Clearly, the identification of Biblical terms or elements found in the Torah or rabbinic literature with recently discovered elements is not an endeavor without its risks.

32   The main argument in favor of this assumption is the verse from Isaiah: *Yotzer OR ubore choshek*. *Choshekh* is a tangible creation, not the mere inherent absence of light.

33   *Torah Shelemah* 54:394. See also *Da'at Miqra* page 6, notes 36 and 38. This opinion, that darkness is likened to *edim* or thick fog, is probably based on the understanding that the first introductory verses of Genesis ch. 2 – the elaboration on the process of Creation – rephrases the first verses of chapter 1. Genesis 1:1 is parallel to Genesis 2:6, etc. In this sense, ואד יעלה מן הארץ ("and a thick fog/mist went up from the earth") might parallel the term "darkness" of Genesis 1:2. We already commented on the parallel between תהו ובהו and ואדם אין לעבד את האדמה.

34   Ex. 10:23.

35   Ramban, Ex. 10:23.

Based on Nachmanides's commentaries, primeval darkness mentioned in 1:2 might be referring to earth's atmosphere in its embryonic state – a primeval and toxic atmosphere. Scientists explain that the early atmosphere of the earth consisted of a dense, thick layer of gases covering our planet, with a very low presence of oxygen. Similarly, planet Venus's atmosphere is depicted by scientists as a "blanket" of carbon dioxide and thick clouds of sulfuric acid, chlorine, and fluorine. Planet Earth, covered by primeval darkness, might have been not just a dark planet, but a planet with an atmosphere unfriendly to life. Like Venus, a dark and hostile-to-life global substance engulfing planet Earth would obviously render it unsuitable for life at this stage. Thus, if *tohu vabohu* conveyed that the planet was uninhabited, desolate, and lifeless, *choshekh* now clarifies the reason for earth's desolation: at this point earth is uninhabitable – it still lacks the basic atmosphere required to sustain life.

With this interpretation of primeval darkness in mind, we understand now why on the very next day, the second day of Creation, the Creator fashioned the *raqia'*, the "clear sky," or earth's definitive atmosphere, displacing *choshekh*, the toxic gases, and bringing the skies closer probably to their present condition.

We will proceed now to the next word, *tehom*, which will hopefully help us to better appreciate the nature of that primeval darkness.

"...OVER THE FACE OF *TEHOM*"

Tehom is probably the most difficult word to translate in the second verse of the Torah. We cannot use the Targum Onkelos, since it just transliterates *tehom* to the Aramaic parallel *tehoma*. In this case we are left without its priceless guidance. Many classic commentaries have not delved into the meaning of this word, as they had done with other terms like darkness or *tohu vabohu*. Most translations rendered *tehom*, almost mechanically, as "deep," "abysses," or "sea abyss."

Following our methodology, we are left with the task of comparing other instances, a total of thirty-six, in which the word *tehom* appears in the Hebrew Scripture to illuminate the meaning of *tehom* in Genesis 1:2. And, as the reader will see, even then, the results are not unambiguous.

In the Torah itself the word *tehom* appears six additional times.

The Flood: The first time the word *tehom* appears in the Torah after verse 1:2 is also in Genesis, in the story of the flood. It appears twice in this section: "In the second month, on the seventeenth day of the month, all the springs of the great *tehom* breached through, and the apertures of heavens were opened" (Gen. 7:11). The flood wasn't just a massive rainstorm falling for forty consecutive days. The Torah explicitly tells us that rain was the secondary cause of the flood. The first cause of the flood was the opening of "all the springs of the great *tehom*." Water, or some other sort of fluid (the text does not mention any specific liquid), coming from the underground in enormous quantities was actually the primary reason for the earth's flooding. In the original words of Rabbi David Aron de Sola, the Torah is describing here "volcanic eruption which opened subterranean fountains and caused the seas to rise."[36] The springs of the great *tehom* closed up again at the end of the flood (Genesis 8:2). In the context of the flood, *tehom* seems to indicate a liquid, or its source, which comes up from underground, i.e., hot-springs, or even submarine seismic movements, which opened and then closed up, allowing water and/or some other sort of liquid (magma?) to come up to the earth surface and "caused the seas to rise." According to this, *tehom* in Genesis 1:2 would be describing water or other liquid coming up from the underground or undersea.

The Red Sea: The word *tehom* also appears twice in the description of the waves of the Red Sea. When the Torah describes the opening of the Red (or Reed's) Sea and the formation of two columns of water, the text says: "The *tehomot* paralyzed [literally, froze] in the heart of the sea" (Ex. 15:5). The dynamic *tehomot* (presumably, waves)[37] stood still, erect, as two columns of water atop the seafloor, to allow the Jewish people to cross the sea.[38] Later on, the *tehomot* covered Pharaoh's army (Ex. 15:8), drowning them to death in the depths of the sea. Here, *tehomot* could have been translated as "depths," except that "depths of the sea" is expressed in

---

36 De Sola et al., *Sacred Scriptures*, Gen. 7:11, p. 30.

37 In the Pentateuch the word *gal* means "a small heap of stones" (for example, Gen. 31:46), while in the rest of the Scripture, it means "sea waves," similar to modern Hebrew.

38 See *Sefer haShorashim*, the Hebrew root t/h/m (תהמ), page 817.

this same text with the term *leb-yam* (Ex. 15:6) – literally, the heart of the sea – or *metzolot* (Ex. 15:8) – the deepest part of the sea – and not with *tehomot*. The word *tehomot* seems to signify the sea waves coming from the depths of the sea or the moving waters of the sea. The sea waves move or become congealed, standing on the sea bed, at the will of the Creator. In this text *tehom* cannot possibly be identified with underground water as in the previous case. Rashi *in situ* states that the word *tehom* is synonymous with "seas."

The Land of Israel: *Tehom* also appears twice in Deuteronomy, when Moses describes the divinely blessed Land of Israel as possessing springs or natural sources of underground fresh water (Deut. 8:7),[39] and especially in the territory of Yosef (Deut. 33:13). In this case, we cannot translate *tehom* as anything related to the sea. The text is clearly describing freshwater springs, which are located under the *ground*, not under the *sea*.

The common point of all these cases is that *tehom* and *tehomot* seem to indicate freshwater, sea water, or any other liquid, coming upward from the seabed, from the sea bottom, or from underground sources. In other parts of the Scripture *tehom* produces noises or voices,[40] probably when the sources of the *tehom* open up and become active. For the most part, and as expressed by Rashi in Exodus, in the rest of the Hebrew Scripture *tehom* is used as a synonym for sea.[41]

The definition of *tehom* is not only important for itself, but is also crucial for a clearer understanding of primeval darkness in Genesis 1:2. The verse states that "[there was] darkness over the face of the *tehom*." Does it mean that darkness covered the sea on the earth's surface, or that darkness covered the surface of the seabed, as the word *tehom*, or abyss, would suggest?

In light of the intricacy of the term *tehom*, I will now present three possible explanations. Each of these explanations has to take into consideration, in addition to the specific meaning of the word *tehom*, the

---

39 Some of them are: The springs in the immediacy of Yam Kinneret, the springs of Gichon, 'En Gedi, Banyas in Tel Dan, Bet-Shean, and the hot springs of Tiberias.
40 Psalms 42:8, 148:7, Chabaquq 3:10.
41 See Jonah 2:6 and Rashi in Exodus 15:8.

textual connection between *tehom* and darkness as well as the usage of the prepositional phrase "over the face of" (*'al-pene*) which precedes *tehom*.

1. Following the traditional understanding of *tehom* as deeps, depth, seafloor (Nachmanides's interpretation is sea-mud), abysses, or irregular formations on the seabed, Genesis 1:2 is saying that primeval darkness was also prevalent *under* the sea, covering the surface of the seabed. Accordingly, the expression "darkness over the abyss" might be expanding the meaning of *tohu vabohu*, saying that lifelessness was the state not just of the surface of the earth, but of the sea as well, from bottom to top.

2. A second possible way to understand *tehom* would result from the more general usage this word has in the Hebrew Scripture, especially in the episode of the splitting of the Red Sea. *Tehom*, as Rashi explained, simply indicates the sea, the sea waves, or by extension, the dynamic behavior of the sea surface. The understanding of *tehom* as "sea surface" in 1:2 is supported by a textual parallel in the book of Proverbs, where *tehom* is again preceded by the preposition *'al-pene*, "over the face of" (*'al-pene tehom*). "When He established the heavens, I [wisdom] was there; when He inscribed a circle *over the face* of the *tehom*" (Proverbs 8:27). *Da'at Miqra* explains that this verse, which connects "heavens" with "*tehom*," refers to the precise point where heavens and *tehom* touch one another; that is, the horizon. The noun *panim* (*pene* is its construct state) is used, without exception, to indicate something external, superficial, visible, not something that lies under several billions of tons of sea water, like the depth of the oceans or seabed. Thus understood, even if *tehom* could sometimes serve to indicate the undersea, the entire expression "over the face of the *tehom*" (*'al-pene tehom*), taken as a whole, would not indicate a location near the seabed, and should rather be understood as above or over the sea surface. The surface, obviously, is the only possible point of contact between heavens and the sea. The preceding preposition *'al-pene* – over the face – indicates, unambiguously, that *tehom* is not referring to a place under the sea, but above the sea. If *tehom* points to the sea surface, then "darkness" might point out the dense atmosphere that was enveloping planet Earth in this primitive state.

3. Based on the flood narrative, and understanding *tehom* as some sort of underground output of the earth – dynamic sea-floors that opened,

closed, and produced noise and huge amounts of liquid – it will be possible to identify *tehom* in Genesis 1:2 with the geological activity scientists have called outgassing. In the initial states of the formation of our planet, all kinds of liquids, vapors, gases, and ashes were coming up from marine ridges, plate tectonics, or other fractures of the earth's crust. The volcanic ashes, smoke, and other gasses coming from underground, reaching and *covering the face of the seas,* will seamlessly fit the description of primeval darkness, i.e., a thick, dark substance enveloping the planet's surface. This idea will also explain the connection of darkness with *tehom. Tehom* would indicate the source of primeval darkness: the dark toxic substance coming up from huge craters or fissures under the sea and the ground. Additionally, understanding *tehom* as some kind of fluid gushing through as a consequence of volcanic or seismic activity will also be consistent with what we said earlier, that the Torah at this point is expanding on the concept of the world's inhospitality. Earth's atmosphere is still completely hostile to life, much like Venus's atmosphere, composed of carbon monoxide, sulphide, sulfur dioxide, etc.

Accordingly, "and darkness over the face of *tehom*" should be understood as "a toxic darkness coming from the underground *tehom.*" Following this interpretation, the whole phrase, "and darkness over the *tehom,*" is prefacing the creation of the second day – the life-friendly atmosphere – by making the reader aware of all the elements that made earth's primitive atmosphere unsuitable for life up till that point.

Finally, this explanation of primeval darkness and *tehom* would sound remarkably compatible with the way scientists explain the early history of earth and how they describe earth's primitive atmosphere, presumably shaped mainly through the effects of massive underground activity, which they called outgassing:

> Where then, did the gasses of our present atmosphere originate? One likely source was outgassing, the release from the interior of the hot, young Earth of water and trace gases trapped in rocks. Compound of hydrogen, carbon, oxygen, and nitrogen such as carbon dioxide, ammonia methane, and a large amount of water worked their way to the surface of the molten Earth.

Even after Earth had cooled and formed a solid crust, outgassing during volcanic eruptions would have continued. The gases found in Earth's atmosphere and hydrosphere...[were] given off by volcanic eruptions and emitted by other sources such as hot springs, geysers, and fumaroles.[42]

Following the opinion that darkness is a substance, and not the mere absence of light, the expression "darkness over the face of the *tehom*" might be indicative of the nature of earth's early dense atmosphere. In a sense, the face of the *tehom* here is equivalent with the face of the planet. The fact that the Biblical text describes *darkness* atop the *tehom* or sea and not atop the planet (the Torah could instead have said: "and darkness over the face of the earth") confirms the Rabbis' theory that at this point there was no dry land on earth, but our planet was completely covered by water.

A planet under water and with a hostile atmosphere cannot yet harbor animals, human life, or vegetation. Darkness, a toxic atmosphere, and *tehom*, the primeval seas covering the planet, are explaining *why* the earth was *tohu vabohu*, or inhospitable.

There is one last question that needs to be addressed before we continue with the next word. If *tehom* is not "abyss" or "depth" but the sea, i.e., the water covering the earth, why would the Torah use in 1:2 the word *tehom* and not the more common term "sea" (in Hebrew, *yam*)? I think that this is because the Torah reserves the term "sea" for verse 1:10 – when the story of Creation reports the *organization* of the seas or oceans on the third day. God then gathered all the waters and separated the waters from the continental land. Then, the Torah mentions seas and oceans. It is as if before being organized into the seas they were called *tehom*. Additionally, (or alternatively) it seems that the Torah would use the term "sea" only when sea stands in opposition to dry land, and at this point, as we soon will see, there was no dry land on the planet. This might also be the reason why at the end of this verse the Torah used the more general word "water" – "and a wind [was] blowing over the face of the *water* [*mayim*]" – instead of the more common word "sea," which the Torah seems to reserve for the

---

42 Edward Denecke, *Let's Review: Earth Science – The Physical Setting*, Barron's Review Course Series (New York: Barron's, 2007), p. 208.

later stage, when water and land are separated and reorganized into two independent entities.

Summarizing, the Biblical expression "and darkness over the face of the primeval sea" seems to be describing the primeval and toxic atmosphere covering the watery surface of the planet. With these two words, *choshekh* and *tehom*, the Biblical text expands or explains the causes of *tohu vabohu* – i.e., the absence of human and animal life on the face of the earth.

We should not be surprised that the Torah starts the story of Creation by describing what planet Earth did *not* have. In this way, the text is preparing us for what is coming up next: during the following two days the Creator will *fix* these two negative elements, *choshekh* and *tehom*. On the second day, the Creator will reverse primeval darkness or the toxic atmosphere, fashioning an atmosphere that supports life. On the third day, God will make dry land appear over the water's surface, displacing the *tehom*. Once that stage is achieved and the earth is ready to host life, God will finally reverse *tohu vabohu*, lifelessness, bringing into existence the first living creatures.

"AND A DIVINE WIND BLOWING..."[43]

The translation of these two words, *ruach Elohim*, is key to understanding (or misunderstanding) Genesis 1:2 and the *entire* sequence of the Creation process.

In Biblical Hebrew *ruach* simply means "wind." But the term *ruach* is a common homonym. It could be also referring to breathing,[44] the soul,[45] or to inspiration (i.e., an invisible intellectual, physical, or psychical mood which *moves*, inspiring or motivating humans – especially prophets). It is often a positive kind of mood, but *ruach* could also be a *ruach ra'a* – a

---

43 It is also possible to understand these words as saying: "A strong wind was violently shaking the waters," probably making huge waves. The word *merachefet* is usually understood as "hovering" but it could also mean "shaking." See Jeremiah 23:9.

44 Gen. 7:22.

45 The same ambiguity (breathing and soul) could be found in the famous verse where the Creator insufflates into Adam a breath or spirit of life (Genesis 2:6). See also Isaiah 42:5 and Ezekiel 11:19.

negative state of mind, or depression – like the mood that at times affected King Saul.[46]

In the Torah, the combination of these two words, *ruach Elohim*, was used in two more instances, expressing a special type of wisdom and inspiration possessed by humans who were particularly inspired by God Almighty. When Pharaoh marveled at Yosef's wisdom (Gen. 41:38) he expressed that Yosef was "a man who possessed *ruach Elohim* [a divine spirit]." When God asks Moses to appoint Betzalel (Ex. 31:3), the architect of the Tabernacle, God assures Moses that Betzalel was granted *ruach Elohim*, this divine spirit which later on was also called *ruach chokhma* – a spirit of wisdom. Throughout the rest of the Tanakh, *ruach Elohim* retains this same connotation: an extraordinary form of wisdom or divine inspiration generally attributed to a prophet.[47] It is in this same vein that the Rabbis have used the term *ruach haqodesh* to refer to divine inspiration.[48]

In our verse, Genesis 1:2, given the absence of any man who could be the subject or recipient of a divine spirit of wisdom, *ruach* cannot possibly be understood as a God-granted inspiration. Obviously, *ruach* cannot mean in this context breathing or soul. The word *ruach* in verse 1:2 was understood by virtually all midrashim and classic Jewish commentaries[49] –

---

46 Judges 9:23, I Shmuel 16:14. *Torah Shelemah* explains that the semantic field of the word *ruach* is much wider, and counted more than thirty different meanings to it. See *Torah Shelemah* 67:341.

47 Ezekiel 11:24, II Chronicles 24:20. *Ruach HaShem* found elsewhere in the Tanakh seems to refer to a wind sent by God, which in a prophetic vision transported a prophet to a different dimension (Ezekiel 37:1). See *Da'at Miqra* there. This is probably the meaning of *ruach HaShem* that Sephardic Jews use for the *hashkaba* prayer: רוח ה' יניחנו בגן עגן; it does not mean "May the Spirit of God bring this soul to the Garden of Eden." Rather, the word *ruach* should be taken metaphorically as a vehicle for the ascension of the soul that departed from the deceased's body. "May the wind sent by God transport and place this soul in [the celestial] Garden of Eden."

48 *Ruach haqodesh* means the inspiration that would rest upon a man visiting the *qodesh*, the Temple (Mishkan or *Bet haMiqdash*, which is also called briefly: *qodesh*). In this sense, we should understand *eretz haqodesh*, Israel, the land of the Temple, and even *leshon haqodesh*, the only language spoken in the Temple, Hebrew.

49 See *Torah Shelemah*, Genesis 54:293, 56:295, 296, and 298, 60:319 and 320. Virtually all midrashim define or refer to *ruach* as a physical wind. Those midrashim that connect between *ruach* and the Divine Presence (*Torah Shelemah* 58:306, 59:311) are actually *derashot* (interpretations) which are not meant to convey the conventional

including Targum Onkelos, Rabbi Sa'adia Gaon, Eben 'Ezra, Maimonides, Nachmanides, etc. – as a physical wind, *not* as a spirit or inspiration. In Genesis 1:2, therefore, the Torah is mentioning two of the physical elements planet Earth was endowed with: water and wind.

Once we know that *ruach* means wind and not spirit, we should ask ourselves what does the pair of words *ruach Elohim* mean? The term *Elohim* usually, yet not exclusively, refers to God Almighty. Although God's proper name is not *Elohim* but the Tetragrammaton (*Yod-He-Vav* and *He*), in the Biblical story of Creation – the first chapter of Genesis – *Elohim* is the exclusive name the Torah uses for God. In that chapter the name *Elohim* appears more than thirty times in reference to God Almighty. In the entire Tanakh the second most used name for God is *Elohim*.

However, the default meaning of the word *elohim* is not "God" but "powerful" or "mighty." And this is true even when the term *elohim* refers to God. *Elohim* should be understood, primarily, as an adjective, not as a noun.[50] It is not God's proper name but God's attribute. The Torah calls God *Elohim* in the exact same way we refer to God in English as "Mighty" or "Almighty."

Elohim, in Scripture, is used extensively in reference to something or someone powerful, magnificent, or with extraordinary authority. Men vested with judicial powers are called *elohim* (Ex. 22:8). Even "gods" or idols with imaginarily attributed powers are also called by the Torah – in the second of the Ten Commandments – *elohim*.[51] An important city, Nineve, is called *'ir gedola lelohim* (Jonah 3:3), a "grandiose" metropolis, due to its huge population. Numerous times, the Torah uses the word *elohim* as a simple adjective that defines a noun, a superlative.

In Genesis 6:2 the Torah refers to certain men called *bene-haelohim* (sons of *elohim*) who are powerful, abusive, and violent people – so much

---

meaning of a word. Most of them are based on the association between the word *merachefet* ("hovering") and its parallel in Deut. 32:11.

50 See Eben 'Ezra 1:1, וזה השם תואר ואיננו עצם, "and this is an adjective; it is not a noun."

51 See also the story of the serpent seducing Eve to eat from the forbidden fruit, assuring her that eating from that fruit will make them like *elohim* (Gen. 3:5). Or when God Almighty tells Moses (Ex. 4:16) that his brother Aaron will be for Moses a mouth to talk to Pharaoh, and Moses will be his *elohim*. In all these cases, the Targum rendered the word *elohim* not as "God" but as "powerful," or the "leading one" (*rabrebin* or *rab*).

so, that it is their corrupt actions that God considers as He decides to bring the flood. The word *elohim* in this case defines a power with negative connotation. The Targum *in situ* rendered the attribute *elohim* as "powerful" (*rabrebaya*), and the Rabbis of the Midrash unambiguously interpreted *bene-haelohim* as "sons of the powerful."[52] In either case, the Torah says that these men abused their power, or leverage, in a world without law and order "to take [as many] women as they wanted" (Gen. 6:2). To prevent a misinterpretation of *bene elohim* as "sons of God," a totally pagan idea associated with idolatry and anthropomorphism, Rabbi Shim'on bar Yochai (Israel, first century CE) "cursed" those who dared to interpret the word *elohim* here as referring to *Elohim* (God).[53]

Once we recognize that the word *elohim* can be understood in two different ways, "God" or "powerful," we can easily appreciate why there are two possible interpretations for the expression *ruach Elohim*. One opinion reads the word as *Elohim*, referring to God Almighty. And another interpretation reads the word *elohim*, as an adjective which portrays the primeval wind as a very powerful wind. Let this be very clear: both interpretations indicate that the word *ruach* should be understood, strictly, as "wind" and not as "spirit."

Many classic commentators (Rabbi Sa'adia Gaon and Radaq among others) indicated that the word *elohim* in Genesis 1:2 is *not* referring to God. It is an adjective ("mighty"), expressing the intensity of the "wind." Their understanding of *ruach elohim* was "a powerful wind."

The Targum and Maimonides, on the other hand, understood the word *Elohim* as referring to God. They explained *ruach Elohim* as "a wind *sent by* God" (or "a divine wind" or "God's wind"). Maimonides says in *More Nebukhim* (2:30) that the motion of the wind is always attributed to God. This idea will be explained in detail in the two following chapters of this section.

---

52 Compare with the events involving the sons of 'Eli haKohen in I Samuel 2:17, among other cases of corruption performed by the sons of the powerful. Alternatively, these *bene elohim* were portrayed as "men of extraordinary beauty," which they would abuse in their corrupt pursuits. See *Torah Shelemah*, Genesis 369:7.

53 See *Torah Shelemah* 370:9.

The most important point for our discussion now is that in the entire Hebrew Scripture or Tanakh, *ruach Elohim* (or *ruach A-donay*, which is also mentioned many times) *never* means "God's spirit." It refers to a divine inspiration, flowing *from* God, to inspire a human being.

The idea of *ruach Elohim* as "God's spirit" or "the spirit of God" is a concept entirely foreign, outrageous, and offensive to normative Judaism. It is a notion that – among other things – would challenge the Jewish principle of monotheism and would border with anthropomorphism, i.e., a personification of God.

The following words by John Gill (1697–1771) in his exposition of the Old Testament (Genesis 1:2) exemplify the mainstream Christian interpretation of these words: "*Ruach Elohim*, the Spirit of God...that is, the third Person in the blessed Trinity, who was concerned in the creation of all things, as in the garnishing of the heavens, so in bringing the confused matter of the earth and water into form and order. This same Spirit "moved" or brooded upon the face of the waters, to impregnate them, as a hen upon eggs to hatch them, so he to separate the parts which were mixed together, and give them a quickening virtue to produce living creatures in them." Non-Jewish commentaries and translators have consistently and unanimously translated *ruach elohim* in verse 1:2 as the "spirit of God," or the "Holy spirit," a concept which alludes to a fundamental theological principle of the Christian church. The holy spirit, in Christian theology, stands for the third element of the trinity – a core Christian belief, which in a sense was born out of this translation.

In Jewish tradition *ruach elohim* was understood either as "a powerful wind,"[54] following the classic commentators, or – as the Targum and Maimonides rendered it – as "God's wind," in the sense of "a physical wind coming from, or directed by God." In this work, we will follow the second opinion, which views *ruach Elohim* as God's wind, divine wind, or a wind directed by God.

---

54 Following Rabbi Sa'adia Gaon's interpretation, we should translate it as mighty "winds." Similar to sea (*tehom*) and water (*mayim*), Rabbi Sa'adia Gaon held that these three nouns should be understood as collective nouns, and be translated in plural.

But why would the Biblical text grant such an exceptional attribute to the wind? Why would the Torah call it a "divine" wind, an attribute that was not given to any other element in the Creation story? As we will see in the next chapter, wind was especially credited in Genesis 1:2 as God's instrument for its crucial function as God's agent during the second and the third day of Creation. Wind played a decisive role in the process of Creation, vital to the formation of clouds and the upper waters of the second day of Creation and in the drying of the land on the third day, which helped the creation of the continents.

Beyond Creation, in the setting of the world's climate wind could not have been of greater importance. Wind is considered to be indeed "the engine of the weather system." Wind is critical to preserving the equilibrium and the balance of temperatures around the globe. "Wind is the heart of the weather machine. Heat and pressure differences bring cyclones, depressions, thunderstorms and hurricanes, all blown across the surface of the globe by the wind."[55]

Wind is essential for the very physical existence of our planet, for the equilibrium of the earth's climate, and for the preservation of water in the world. "Without wind our beautiful earth will be transformed into a cauldron of extremes. The heat of the tropics would increase inexorably, while toward the north and south the planet would freeze beyond the point at which life could survive. Instead we have wind. The circulation of air around the planet, ultimately mixing hot and cold, wet and dry, to create the rich confection of cloud and clear sky, rain and storm that make up the weather that we all accept as part of our lives."[56]

The reason many of us are not aware of the crucial role the element wind played in the story of Creation, a role which the Biblical text was careful in emphasizing by calling it *ruach Elohim*, is the Biblical translations we all use. Following allegorical or theological exegesis, translators – incredibly, *most* of them! – neglected the plain meaning of the Hebrew text (*peshat*)

---

55 John Lynch, *The Weather* (Richmond Hill, Ontario: Firefly Books, 2002), p. 16.
56 Ibid., p. 37.

and the bulk of classic rabbinical tradition, rendering *ruach Elohim* as "God's spirit" or something of that sort.[57]

The role of wind will be examined in greater depth in the next two chapters.

"...Over the Surface of the Water"

Liquid water (and life) is what makes our planet exceptional and unique in our solar system, and most probably in the whole universe. According to a rabbinic tradition recorded in the Talmud,[58] water was not a scarce element in our incipient planet. On the contrary, earth in its primitive state was, literally, a water planet. Based on the tradition that planet Earth was covered by water before dry land surfaced, our Rabbis formulated a blessing to be recited every day when we step on solid ground: ...*Roka' ha-aretz 'al hamayim*, "Blessed are You, HaShem our Lord, King of the universe, Who extends the dry land over the waters." Contrary to what ancient civilizations believed, but compatible with what modern science affirms, this blessing states unambiguously that water was there *first*, before land, and not the other way around.

Keeping in mind that the primeval planet was completely covered by water, we can better appreciate how the Rabbis understood and used the words *tohu vabohu*, alluding to our planet's desolate state when (but mainly *because*) it was covered with water.[59] The Rabbis coined a special expression to articulate that, should human civilization as a whole fail to listen to God's words, God would erase "humanity" and bring the planet back to its primitive lifeless state. They said that God would then *machazir et ha'olam letohu vabohu*,[60] "bring the planet back to its original inhospitable

---

57 Even my favorite English translations, *The Living Torah*, by Aryeh Kaplan, and *The Sacred Scriptures in Hebrew and English*, by David Aron de Sola and Morris Raphall, in a way that escapes my understanding, translated *ruach Elohim* as "God's spirit"!

58 Talmud Babli, *Chagiga* 12a.

59 Radaq, Genesis 1:2, explaining *tohu vabohu*, said that "the earth was void of any living creature, because it was completely covered by water" (כי היתה כולה מכוסה במים ...ריקה מכל בריאה).

60 See, for example, *Midrash Shir haShirim Rabba*, parasha 1: "Had they not consented to receiving the Torah, I would have brought the world back to a state of *tohu vabohu*," (מחזיר את העולם לתהו ובהו), and many others.

and desolate condition." What would God do to produce that state? God would not bring an apocalyptic chaos or a universal plague, but He would, somehow, make the world inhospitable by covering it in its entirety with water. This retribution was exacted already once, when God brought the flood. Upon seeing that men's behavior was corrupted (Genesis, ch. 6), the Almighty decided to punish the human race specifically with the flood – not with any other cataclysm or plagues as He did in other instances, for example, when He punished Sodom and Gomorra with a deadly sulphuric rain, or the Egyptians with ten devastating plagues in the story of the exodus. At the time of the flood, God did not want to destroy the planet itself, but to make the world unsuitable for life. The flood made the earth once again uninhabitable – *tohu vabohu* – for humans and animals, by covering dry land. Thus covered with water, mankind's food and oxygen supply – vegetation – was destroyed, rendering human survival impossible.

The notion that our planet was originally covered by water is also alluded to in the book of Psalms, in *Barekhi nafshi* (Psalm 104). This is a Psalm the Rabbis and Biblical commentaries saw as parallel to the narrative of the story of Creation.[61] The psalmist portrays the process of Creation in a poetic narrative that, among other things, describes the primeval world as a world under water. The primeval planet would have consisted entirely of sea waters – interestingly, called in this Psalm *tehom*. The *tehom* – or, as we explained, the primeval sea – is depicted as covering even the highest of peaks: "You covered [the earth with] the *tehom* like a cloth; over the mountains, the waters would stand"[62] (Psalms 104:6).

The last part of verse 9 of Psalm 104 is even more explicit about the primitive watery state of the earth: "A boundary [for the waters] You set, not to be trespassed, lest they [the waters] would *come again* to cover the earth."

Geological evidence found in the last few decades points out that the earth was once covered by water (and according to the Torah, twice: the second time, at the time of the flood). Geologists also maintain that, during what is known in science as the pre-Devonian era, the sea level

---

61 Eben 'Ezra, Gen. 1:2.
62 Radaq, Psalms 104:6.

was high worldwide. "Panthalassa," scientists claim, was a universal ocean that covered the planet while land lay submerged under shallow seas. Even earth's great deserts were once covered by water.

Water – ocean water, fresh water, water on the planet's surface, or above the surface, or underground – is what makes our planet unique. Water is extremely important in the Biblical story of Creation. And we will consecrate the entire next chapter to it. We will see that the Creator used water as raw material for His creative activity. And although water is presented in Genesis 1:2 as part of the problem, i.e., one of the reasons of *tohu vabohu or* absence of life, water will be used by the Creator as the first source of life, displacing *tohu vabohu.*

SUMMARY

After Genesis 1:1 announced that God created heavens and earth, we might have expected a grandiose description of our planet: its beautiful landscapes, a clear sky, and a dry land blooming with life. That would probably have met our human expectations of a divine and perfectly created world.

But instead, the Torah paints an image of the just-born planet that is somber and lugubrious. Planet Earth is in its primeval state, lifeless and still unsuitable for life. Above the planet's surface, we find a blanket of "darkness." A toxic darkness. A Venus-like atmosphere devoid of oxygen. There is no stable weather system as the one we know today, which would sustain life. The planet's surface is not better. Earth is covered by *tehom*, the primeval waters or sea. A sort of Panthalassa. There is no dry land where plants would flourish and animals or mankind could live and procreate. At this stage, earth is a dead planet, like Mars. Nothing like what it is today. Life is still not here. As we will later see, it will take four Creation-days to get the planet ready for harboring life.

In the second part of verse 2, however, we find a *ruach Elohim*, a wind. It is the most primeval form of energy, which will soon become one of God's agents in forming the atmosphere and the weather system, displacing the primitive toxic darkness. Later on, the wind will be used by God to separate the land from the primitive seas. Wind will become God's main instrument for generating the basic environment that will support life.

In modern days we are able, more than any other time in the history of humankind, to better appreciate the accuracy and precision of the Torah in its description of our planet in its primeval state. When discussing the early state of our planet, modern scientists have used terms that are remarkably similar to those used by the Biblical text. For J. D. Macdougall, for example, the incipient planet Earth looked *so* akin to the one described in verse 1:2 that, if not for Macdougall's explicit confession of his unfamiliarity with the Biblical narrative,[63] one would be convinced that he borrowed the following words from the Torah: "Thus the earliest days of earth history must have been very chaotic...the earth would have been very unfamiliar and *inhospitable* for time machine human visitors. By this time there would probably have been liquid *water on the surface*, but there was *no visible life* – no plants, no animals – and *the atmosphere was unbreathable* because it contained no oxygen. There were *no large continents* as we know them today...."[64]

Except for God's wind, Macdougall's description covers Genesis 1:2 in its entirety!

---

63 J. D. Macdougall, *A Short History of Planet Earth* (New York: John Wiley and Sons, 1996), p. 13.
64 Ibid., pp. 20–21. Italics added.

CHAPTER 5

THE BLUE PLANET

The first verse of the Torah, "In the beginning, God created heavens and earth," announced that God created the universe from nothing. The verse singles out our planet, recognizing it as a creation worthy to be distinguished from the rest of the universe. In the next sentence, Genesis 1:2, we realized what makes earth different.

First, "earth" is different from "heavens" because unlike the rest of the universe, our planet was not completed upon its Creation. The Torah describes earth in its primeval state with the words *tohu vabohu*, "uninhabited and inhospitable." God deliberately created it without life and lacking the basic physical conditions needed to host life. A slow and progressive process of adjustments and adaptation would still be necessary to transform earth from a desolate world into a living planet. And second, our planet is unique in that it contains water, the most essential element needed to become the greenhouse of life.

In this chapter we will see that in the Biblical story of Creation, the Creator chose to start the adjustment of the planet by creating the *raqia'*, the suitable-for-life atmosphere, by dividing the primeval waters. Although not explicit in the Biblical text due to its deliberately extraordinary brevity, the attentive reader will find in the development of the story of Creation a sophisticated step-by-step progression, in which each element mentioned by the Torah is instrumental at a later stage for creating or recreating the next element.

There is a reason why wind, water (Gen. 1:2), and – later on – light (Gen. 1:3), are highlighted in the story of Creation. They are indeed the materials and the tools that will serve as God's agents for His creative activity in the following days. Accordingly, we should be able to find that God utilized the elements created before the second day as instruments for His creative activity in the second day. Also, we should be able to find (explicitly or not) that in the creative processes of the third day, God utilized elements from the first and second days.

To begin with, we will try to identify and briefly analyze the sequential process of Creation, which started with wind and water and culminated with the formation of earth's biosphere.

THE SECOND DAY OF CREATION

Though lifeless and inhospitable, planet Earth contained from its inception the most critical element needed to produce and sustain life: water. Water – at this stage it is only seawater – is used by God as a raw material, the most predominant one indeed, throughout the process of Creation. No other element in the story of Creation was transformed, retransformed, and reutilized by the Creator as much as seawater. The Rabbis coined a special expression for the multiple transformations and uses of water during the initial days. They called it *melekhet hamayim*,[1] the "work done with [or 'on'] water." The Biblical text (Gen. 1:7) reports that during the second day the *raqia'* was made by dividing the water into two categories: upper waters and lower waters. During the third day (Gen. 1:9–10), seawater was separated from dry land, allowing vegetation to appear. On the fifth day (Gen. 1:20), water was used by God for the creation of the first living creatures.

The fact that the role of water in Creation was so decisive is indicated by its mention in the second verse. Actually, the presence of water was acknowledged there twice. The second time is at the very end of the Genesis 1:2, "over the face of the water," and the first time, implicitly, is in the preceding phrase, "over the face of the *tehom*," indicating that the planet was entirely covered by the water of the primeval seas. Still, it seems to me that not enough attention has been paid to the crucial role of water on the Creation process. There might be a few practical reasons why.

1. As observed by Rashi (on Gen. 1:1), similar to wind and darkness, there was no particular divine utterance associated with the creation of water. Unlike what happened with the creation of light, God did not say: "Let there be

---

1   *Bereshit Rabba* 4, *vaya'as Elohim*. See also Rashi there.

water." Water appears as part of the elements planet Earth was initially created with.

2. Additionally, we might fail to identify the sequentiality of the processing and reprocessing of water because of the creation of light. Immediately after primeval water is mentioned (Gen.1:2), God creates light (Gen.1:3), thus *apparently* interrupting the textual flow of what would have been expected as the natural thematic continuum: presence of water (Gen. 1:2) and then, the separation between upper and lower waters (Gen. 1:6–7). In other words, while the second verse describes – and emphasizes – the presence of water on earth, Genesis 1:3–5 divert our attention from water, interpolating the creation of light which *apparently* does not add anything to the sequence: water, followed by the division of water. Without any explicit reason, light breaks the continuity of the story of water, leading the inattentive reader to not connect the dots between 1:2 and 1:6–7.

To better appreciate the continuum of the narrative of the processing of water (*melekhet hamayim*) and the critical role of light in that scheme, we will need to explore first what really happened during the second day and what this "separation between the waters" consisted in. Then, we will be in a better position to reexamine the connection between water, light, and division of water.

THE WATER CYCLE

Genesis 1:6
And God said, 'Let there be an expanse [*raqia'*] in between the waters, and let it divide waters from the waters.'

The second day reports the division of waters into two different categories: water[2] under the sky and water above the sky. At this point, the Torah

---

2   In Hebrew *mayim* means "water" or "waters." I will be using the singular and plural without distinction.

says nothing about the nature of these two types of water, except that one will be above, in the sky or *raqia'*, and the other, below. We might safely assume that the lower waters are the waters of the oceans, as this is explicit in Genesis 1:10. But what are those upper waters?

As we will demonstrate, the upper waters are the reservoir of water in the sky in the form of clouds. Based on the Midrash, Maimonides describes the *raqia'* as being created from the water.[3] On the second day, he says, the physical laws of water were established: "Part of the water was separated, somehow, over the air."[4] To explain precisely how the *raqia'* was formed out of the water and Maimonides's idea of the separation between upper and lower waters, I will quote the commentary of Rabbi Moshe Chefetz.[5]

Rabbi Chefetz identified the upper waters with vapors, formed by the effect of the evaporation of the lower waters. In his book *Melekhet Machashebet*, Rabbi Chefetz explains that according to the Rabbis the word *shamayim*[6] is composed of two Hebrew words: *esh*, "fire" or "heat," and *mayim*, "water." *Shamayim* is then the product of *heat* and *water*. Rabbi Chefetz then explains the meaning of Genesis 1:6, "Let there be an expanse [*raqia'*] in the midst of the water." Accordingly, God's command could be paraphrased as "Let there be in the water [*betokh hamayim*] air of a moving nature, which is light and expands up [i.e., vapor]."[7] In Rabbi Chefetz's opinion, *raqia'* does not allude to the expansion *of the space* in and of itself, but, as per Maimonides, to the expansion *of the water* transformed into vapors, which will create the *raqia'*: "Same as it happens when water is

3   *More Nebukhim* (Schwarz, p. 365). Based on *Bereshit Rabba* 4:2.
4   *More Nebukhim* 2:30: חלקם הובדל בצורה כלשהי מעל האויר. The identification of the upper waters with the clouds was also ratified by Rabbi Yitzchaq Shmuel Reggio in his commentary to the Torah (Gen. 1:6): חלקם נקבצו למעלה והיו ענן (*Torat haElohim* [Vienna, 1821], p. 4).
5   *Melekhet Machashebet*. First published in Venice, 1710. I'm using the Warsaw edition, 1914, pp. 10–11.
6   Notice that in the context of the second day, *shamayim*, "heavens," should not be confused with "heavens" of Gen. 1:1. In the second day *shamayim* is the visible sky above us, while in 1:1, *shamayim* is everything in the universe other than planet Earth. Maimonides makes this point explicitly in *More Nebukhim* 2:30 (Schwarz, p. 366).
7   This is the Hebrew text with Rabbi Chefetz's original words: יהי בתוך המים אויר וגוף מתנועע דק ומתפשט....

placed on fire, the water easily gets transformed into vapor."[8] When that vapor encounters cold temperature, the vapor will turn again into water or rain.

In other words, on the second day, the physical laws that allow water and vapor to exist as two separate entities were established and somehow made functional. For Rabbi Chefetz, the separation between the two waters is the differentiation between water in a liquid state (water in the ocean) and water in a gaseous state (vapor, moisture, humidity, and clouds),[9] achieved as an effect of heat. This separation put in motion, for the first time, what is known today as the cycle of water.[10] Evaporation separates a fraction of seawater (lower waters) turning it into water vapor or clouds (upper waters).

Modern scientists also describe clouds as *water* suspended in the air: a "visible mass of water droplets, ice crystals, or a mixture of both that is suspended in the air, usually at a considerable height."[11] The beautiful words of John Lynch fit perfectly the Biblical definition of upper waters, or water above the sky: "We live on a water planet. The seas dominate the world, but there is also an ocean around us and an ocean above us."[12] It would be hard to find a better description of the division of the waters, describing clouds as upper waters, than "an ocean around us and an ocean above us."

Life, in all of its variations that we know today, cannot be possible without the water cycle. The second day portrays the creation of that vital-for-life mechanism: evaporation and transportation of water leading to the formation of the upper reservoirs of waters (clouds), and eventually leading to rain.

---

8   In Hebrew: כאשר יעשו המים על האש בנקל יתהפכו לאויר והאויר ההוא הנהפך אם ימצא קור בנקל ישוב למים כבראשונה.

9   Rabbi Chefetz also explains that the particle 'al (*me'al hashamayim*), which is usually translated as "above the sky," is found elsewhere in the Pentateuch used as a preposition which indicates closeness or alongside, etc., and not necessarily "in a higher place." As examples he brings: *ve'al charbekha tichye*, "and *by* your sword you shall live" (Gen. 27:40); *vayabo-u ha-anashim 'al hanashim*, "then, the men came *with* the women" (Ex. 35:22).

10 See next chapter.

11 *Encyclopedia Britannica* (Macropedia), 15th ed., s.v. "cloud."

12 John Lynch, *The Weather*, a BBC edition (Toronto: Firefly Books, 2002), p. 84.

In modern words: "Water flows from one reservoir to another, often undergoing a dramatic physical change…. Within the system, water is constantly recycled as evaporation, condensation, precipitation, and run-off cause it to flow between the various reservoirs. Our weather consists of a constant interplay of water as vapor, liquid, and solid ice…."[13]

Rabbi Menashe ben Israel explained that the division between the lower and the upper waters resulted in "the formation of rain."[14]

To be ready for life, our planet needs freshwater. Precipitation is the sole and exclusive source of earth's fresh water. To produce rain we first need the primeval water mentioned in Genesis 1:2. Ocean water is the raw material of freshwater. Without the ocean's water, rain would not be possible. Oceans worldwide are responsible for 90 percent of the atmosphere's moisture and, in turn, for the water that will be delivered back to the earth as precipitation. Ninety percent of rainwater will fall back onto the oceans or, as Rabbi Yochanan said, the overflowing waters of the *raqia'* formed on the second day are transformed into "thick drops, which come down into the salted waters" of the oceans.[15]

Only 10 percent of freshwater falls on continental land. Every year, "about 9,500 cubic miles (40,000 cubic km) of water evaporates from the ocean and falls on land. This yearly flow is about ten times that of the Amazon River and in theory is enough to support at least five times the current number of people on earth."[16]

Freshwater is water with low concentrations of dissolved salts. Out of all the water on earth, only 2.75 percent of it is fresh water. From it, 2.05 percent is water that is frozen in glaciers, and 0.68 percent is groundwater. And just 0.0101% of it is surface freshwater gathered in lakes and rivers. As far as we know, the sole natural source of freshwater *in the universe* is precipitation from the atmosphere, in the form of mist, snow, and mainly rain. Freshwater is the essential elixir of life. The Torah devoted a whole day

---

13 Bruce Buckley, Edward J. Hopkins, and Richard Whitaker, *Weather: A Visual Guide* (Toronto: Firefly Books, 2004), p. 16.

14 Ben Israel, *Conciliator*, p. 3.

15 See *Torah Shelemah* 95:455. See also *Torah Shelemah* 101:483 and 102:485 for other midrashim that explicitly identify upper waters with rain.

16 James F. Luhr, ed., *Earth* (New York: Smithsonian/DK Publishing, 2003), p. 130.

to describe its formation. The second day was dedicated entirely to depict the conversion process of primeval ocean water into the most precious liquid in the entire universe: rain.

LIGHT AND HEAT

Once we realize that the second day of Creation is referring to the onset of the water cycle, we may finally understand that the interpolation of "light" between the first reference to water in Genesis 1:2 and the description of the evaporation of water in Genesis 1:6 and Genesis 1:7 was absolutely necessary.

The nature of primeval light (the light whose creation is reported in Gen. 1:3) is a matter that will be further analyzed in the third section of this book. What needs to be beyond doubt is that this light also possessed the property of heat (in Hebrew *esh* or *chom*). Maimonides explicitly acknowledged the property of heat derived from primeval light. In *More Nebukhim* he asserts that *OR*-light and *choshekh*-darkness are the physical cause in bringing something to its existence or to its termination, "because of the heat and cold that they produce."[17] We will also corroborate this property of *OR*-light in the following chapter, when analyzing Psalm 104.[18]

Once we take into consideration the three elements mentioned in anticipation of the creative activity of the second day – wind, water, and light – we can easily understand that on the second day something else was generated besides (or because of) the water cycle. That is, the weather system.

The weather system is probably the most basic necessity for life to exist. It ignites the processes of renewal of water, transforming the abundant seawater into the vital-for-life freshwater, and allows the conservation of water in its liquid form. "The weather system is in us and all around us...it is the thin veil that shrouds our planet and defines the limits within which

---

17 *More Nebukhim* (Schwarz, sec. 2, ch. 30, p. 367), בשל החום והקור שבעקבותיהם .... This text
   is also quoted by Radaq in his commentary to Genesis 1:3.
18 Menashe ben Israel also mentions the property of heat in primeval light. See
   Conciliator, question 2, p. 4. The nature and identity of primeval light will be the main
   subject of the third section of this book, and the heating property of primeval light
   will be, hopefully, properly demonstrated.

we can stay alive. The temperatures below and above which our bodies will cease to function, the forces of wind and flood that we can withstand, or the electrical charge that can instantly destroy us."[19]

Now, let us ask ourselves: What are the basic components of the weather system? What elements would we expect to see in an initial inventory of earth, which are necessary for the operation of earth's climate? According to John Lynch, in his book *The Weather*, we are looking at three basic elements: (1) wind, which is considered the engine of the weather system; (2) water, which is the fuel of the weather system; and (3) heat, which is the energy that creates the ignition of the system.[20]

Lo and behold, these are exactly the three elements the Torah describes in its second and third verses! Genesis 1:2 acknowledged the presence of *wind* ("powerful winds" or "God's wind") and *water* that covered the face of the planet. And in verse 1:3 we find the third critical element to produce evaporation: *light* or *heat*.

We are now able to appreciate that, far from being an arbitrary interjection, the creation of light was a sequential prerequisite absolutely necessary for the creative activity of the second day. Light is what started the vaporization cycle,[21] later producing, by the Creator's command, the separation between the ocean-water and the sky-water.

It is with wind, water, and heat that clouds were formed. Light-heat evaporates the seawater. Once water is made into vapor, the winds form the clouds. This step represents the core of the weather cycle: "The most direct and obvious reminder of moving air's simple ability to create the weather is clouds. Clouds consist of moist air that has risen, cooled, and released tiny droplets of water that are enough to remain airborne…. Clouds bring rain, snow, thunder, and lightning, they are made by wind and they help to make wind."[22]

---

19 Lynch, *Weather*, p. 11.
20 See Lynch, *Weather*, p. 84: "If the wind is the engine of the weather and the heat from the sun is the energy that creates the ignition, water is the fuel."
21 See also *Me'am Lo'ez*, Tehillim 104. In Hebrew *UR*, which means heat, is written exactly like *OR*, light.
22 Lynch, *Weather*, p. 18.

With the combination of these three elements, the Creator set in motion a system that produced the elixir of life: freshwater. "Imagine an entire planet where the universe's finest liqueur is boiled out of fermenting seas by a brilliant yellow star, distilled in the skies and rained back down on the land, forming lakes and rivers of the inebriating brew. The planet, of course, is Earth, and the liqueur is freshwater."[23]

The *Raqia'*: Earth's Atmosphere

Evaporation, the act that divided gaseous water (upper water) from liquid water (low water) started the onset of the water cycle and generated the weather system. But at least one more thing happened on the second day as a consequence of this division of waters: I'm referring to the clearing of the primeval toxic darkness (*choshekh*) and the formation of a new life-friendly atmosphere.

> Genesis 1:7
> And God made the expanse [*raqia'*], and He separated between the water above the expanse and the water below the expanse; and so it was.

This verse connects the separation of the waters, through evaporation, with the formation of the *raqia'*. *Raqia'*, or expanse, indicates what we call today the atmosphere, i.e., the 100-mile extension above earth that contains nitrogen, oxygen, carbon dioxide, and the basic elements required for life.

To the best of my knowledge, the first rabbi who explicitly called the *raqia'* atmosphere[24] (more precisely, *atmosfera* in Italian) was Rabbi Isaac Shmuel Reggio (1784–1855), who also, following in the footsteps of Maimonides and Rabbi Moshe Chefetz, mentions that the *raqia'* should be seen as the result of the expansion of the water.[25] In his commentary

---

23 Larry O'Hanlon, "Freshwater: Earth's Life Force," for the program *Planet Earth*, Discovery channel, http://dsc.discovery.com/convergence/planet-earth/guide/freshwater.html.

24 Later on Rabbi Hayim Pereira-Mendes (1857–1932) also called the *raqia'* atmosphere (in English). See *Jewish History, Ethically Presented* (New York, 1896), p. 5. See also *Da'at Miqra*, Genesis 1:6–7.

25 Reggio, *Torat haElohim*, p. 6: כי מהבדלת המים נולד הרקיע.

to the Torah on Genesis 1:6 he comments on *raqia'*: "That is, the pure air that surrounds the entirety of the terraqueous globe and it is called in the vernacular *atmosfera*...and this air was created on the second day to give sustenance to the plants, which were created on the third day, and for the living creatures created on the fifth and the sixth days."

Coincidently, contemporary geologists believe our earthly atmosphere consisted initially of a blanket of clouds formed by evaporation. Water vapor and other gases once chemically bound inside the planet erupted from the surface in huge quantities. Accordingly, heat "produced a huge amount of vapors coming up from the earth. These vapors produced a huge 'blanket' of clouds, which eventually cleared the primitive toxic atmosphere."[26] In other words, scientists also attribute the formation of our atmosphere to a process that began with the evaporation of water (by heat, water, wind). The reduction of carbon monoxide in the atmosphere and the presence of oxygen was initiated by the emission of water vapor (photosynthesis pertains to a later stage).[27]

The creation of the *raqia'* caused the displacement of *choshekh*, endowing our planet, ever since,[28] with a clear and life-friendly atmosphere. For a proper understanding of Genesis 1:6 and 1:7 one should bear in mind that the process of division of the waters (vaporization) was responsible for the creation of the *raqia'*, and simultaneously, the new *expanse* was responsible for allowing the process of evaporation-precipitation. The water cycle requires the existence of the thick layer of the atmosphere to have temperatures above the melting point of water, near and above the earth's surface.

This is a summary of the events that took place during the second day of Creation:

1. The creation of earth's present atmosphere (*raqia'*), which displaced primeval darkness. That unfriendly-to-life

---

26 Robert D. Ballard, *Exploring Our Living Planet* (Washington, DC: National Geographic Society, 1983), pp. 24–25.

27 Ibid., p. 23.

28 "Ever since" is a paraphrase of "*vayhi khen*," as we will see in the next section.

primitive atmosphere was cleansed by the division of water, that is, evaporation and later on, precipitation.

2. The production of freshwater from salt water. At this point, however, rain, freshwater, or even clouds are not explicitly mentioned in the Biblical text. We will elaborate on this matter in the next chapter.

3. The organization and activation of the weather system, which also began with the evaporation cycle. We can clearly identify in verses Genesis 1:2 and 1:3 the three main components of the weather system: wind, water, and heat.

All these complex processes are portrayed in an exquisitely brief narrative consisting of just three sentences, in a mere thirty-eight words.

Due to the brevity of the narrative (the second day has the shortest text of the six days of Creation) and the absence of the key words: clouds, freshwater, wind, atmosphere, oxygen, etc., the modern reader might underrate the crucial importance of this day for the existence of life on earth. For today's scientists, nothing on earth is more crucial to its habitability, nothing is more inherent to its identity as a life-harboring planet, than the constant movement of waters. "Indeed the main activity of the planet might be regarded as being the transport of water, and water's journey through both time and space is as surprising and profound as are its effects upon us."[29]

If not read carefully, the Torah seems to be focusing its attention exclusively on the formation of the *raqia'* as an empty "expanse," rather than on the creation of the life-supporting atmosphere. As we will see in the next chapter, it is mainly thanks to the Psalms that we can safely determine the identity of the upper waters as rain-producing clouds.[30]

---

29 Lynch, *Weather*, p. 84.

30 Most of the commentaries that identify upper water with clouds, rain, etc., are based directly or indirectly on Psalm 104:4.

THE THIRD DAY OF CREATION

The creative activity of water continued during the third day of Creation.

Water's role in the process of Creation (*melekhet hamayim*) did not come to an end on the second day. Our Rabbis pointed out that, unlike all other days, on the second day of Creation the Torah did not say "and God saw what He had created, and it was good" (*vayar Elohim...ki tob*) – an expression the Torah uses for all other days of Creation, and notably twice on the third day. The Rabbis explained that water still needed to be reprocessed by the Almighty, as Creation went on. In their own words: "The Scripture did not say 'it was good' [in the sense of it having attained completion] on the second day, because the work of water was still unfinished."[31]

Two creative events on the third day are directly or indirectly connected with water, more specifically with *fresh* water, the brand-new product of the second day. These two events should be considered, too, part of the yet unfinished creative activity with water.

> Genesis 1:9
> And God said, "Let the waters under the sky be gathered into a single place, so that the dry land may show up," and so it was.

> Genesis 1:10
> And God called the dry land "earth," and the gathering of the waters He called "seas"; and God saw that it was good.

In these two verses, the Torah reports again an act of separation. But whereas on the second day upper water was separated from lower water, now the lower waters are separated from dry land. This is the creative event that must have brought our planet closer to its present distribution of the 70:30 ratio of oceans to dry land.

FRESH WATER AND EROSION

The Rabbis considered rain one of God's most important blessings to mankind. In the second blessing of the *'Amida*, we praise God for His might

---

31 Cited by Rashi, Genesis 1:7, ‏לא נאמר כי טוב‎.

(*geburot*), singling out His power to produce rain to support and maintain life. In the wintertime's 'Amida, we dedicate one entire blessing to asking God for rain, the main source of livelihood.

In the Creation process, the comprehensive role of rain might be uncovered by (1) having in mind the identification of rain with the upper waters, following the reference of Psalm 104, as we will see later on, and (2) reading the Creation story as a successive progression, where each new element appears to be brought into existence for the sake of the next step of Creation. Water and wind (Gen. 1:2) and heat (Gen. 1:3) are *implicitly* used by God to create the mechanism of rain (1:6–7). And together with wind, rain, the new product of the upper waters, is *implicitly* used by God to bring about the events of the third day (Gen. 1:9–12).

How so?

On the third day, God separated land from water. Water receded and dry land emerged. Although nothing is explicitly said about the precise way God dried the oceans that covered the planet surface, Eben 'Ezra indicated that the reason why the wind is called "God's wind" (Gen. 1:2) is because the wind was an agent of Creation, activated by God's will, to dry the water.[32]

Eben 'Ezra's explanation is critical for the main theory of this chapter and the next, for the reasons that follow.

According to Eben 'Ezra we may infer that God operates through "natural" agents, and that God uses the elements He had previously created to further pursue His creative activity. We may also infer that God used those natural elements as agents of Creation, even though *they are not explicitly mentioned* in the Creation story.

Back to the wind drying the seas, the Rabbis compared the drying of earth's land with the drying of the Red Sea,[33] when the Jews were leaving the Egyptian captivity. In the story of the exodus the Torah explicitly mentions that God brought "a strong wind" (*ruach kadim 'aza*) that blew on the waters of the Red Sea during a whole night to dry the seawater.[34]

---

32 Eben 'Ezra on Gen. 1:2: בעבור היותו שליח בחפץ השם לייבש המים. Rashbam, Rabbi Shmuel Ben Meir (1085–1158), had a similar approach to the role of wind; see his commentary to Gen. 1:2.

33 See *Torah Shelemah* 109:517, and many others.

34 Ex. 11:21.

Following this pattern I would propose that, like wind, rain too was used by God as a Creation tool. Rain, the product of the second day of Creation, might have also played a major role during the events of the third day in the formation of the new continents' landscape: mountains, rivers, lakes, valleys – all topographical transformations whose development is not recorded elsewhere in the Creation narrative of Genesis.

Similar to the way wind was used by God to dry up the land, rain might have been used to shape its landforms. Scientists explain that rain is not only responsible for the existence of rivers, lakes, and huge underground deposits of drinkable water. Thanks to science's present discoveries in the area of geology and earth studies, we know that freshwater is critical for the *activation* of the forces of erosion. Precipitation has directly and indirectly affected earth's geological and marine structures, and has sculpted the landforms of our planet more than any other natural element. "The water cycle is taught to every schoolchild, for good reason. Not only does the water cycle give us the water we drink and use to grow food, it is also the carver of coastlines, sculptor of mountains, *and the burier of seas* [italics mine].... Without fresh water Earth's land masses would be barren, the continents might be in different locations, mountains would be far taller, and life virtually impossible."[35]

Today, we might be able to understand the role of water in the Creation process as one of God Almighty's agents, not only in its critical role as God's agent in bringing life to existence (Gen. 1:20) and maintaining life and vegetation, but also in its role of shaping the planet's landscape on the third day.

FRESHWATER AND VEGETATION

Still exploring the events of the third day and how they were affected by the events of the second day, we will analyze the next act in the sequence of Creation, after the division between land and sea: the emergence of vegetation.

---

35 O'Hanlon, "Freshwater," http://dsc.discovery.com/convergence/planet-earth/guide/fresh-water.html.

Genesis 1:11

And God said: "The earth shall send forth vegetation. Seed-bearing plants and fruit trees that produce fruits with seed in it, according to their various kinds." And it was so.

Genesis 1:12

And the land produced vegetation: plants bearing seed according to their kinds and trees producing fruit with seed in it, containing their own kind of seeds.

Maimonides points out that these two elements, rain and vegetation, form one sequence. He quotes the Rabbis, who said, "Vegetation did not grow until it had started to rain."[36]

Plants, indeed, provide another excellent example of the sequence of Creation in progressive steps. In order to have humans, the ultimate goal of the creation of our planet, you need food. Plants – not animals – were humans' first God-given food. Let me quote on this matter the words of Rabbi Menashe ben Israel. Two Talmudic Rabbis, Rabbi Yochanan and Rab, agreed that, at first,

> animals were not permitted to Adam as food.... After God had blessed Adam and made him supreme over every animal, although he had dominion over them, it was not as an absolute master [allowed to take animals' lives]...for God had already dedicated the food by which everything should be maintained: as he said to them, "Behold I have given you every herb-bearing seed which is upon the whole face of the earth, and every tree

---

36 *Bereshit Rabba* 13:1: תני רבי חייא אלו ואלו לא צמחו עד שירדו עליהם גשמים. Genesis 2:5–7 apparently states that rain started only after the Creation of man, and not on the second day as I contend. However, these verses could be understood, without exegetical effort, in a way that coincides with our interpretation that the second day actually describes the water cycle, including the appearance of rain. See the commentary to *Midrash Rabba haMebo-ar*, Gen. 13:1, which explains that Gen. 2:5–7 refers to the rain falling specifically on the Garden of Eden and at that precise moment, not to the rain falling on the rest of the planet. As the Rabbis explained, God loves the prayer of the righteous and withheld the rain "in the Garden of Eden" so Adam would have to pray for rain.

in the land which is the fruit of a tree yielding seed, to you it
shall be for food" (Gen. 1:29).[37]

Adam and Eve were given plants, not animals, as their food.

AND THEN, MORE...

Vegetation is vital not only as a source of edible food but also as a source of
another indispensable resource that supports the existence of life: oxygen.
Plants are the lungs of our planet. They absorb the toxic gases (carbon
dioxide) from the atmosphere and transform them into oxygen by a process
called photosynthesis. To have any form of complex life you need oxygen.
"The animals we eat gain their protein and fat from plant food. Carbon
dioxide in our atmosphere is the fundamental foodstuff for every plant,
animal, and human on planet earth."[38]

There is a marvelous correlation between the second and third day
of Creation. The two most important resources you need for any form
of complex life to exist are freshwater and oxygen. On the second day of
Creation, God creates the atmosphere and thus puts in motion a process of
separation of waters that will go on, continuously, for good. The separation
of the waters creates the atmosphere, but it serves a higher practical purpose.
This perpetual process – separation of the water, leading to evaporation
of salted water, leading to production of freshwater – guarantees that
earth will never lack freshwater. Clouds and rain will *replenish* the most
important life resource.

In a similar way, during the third day, God creates vegetation, ensuring
the recycling of the other vital resource for animal and human life. Humans
and animals take oxygen to burn food and throw out carbon dioxide as
a waste product. Plants work the other way around. They use very little
oxygen. They take in carbon dioxide to make food and produce oxygen

---

37 Ben Israel, *Conciliator*, question 10, p. 19. Rabbi Menashe ben Israel also points out
that according to the Biblical text, God gave humans plants and seeds for food while
to animals only the plants. Perhaps this means that humans were endowed with the
potential to develop the seeds, i.e., agriculture. The consumption of animals was
explicitly permitted to humans only after the flood. See Genesis 9:3.

38 Gabrielle Walker, *An Ocean of Air* (Orlando, FL: Harcourt, Inc., 2007), p. 68.

as their waste product. "As fast as humans and animals use up oxygen by breathing, plants return it to the atmosphere. It is almost as if living plants are working to make the world habitable for us – as if the most important component of our atmosphere [oxygen] has been made by life, for life...."[39]

Going back to the idea of successive Creation. In order to have vegetation you need:

1. Water, which planet Earth was created with.
2. Light/*OR*, which appeared on the first day, also for photosynthesis to take place.
3. Rain, or freshwater, which surged on the second day as a consequence of the evaporation of seawater (by light) and the formation of clouds (by wind). Without freshwater, there is no vegetation.
4. Dry land – soil with mineral and nutrients – which appeared in the first part of the third day, when God separated the water from dry land.

Vegetation, which was brought to existence on the second half of the third day, is the first organic element and marks the culmination of the creative cycle produced by God using wind, water, and primeval light. Vegetation is indeed the initial link of the food chain and the source of oxygen production for humans and animals. Animals will come next, followed by humans.

Although the Torah does not refer explicitly to a progression or a sequence in Creation, the Rabbis pointed out that, counterintuitively, man was not created first. Man is the last and ultimate creation, and everything preceding him was created *for* him. Following this idea, we should expect to find a progressive development of Creation. God Almighty treated man as a good host would treat a guest. Before God welcomes man into His world, God sets a table ready for man, so when man appears, he has everything he needs for his sustenance and livelihood.

---

39 Ibid., p. 45.

THE FIFTH DAY OF CREATION

On the fifth day of Creation, more creative work was done by God through (or *with*) water.

> Genesis 1:20
> And God said, "Let the water bring forth living creatures, and let birds fly above the earth across the expanse of the sky."

In this verse ocean water *explicitly* becomes God's instrument in the production of life.

In the Biblical story of creation, life was not generated spontaneously or ex nihilo by God's direct command, as it was in the case of heavens and earth in Genesis 1:1. The Torah describes unambiguously that the Almighty used water as His medium of choice to bring forth (or to fashion) the first living creatures. That is: amphibians, insects, reptiles, invertebrates, fish, birds, and other non-mammal animals (mammals were created from the earth on the sixth day, as mentioned in Gen. 1:24).

Notice that God did not talk *to* the waters, as if waters were an animate being. The Torah is very clear that life did not surge from water spontaneously. Despite its wide use in Creation, water is a mere tool of God's choice, an inanimate passive element, without any independent will or power.

Incidentally, it seems that today's scientific community should have no objection to the idea expressed in Genesis 1:20, that the first living creatures originated in the oceans. Many scientists believe that life originated beneath the surface of the ocean at the deep sea hydrothermal vents. The hydrothermal vents were first discovered in 1979. They release hot gaseous substances from the center of the earth at temperatures exceeding 572° F. Previously scientists were sure that life could not exist deep beneath the surface of the ocean. Next to the hydrothermal vents, however, they found ecosystems thriving in the depths of the ocean. These ecosystems contained various types of fish, worms, crabs, bacteria, and other organisms that had found a way to survive in a hostile environment without energy coming from sunlight. Because life had been found to exist where it previously was thought impossible, many scientists began to speculate as to whether or not this was where life actually originated on the earth.

John Corliss of Oregon University proposed that "hydrothermal vents provided the necessary ingredients and conditions such as hydrogen sulfide and methane gases, metal, heat, and raising watery solutions to create life from non-living matter. These researchers see the vents as manufacturers of the building blocks of life, amino acids, and incubators for changing amino acids into living cells that survived and grew as chemoautotrophs.[40]

THE *HIF'IL* VERBAL FORM

We will now introduce a particular verbal form in the Hebrew language: the *hif'il*. This form, used in the Torah to describe some of the acts of Creation, will help us clarify that God's transformative activities during the Six Days of Creation occurred through agents. The *hif'il* is the verbal form that indicates a causative. In some cases, A, the subject, is using B to do or to cause C. For example, the Hebrew *hif'il* verb *lehar-ot* means "to show," but should more precisely be translated as "to cause to see." That is, A causes B to see or understand C.

Another example is the verb *lehotzi* (to bring out): The blessing over the bread says: "Blessed are You, Lord, our Almighty-God, King of the universe, [Who causes] bread to come out from the ground" (…*hamotzi lechem min ha-aretz*). Evidently, it was man who harvested the grain, made the flour, and baked the bread. A Jewish individual, however, declares that God is the One Who ultimately created the grain, watered the fields, and granted man the wisdom and ability to bake the bread. In other words, what normally is seen as "*man* made the bread, *with God's help*," Jews see as "*God* made the bread, *through man's agency*." Thus, the blessing is addressed directly to God.

This verbal form is used extensively in the Hebrew Scripture and Jewish liturgy to describe God's performance and involvement in nature (because, of course, God is not *part* of nature). In the Creation process, the verbal form *hif'il* is widely used, particularly in the creation of life forms.

In Genesis 1:20, use of the Hebrew verbal form *hif'il* shows that God used water (or the oceans) as an *agent* of Creation. Here, the *hif'il* form

---

40 See R. V. Fodor, *The Strange World of Deep-Sea Vents* (Berkeley Heights, NJ: Enslow Publishers, Inc., 1991), p. 51.

serves to signal that God (A) caused the water (B) to produce life (C): "And God said, 'Let the water bring forth [*yishretzu hamayim = hif'il*] living creatures.'" That is, God produced life through the instrumentality of water.

Later on, God, Who already created vegetation using the soil (Gen. 1:12), also produced (or fashioned) more complex living organisms, mammals, out of the earth: "Then God said, 'Let the earth bring forth living creatures after their kind: cattle, animals, and beasts of the earth after their kind; and it was so" (Gen. 1:24). Oviparous animals, mammals, and man's *body*, were produced by God's command from the dust of the earth. Again, in these two cases the Torah used the *hif'il* verbal form (*tadshe ha-aretz, totze ha-aretz*), "let the earth bring forth," to indicate this type of dynamic between the Creator and His agents of life: water and the earth.[41]

SUMMARY

Progressive creation means that God systematically used the natural elements He had previously created for the next level of the Creation process, further improving and re-shaping the planet.

We can demonstrate the existence of this process from the first to the third day of Creation. It consisted of the following steps.

1. God created the heavens and planet Earth out of nothing.
2. At its initial stage, planet Earth is lifeless. But it contains the most fundamental among the building blocks necessary for it to become a biosphere: water. The planet is also equipped with a singular source of energy, a creative agent God will use, which is prominently named "God's wind." Water is the raw material. Wind, the engine.
3. The third element, light, is also a source of energy. As any other type of radiation, primeval light acted as a source of heat as well.

---

41 It is worth noticing that unlike all other living creatures, man was not created by proxy, i.e., God did not order the earth or the water to produce man, as He did when He created plants and animals (1:12, 1:20, 1:24). God created man from the earth by a direct action. Accordingly, the creation of Adam is not described by a *hif'il* verb but by a direct verbal form, *vayibra* (1:27) and *vayitzer* (2:7).

4. Water, wind, and light are the three essential elements God will use to (1) generate the water cycle, (2) set the weather system, and (3) create the earth's atmosphere. These three systems were initiated by one single process: water evaporation, or in Biblical terms "the separation between lower and upper waters."

5. By God's command, on the second day, water, wind, and light formed the clouds, the weather system, and the atmosphere (*raqia'*), inaugurating the process that culminated in rain.

6. Wind and rain were part of the elements used by God to perform the creative activity of the third day. Through wind, the Creator separated the land from the seas (and organized the seas).

7. Later on, in the same third day, the newly created rain irrigated the dry land. The Creator now brings forth vegetation out of the fertile soil.

8. Vegetation is viewed by the Hebrew Scripture as the living organisms' fuel and food (Gen.1:29), not necessarily a purposeful form of life in and of itself. Vegetation is the last step of the first Creative process (the preparation of this planet to host life) and the first step of the next creative process (the generation of life).

Interestingly, scientists too report a sort of progression on early earth, from the formation of the atmosphere until the appearance of life.

[1] Earth's primitive atmosphere held no free oxygen. It was mostly water vapor, nitrogen and carbon dioxide. The sun's deadly ultraviolet radiation blasted the planet. [2] But water vapor meant rain, and rain washed sediments and chemicals into the sea, enriching it. The oceans were ready for life.... [3] The plants produced oxygen, a by-product of photosynthesis... as green plants spread, they leaked free oxygen into the seas and the atmosphere...as atmospheric oxygen increased, oxygen molecules linked to form ozone in the stratosphere. [4] The ozone layer screened out much of the sun's lethal ultraviolet

light and for the first time, dry land was safe for life. On an earth reshaped by life itself, they paved the way for the first [5] amphibians.[42]

Notice the progression and order described in the above text, and its remarkable similarity with the Biblical order:

1. Toxic atmosphere, darkness, and ultraviolet radiation (Day One in the Biblical story)
2. Water vapor, clouds, rain = atmosphere (Day Two)
3. Vegetation (Day Three)
4. Normal filtered sunlight (Day Four)
5. First animals (Day Five)

In the next chapter we will focus on identifying this progression and God's agents of Creation.

---

42 Ballard, *Exploring Our Living Planet*, pp. 24–25. The numeration is mine.

CHAPTER 6

AGENTS OF GOD

In the present chapter we will provide additional support for the identification of *upper waters* with *rain*, and *primeval light* with *heat*. The theory of the sequence of Creation we presented in the last chapter was based chiefly on this identification. We will also analyze in greater depth the role of wind-*ruach*, water-*mayim*, and light-*OR* in the Creation narrative.

The key to our analysis is a very revealing chapter in *Sefer Tehillim* – Psalm 104.

The Rabbis observed that the description of Creation given by the Torah in Genesis is extremely brief. They explained that Biblical brevity, particularly in the case of Creation, was not unintentional. Delving into the details of the making of the world is a pretension far beyond our limited human mind. The Rabbis claimed: "The process of Creation cannot be [fully] revealed to flesh and blood [i.e., humans]; therefore, the Torah succinctly stated, 'In the beginning, God created [heavens and earth,' without further elaboration]."[1]

Indeed, the first chapter of Genesis dedicated merely thirty-one verses to describe the entire process of creation of the universe, the preparation of planet Earth to host life, and the creation of all living organisms.

But that brief narrative was supplemented with more detail, depth, and color in Psalm 104, a Biblical poem known in Hebrew as *Barekhi nafshi* ("May my soul bless [HaShem-God]"), traditionally attributed to the writings of King David. In Jewish liturgy, this Psalm is read on Rosh Chodesh, the commencement of the new month, which represents the beginning of a

---

1 See *Torah Shelemah*, Gen. 19:80. A similar idea is expressed by *Midrash Rabba* 1:6 in the name of Rabbi Yehuda bar Simon, based on the verse from Daniel 2:2: הוא גלא עמיקתא ומסתרתא. Whatever was concealed in Genesis was later on explained in the *Nebi-im*, the Prophets.

new cosmic cycle. *Barekhi nafshi* provides us with rich details of the events that took place during the creation of our planet. Numerous times the Rabbis referred to and used *Barekhi nafshi* as the clarification of Genesis, chapter 1. In the Midrash, the Rabbis highlighted the correspondences between these two texts and said: "Many matters were written by Moses on the Torah that were inaccessible, and David came and clarified them."[2]

Our Rabbis formulated a general methodological rule in the study of the Torah, which perhaps could be referred to as Poor Text–Rich Text: "The words of the Torah are poor in one place and rich in another place."[3] With this statement, the Rabbis meant to say that in one context the Hebrew Scripture might deal with a subject in very succinct terms, while in another place it provides a richer, detailed account on the same subject, leaving it up to the serious student to make the necessary effort and connect the dots.

Barekhi nafshi is perhaps the best expanded commentary and a superlative supplement to the Biblical story of Creation. It is the ultimate example, perhaps, of how a Biblical text explains itself.

INTRODUCING *BAREKHI NAFSHI*

Before we analyze the beautiful ideas of *Barekhi nafshi* and the invaluable information it adds to the succinct Biblical description of Creation, I would like to show the structure of this Psalm and its correspondence to the story of Creation:

> **Verse 104:1 – The first act of Creation (Genesis 1:1)**
> God, the Creator of heavens and earth, conceals Himself, thus becoming what we will call the undercover Creator.
> **Verse 104:2 – The first day of Creation**
> Light and stretching of the heavens.
> **Verses 104:3–4 – The second day of Creation**
> The formation of the firmament. Clouds, rain, wind, and heat. The weather system. Identifying two of God's agents.
> **Verses 104:5–18 – The third day of Creation**

---

2   See *Torah Shelemah* 41:242.
3   Talmud Yerushalmi, *Rosh HaShana* 3:5.

Dry land and fresh water. Earth landforms. Vegetation and trees as food and shelter for animals.

Verses 104:19–23 – The fourth day of Creation

The sun, moon, and stars.

Verses 104:25–26 – The fifth day of Creation

Sea creatures.

Verses 104:20–24 and 27–30 – The sixth day of Creation

Mammals, and man. God sustains Creation, providing food for all creatures.

From 104:30 to the end of the Psalm, King David praises the Creator and pledges to sing to and to praise Him for the rest of his life.

In the following lines we will analyze the verses from this Psalm that will help us to better understand the first three sentences of the Torah.

Psalms 104:1 – The Divine Hide–and–Seek

HaShem, My Lord, You are overwhelmingly great, You covered Yourself with glory and splendor.

As it transpires from Rashi[4] and other commentators, the first verse of the Torah (Gen. 1:1) makes it clear that the purpose of the Biblical Creation story is not to inform us of the exact date of birth of the universe, the physics of the Creation process, or the biochemical structure of God's creatures. The most important idea *Bereshit* conveys is that the world is not there by happenstance, cosmic randomness, or by the effect of some mythological gods' prowess. Genesis 1:1 and the rest of the first chapter announce that our world is the work of God, the Intelligent Creator of heavens and earth, of all forms of life, and, of course, of the human race.

All other technical information provided within the Creation narrative is not the main point of this narrative. *What* God created and *when* God created it is just ancillary information, incidental to the greater scheme

---

4   First commentary of Rashi, Gen. 1:1. The aim of the Biblical narration is to convey that God is the exclusive Creator of our world. Rashi, following the Midrash, applies this notion to advocate for the right of the Jewish people to possess the Land of Israel.

of the Torah. The reason for disclosing some of those details is to allow us to admire and praise God, the Supreme Creator, as King David was inspired to do, by uncovering the fascinating world that God fashioned. The Torah does not seem to consider it necessary to promote the quest leading to discovery of scientific truth, i.e., what precisely happened at the time of Creation. After all, as we said several times, even if we had enough information about those first instances of Creation (which we do not), it would be impossible for us, human beings, to comprehend those facts – which pertain to a reality that is fundamentally different from ours (try, for example, to picture in your mind a reality *pre* Genesis 1:4, where light did not automatically displace darkness).

Barekhi nafshi follows the same path. Its focus is not on teaching us the mysteries of the Creation process. It poetically praises God's wisdom and power in the making of this world. What it encourages us to discover is not the process of Creation itself, but Him, the Creator.

That is why, while dealing with some of the particulars of Creation, the specific focus of *Barekhi nafshi* is God. The first part of *Barekhi nafshi* (Psalms 104:1–4) deals with one very profound question, a matter that confuses the simple man of monotheistic faith. How is it that we do not *see* God, the Almighty Creator? The God of Israel is Omnipresent. In the words of the prophet Isaiah (6:3), "His glory [Presence] fills up all of earth." He created the world, He controls it, and He is constantly guiding it. How is it possible, then, that we do not see Him anywhere? What is the reason for God's invisibility vis-à-vis God's permanent providence over Creation? Genesis and the Pentateuch at large never referred directly to this matter. But King David devoted the first verses of his poem to answer why we cannot see God or, more accurately, what ways we should be seeking to find Him.

This subject matter is clear from the very beginning of the Psalm: You, God, overwhelmingly great, You hide from us, clothing and veiling Yourself with glory and splendor. Then, in the verses that follow, King David focuses his attention on God's modus operandi, showing us that God creates and hides. God runs the world, while remaining unseen. God is invisible to us because He works "undercover." God has absolute control over His universe, but He manages this world "by proxy" – through a myriad of agents or "angels."[5] Angels, in the form of natural forces, were used by God in the Creation process, and are continuously activated (in the *hif'il* verb sense) by God to maintain His Creation. God remains simultaneously unseen and in control of the universe, by acting through His agents. In the following verses we will meet some of God's agents.

Psalms 104:2 – From Behind the Screens

[God] dresses Himself up with light, as with a garment; [He] stretches heavens like a curtain.

The elements light (*OR*) and heavens (*shamayim*) are an obvious allusion to the main creations of the first day.

Beyond serving as poetic motifs, the Rabbis read the analogies between *light* and *garments*, and *heavens* and *curtains*, as great philosophical insights into the depths of the narrative of Creation. This verse, which elaborates on the ideas of the previous verse, is not referring to God's creations, but to God the Creator, and it explains the reasons we do not see the Creator of the universe. God makes Himself invisible, by hiding behind a robe of *light* and a veil made of *heavens*. In other words, from our perspective as inhabitants of the earth, light and heavens are a screen, hiding God's presence from us. We lift our eyes, searching for the Most High, but all we see is the luminous sun and the skies. Our sight cannot pierce through the multiple screens (or dimensions) which conceal God's presence. The Creator of the universe remains unseen, out of sight. Voluntarily eclipsed. He cannot be spotted. When police detectives watch a suspect from outside an interrogation room, the suspect looks at them but all he sees is a mirror. Similarly, King David explains that although God sees us, knows our actions, our thoughts, and our intentions, we cannot possibly see Him. All we see is light and heavens.[6]

---

5 Maimonides, in *Hilkhot Aboda Zara*, ch. 1, elaborates on the concept of God's servants and the risks of missing God as the ultimate cause. He explains that ancient pagan men, prior to Abraham, abandoned the worship of the invisible King (God Almighty) to serve and worship His more visible ministers (agents, i.e., the sun, the moon, wind, etc).

6 It is possible that in Psalm 104:2 *light* alludes to daytime and *heavens* to nighttime, as

Light, as well as many of God's agents, might in itself be so overwhelming to a human being that its incomprehensibility makes it clear to us why the infiniteness of its Creator is beyond our reach. Elaborating on this idea, the Talmud Yerushalmi (*Cholin* 59b) tells of a clash between a pagan man and a Jewish scholar. A Roman emperor pretentiously demanded from Rabbi Yehoshu'a ben Chananya (second century CE) to see the God of Israel. "That is impossible," retorted the Jewish sage. As the emperor insisted, R. Yehoshu'a took him outside, to the summery daylight, and asked him to stare at the sun. "I cannot," said the emperor. Rabbi Yehoshu'a had persuasively made his case. "You cannot withstand glancing at one of His servants – how much more so with seeing His own glory!"

God clothes Himself with a layer of light. Any form of God's direct revelation would be unbearable for humans. God's concealment safeguards us, not Him. In the covenant at Sinai (*ma'amad Har Sinai*), at the time the Jewish people received the Ten Commandments, God revealed Himself with His voice, announcing the first two commandments. The people of Israel were literally overwhelmed to death by that experience, and in panic requested Moshe's agency for transmitting the rest of God's commandments (Exodus 20:15–16).[7] Attending this request, God then spoke to the people of Israel by Moshe's mediation. Moshe became God's human instrument, His agent for giving the Torah to Israel.

Similarly, in the aftermath of Creation, innumerable screens made of God's natural agents conceal God's overwhelming presence from us. These screens set the limits of our sight when we lift our eyes seeking the Almighty Creator. King David teaches that a person should not confuse God's invisibility with His absence. From this verse we might better understand why we, or science and scientists, when examining Creation, will never encounter God directly; rather – inevitably – we encounter any of His numerous agents. God is invisibly omnipresent. We may find Him not with our eyes, but with our minds.

---

two screens that complement each other. The motif of heavens as nighttime is clearly seen in Psalm 8: "When I see Your heavens…the moon and stars…."

7   This is why the first two of the Ten Commandments are presented in the first person (God speaking directly), while the rest of them are in the third person (God speaking through Moshe).

Psalms 104:3 – Upper Water and Clouds

He Who made the beams of His upper chambers with water...

The previous verse described God's voluntary eclipse. It explained that the creations of the first day – heavens and light – conceal His presence from us. God is out of our sight, behind a dimension of celestial brightness.

Verses 104:3 and 104:4 present more illustrations of God's undercover operation. Verse 104:3 tells that God operated by means of His agents when He created the world and, similarly, He has continuously been managing the world through His agents ever since. Verse 104:3 describes the events of the second day of Creation, shedding light, incidentally, on the identity of some of the elements created during that day: *raqia'*, upper waters, lower waters.

The sky – clearly alluding to the *raqia'* of the second day – is called in this Psalm "His chambers" (*'aliyotav*),[8] and serves as yet a third divine screen that hides God's presence. According to the psalmist, we do not see God dwelling inside His chamber. Instead, we see the sky, the clouds, the rain. They are the visible walls of God's chambers. God's chambers (*'aliyotav* literally means upper chambers) are, of course, the upper waters of Genesis 1:7, explicitly depicted here as clouds and rain. God's chambers in this metaphor are – figuratively speaking – the control center where the operations of rainfall are programmed and activated by the Creator. We cannot see the Operator, but we see the operations center and in our minds we recognize God's existence by the effects of His commands.

King David then describes how God activates the process of rain.

He makes the clouds His chariot...

Now, finally, we have a concrete description and a conclusive definition of the upper waters mentioned on the second day. Although in the Torah there is no explicit mention of the presence or formation of clouds, this Psalm – incidentally, but unambiguously – identifies the new creation of the second day of Creation as clouds. The upper waters made on the second

---

8   Notice that the word *shamayim*, "heavens," is not used here, but rather *'aliyotav*, probably an allusion to *raqia'*. See following note.

day are in fact the natural water reservoirs stored in the clouds, suspended high in the atmosphere, which are destined to return to the earth's surface in the form of rain and snow.[9]

The clouds – in Hebrew *'abim* – are compared to God's chariot. Not to say, of course, that the clouds *transport* God, but that they are *driven by* God.[10] In other words, God controls and directs the clouds to produce rain. Although invisible and hidden in His celestial chamber, God, this verse carefully asserts, is in absolute control of His Creation. He is behind the wheels of Creation, driving the clouds to produce rain. God is the unseen driver of Creation. We see the chariot, we perceive its purposeful direction, but we cannot see the Driver.

…He Who rides on the wings of wind.

How does God Almighty drive the clouds? …*Riding on the wings of winds.*[11] In this verse, King David describes what the Rabbis will later term *morid hageshem*[12] ("[He] Who causes the rain to fall"). The word *morid* is also constructed in the causative *hif'il* verbal form, meaning: God causes rain to fall by the effect of winds and clouds. Very elegantly, King David started from the final product: water/rain (God's chambers made of water), then continued with the most immediate cause of rain: clouds (clouds, as God's chariot), and concluded with the first divine agent, the mover of the clouds: wind. God Almighty directs His wind riding on its wings. Accordingly, 104:3 is saying: "God produces rain by driving the clouds, through His wind…." Clearly, a wind driven by God, alluded to in this verse, is the divine wind (or God's wind) of Genesis 1:2.

King David carefully emphasizes that God is present in every step of the rain process, and yet, remains invisible – in His impenetrable chambers.

---

9   The identification of the term *'aliyotav* (His upper chambers) with rain becomes absolutely evident when *'aliyotav* is used again in verse 13: *Mashqe harim me'aliyotav*, "He waters the mountains from His upper chambers."

10   See Radaq on this verse.

11   According to Radaq, the term *mehalekh* is associated with driving, riding, and shepherding animals.

12   Ezekiel 24:36.

Psalms 104:4, Part 1– God's Secret Agents

He makes winds His angels; [His servants – a burning fire].

Still within the framework of the second day of Creation, our verse refers to *wind*, and further mentions a mysterious *fire* never mentioned explicitly in Genesis, chapter 1.

Wind and fire are called here *mal-akhim* and *mesharetim*, (God's) angels and servants. In Biblical Hebrew, the term *mal-akh*, "angel," means agent or proxy. It could refer to an agent of God or to an agent of man.[13] Such an agent could be human or of any other sort.

In the second verse of the Torah, *wind* is mentioned explicitly as one of the elements included in the description of planet Earth's initial inventory. Our verse 104:4 confirms our contention that the mysterious *ruach Elohim* mentioned in Genesis 1:2 should not be understood as a *divine spirit* but rather – as the Targum, Sa'adia Gaon, Maimonides, and other commentaries understood it – a physical wind, acting as an agent of God in Creation and beyond.

Ruach Elohim, we said, could be interpreted as a mighty wind (*elohim* acting as the adjective *mighty*), or as God's wind. King David's identification of wind with God's *mal-akhim*, or agents, conforms beautifully and precisely with the idea of God's wind or a wind directed by God, the way Targum Onkelos and Maimonides understood it.

Of course, wind is not a tool used by God just in the creation of the world. Wind, as Maimonides explained, is God's instrument of choice in the continuous control and maintenance of earth's climate and beyond.[14]

God's usage of proxies, tools, and instruments is common. Beyond the context of the narrative of Creation, God's acting through agencies is prevalent throughout Biblical literature, rabbinical thinking, and Jewish

---

13 *Mal-akhim*, usually understood as "angels," must be comprehended as agents, messengers, proxies, or emissaries. Ya'aqob Abinu (Jacob) sent *mal-akhim lefanav*, messengers ahead of him to his brother Esau (Gen. 32:3). The English word "angel" comes from the Greek *aggelos*, which has a similar meaning to the Hebrew *mal-akh*: messenger, agent.

14 Psalm 148:8 also has the wind as God's loyal servant: רוח סערה עושה דברו.... See Rashi and Radaq there.

liturgy. The Rabbis stated that God constantly uses a multitude of agents to perform His will (*harbe shelichim laMaqom*).[15] Acting through agency is the norm in God's interaction with His world in the day-to-day operation, not just in His miraculous interventions.

On this latter point, take for example every one of the plagues brought by God upon Egypt at the time of the exodus – each and every plague was an agent of God, carrying forth God's message to Pharaoh, Egypt, and the people of Israel.

The very last plague, death of the firstborn, was explicitly described by the Torah as performed by God's agent or intermediary. God sent a *mashchit*[16] (which was traditionally identified as an angel of death) to inflict the ultimate punishment on the Egyptian firstborns, while God Himself (so to speak) protected the Jewish homes – "[God] protected the homes of the Children of Israel in Egypt" – from His own agent, the *mashchit*'s deadly blow.[17] The Torah singled out this event as a singular one in which God, exceptionally, acted directly and without any agency. As the Haggada of Pesach says: "I [protected you], and not an angel; it was I, not an intermediary." During the last plague God shielded the people of Israel, protecting them against one of His own agents. The fact that this plague was singled out as unique leaves no doubt that God's normal way of acting is through His agents.[18]

---

15 For a wider use of this maxim see Nachmanides's commentary on Gen. 37:15.

16 Ex. 12:23. Read this verse carefully in light of the next note.

17 This is how the verb *pasach* in 12:23 and other related verses should be understood. The Targum Onkelos translates *pasach* as "*chais*": cared, watched, or protected, as in the rabbinic expression אדם חס על ממונו, "A person protects and takes good care of his assets." *Protection* rather then *passing over* is the idea we celebrate on the night of Pesach, which is also called *lel shimurim*. Accordingly, God sent His agent *mashchit* – angel of death – to punish the Egyptians, while God Himself protected (*pasach*) the houses of the Hebrews, preventing His agent to inflict his lethal blow on the firstborn Jews. In the Biblical text, this type of confusion about the identity of the subject, God or one of His agents, is not uncommon. See, for example, Gen. 18:3 and the debate among the commentaries on the identity of the addressee of the patriarch Abraham.

18 That is the reason why, according to tradition, Moses – God's noblest human agent – is not mentioned in the Haggada: to emphasize that it was God Who directly and without any agency protected the Jewish people at the time of the death of the firstborn, the final and most lethal plague.

Wind acting as one of God's agents is not a concept unique to the creation of the world. The Torah tells explicitly about how God used the wind as an agent in the exodus from Egypt. God brought an eastern wind (*ruach qadim*) to bring the locusts into Egypt and, later on, to drive them away once the devastating insects had finished their voracious mission.[19] At the time of the exodus, when the Children of Israel needed to escape from Egyptian bondage, God split the sea for them. Interestingly, the Torah does not say that God acted directly upon the waters. God used, yet again, a powerful wind (*ruach qadim 'aza*) to dry up the sea-bottom and thus split the water,[20] allowing the people of Israel to cross to the other side on dry land.

In the Creation story, the presence of wind on planet Earth is carefully and especially acknowledged (*ruach Elohim*) in Genesis 1:2 as God's instrument or agent. During the second and third days, wind performed its creative mission as God's secret agent. *Barekhi nafshi* mentions wind in its description of the second day, and thereby uncovers the secret but critical role wind played in the first days of Creation. Wind was instrumental during the formation of the water cycle, helping (or causing) the process of rain, which took place during the second day. Wind transfers water molecules away from the evaporating surface, maintaining the atmosphere's moisture, hence triggering the formation of clouds. In a sense, wind was the most critical medium the Creator used for the formation of earth's atmosphere and the entire weather system.

Based on this Psalm, among other sources, the Rabbis also viewed wind as the basic agent God presently and constantly uses to produce rain, the source of livelihood. The Rabbis introduced to Jewish liturgy a praise to God Almighty, Who "makes the wind blow, and causes the rain to fall" (*mashib haruach umorid hageshem* – again in the *hif'il* form). The Rabbis could have credited the production of rain to the effect of other more visible or noticeable elements, like clouds, thunder, or lightning. But they recognized

---

19 Ex. 10:13, 19.
20 In that order: first He dried the sea, and then, as if consequently, the sea stood as two walls. See Ex. 14:21.

that rain comes specifically as the effect of the wind, God's agent in creating and maintaining the weather system.[21]

Why did the Biblical text not acknowledge the use of wind or other agents of Creation more directly? First, I would contend that the Scripture did acknowledge the exceptional role played by wind when in Genesis 1:2, it mentioned wind as "God's wind." It may be, then, that the omission of "wind" from the rest of the Creation story could be attributed simply to Biblical brevity (and brevity, as we have had the opportunity to mention, is the norm in the account of Creation). Or perhaps, by not explicitly acknowledging the role of wind during the second or third days, the Torah wished to highlight that, although God employs His agents, we should not *confuse* them with the Creator responsible for them. Perhaps, in light of the primary objective of Genesis – which is to show us that it is God Who created the world and equipped the world with everything necessary for life – the Torah presents the Creation process as performed directly by the Creator, even in those instances where, upon reading the text very carefully, we can appreciate that He acted through natural forces.

The book of Psalms, nevertheless, is more explicit. *Barekhi nafshi* focuses its attention on the agents God used, explaining God's continuous providence (*hashgacha*) over the world against the backdrop of His invisible omnipresence. *Barekhi nafshi* is a priceless postscript to the narrative in Genesis. It reveals the details of the Creation process, enriching our awareness of God's presence and His modus operandi in the world.

---

21 *More Nebukhim* 2:30 (Schwarz, p. 364) points out that the wind is God's agent par excellence: "The blowing of the wind is always attributed to the Creator." See the numerous examples Maimonides presents there.

Psalms 104:4, Part 2 – Heat and Water Evaporation

[He makes winds His angels;] His servants – a burning fire.

One of the most critical contributions of Psalm 104 to the understanding of the first chapter of Genesis is the identification of primeval light (in Hebrew, *OR*) mentioned in Genesis 1:3 with fire or heat (*esh*) – acknowledging it as God's second agent of Creation. *Fire* in Psalm 104:4 can only parallel the light of Genesis 1:3, an unambiguous indication of the heating quality of the primeval light.[22] By tradition, we know that the kind of fire obtained through combustion was attributed by the Rabbis to Adam's inventiveness, and not to God's direct Creation in Genesis.[23] Therefore, the "fire" alluded to in Psalm 104:4 as one of God's creations, particularly within the framework of the second day, and portrayed as one of God's agents of Creation, cannot be the flames we commonly think of as "fire."[24] We must necessarily conclude that "fire" mentioned in Psalm 104:4 refers to the primeval light (*OR*) of Genesis 1:3.

The nature of this primeval light is a matter that we explore in the next section of this book. Nonetheless, we can now verify that, as we had previously assumed, just like any other source of electromagnetic radiation the light of Genesis 1:3 was not just a source of luminosity, but of energy and heat too.

The word *esh* is also used as "heat" in Psalm 148:8: "heat and hail, snow and vapor," whereby *esh* – clearly *solar heat* and not *fire* – is counted among the elements of the weather system, together with hail, snow, and vapor (i.e., mist).

---

22 There is evidently a relationship between *OR* ("light") and the word *UR* ("fire"), which in Hebrew is written the same way. *UR* appears several times in the Hebrew Bible as *fire*; see Isaiah 31:9, and others. As for the word *OR* as *fire* or *heat*, there is one verse (Malachi 1:10) where *OR*, in the form of the verb *ta-iru*, refers to the ignition of fire on the altar.

23 Talmud Babli, *Berakhot* 12a.

24 That is, the triggered combustion of a carbon-based compound, and the consequent rapid oxidation that releases heat and light.

Heat is a property of any light or electromagnetic radiation. Following the pattern we have already found in the Creation narrative, we do not expect the text of Genesis to explicitly identify heat as one of God's agents. However, similarly to what we saw with wind, the fact that *Barekhi nafshi* explicitly acknowledges heat (*esh*) as one of God's agents within the context of the second day of Creation clearly indicates that in the process of the division of the waters, heat played a crucial role in the separating between liquid water and vapor, allowing the progression of the Biblical sequence of Creation:

> **Wind + Water** (Gen. 1:2) + **Heat/OR** (Gen. 1:3) → **Vaporization/ Clouds/Rain** (Gen. 1:6–7) → **Vegetation** (Gen. 1:12)[25]

Verse 104:4, "He makes winds His angels; His servants – a burning fire," exposes wind and heat as the two hidden agents used by the Creator to produce the atmosphere and the events of the second day. Light/heat[26] was also used by the Almighty as an agent in the creation of the *raqia'* on the second day; in a similar way wind was used by God to dry up the land during the third day. And, probably, in the same way wind was instrumental to form the clouds during the second day, heat was operational in drying up the continents during the third day.

Psalms 104:8 – Freshwater and Erosion

They went up the mountains, they flowed down the valleys, to the place You founded for them.

Verse 8 of our Psalm *might* be suggesting the activity of a third agent employed by God in Creation, in addition to wind and heat. This verse

---

25 The role of evaporation or mist on vegetation seems to be explicitly recorded in Genesis 2:6: "And a mist came up from the earth and watered the whole surface of the ground."

26 *Bereshit Rabba* 4:7. Rab says that the Almighty combined *esh* (heat) and *mayim* (water) to make the sky. A similar explanation was given by Rabbi Yochanan, except that according to him the water the Almighty took was in the form of snow (שתי פקיעות של אש אחד של שלג); ibid. 10:3. This was probably the source of Rabbi Chefetz in *Melekhet Machashebet*.

seems to hint that rain acted as one of God's tools in the Creation process as well. The Rabbis saw rain as one of God's most blissful mediums in providing sustenance to His creatures. Similar to wind, in the second blessing of the 'Amida (Jewish silent prayer), rain is one of the key elements for which we proclaim God as the Compassionate Provider for all living creatures (*mekhalkel chayim bechesed*).

Following the pattern we found in the case of wind and heat, rain too should not be expected to be acknowledged *explicitly* as an agent of Creation. Actually, it is only thanks to *Barekhi nafshi* that we are able to identify rain as the upper waters of Genesis to begin with. The Torah never mentioned precipitation (in Biblical Hebrew, *matar* or *geshem*) in chapter 1. It talked, simply, about the separation of the waters. As we have showed, understanding this verse as alluding to rain conforms to our understanding of the Creation narrative as a successive progression, whereby each element is created as a basis for the creation of the following element. Water and wind (created during the initial act of Creation), needed heat (created on the first day) to produce rain (created on the second day). Rain, therefore, might have been an instrument for the development of the events of the third day. On the one hand, as we have already seen, rain is vital for vegetation, created on the second part of the third day. That fact alone will be enough to justify the successive progression water → heat (first day) → rain (second day) → vegetation (third day), viewing the role of rain as a prerequisite for vegetation.

However, I would like to argue in the following lines that verse 104:8 *might* assign to rain an additional role in the cataclysms that shaped the continents and their features on the first half of the third day, when the story of Creation reports the emergence of the land over the surface of the oceans. When the Creator ordered the waters to recede, to gather into the ocean and allow the dry land to be seen, the Torah succinctly says "and let dry land be seen." Consistent with Biblical brevity, nothing is mentioned about *how* God moved the water, *how* God brought up the land, and *how* dry land acquired its present landscape.

Some rabbis, we have seen, explained that God used wind to separate the sea from the continents. But what about the continental landforms? What medium was employed by God Almighty to bring up the dry land

and shape the present earth's landscape of mountains and valleys? Carefully analyzing verse 104:8 we might find an allusion to the role of rain in the process of landform development.

The words of this verse are quite difficult to understand. The verse is at the center of a detailed narration of the geological events that took place during the third day of Creation, resulting in the emergence of dry land. It is worth noticing, incidentally, that Psalm 104 dedicates to the third day the most elaborate and longest narrative, containing the largest number of verses of our Psalm: fifteen. For our analysis of 104:8, it is important to bear in mind that water is overall the main subject of the third day. Twelve of the fifteen verses dedicated to the third day deal with water's role in Creation (remember m*elekhet hamayim*?).

To begin with, let us analyze the context of our verse.

Psalm 104:6, "You covered it [the earth] with the primeval sea as with a garment; the waters stood above the mountains," portrays a state of the planet in which water is covering it entirely. This is compatible with (or perhaps one of the sources of) the rabbinic tradition that at its incipient stage, our planet was completely covered by water.[27] In 104:7, "From your rebuke they [the waters] would flee; from the sound of Your thunder they [the waters] would hastily escape," something of cataclysmic proportions happens. The verse describes the receding of the water, which produces some unimaginably forceful thunder and noise.

Verse 104:8 now continues: "They went up the mountains, they flowed down the valleys, to the place You founded for them." In order to understand what this verse is saying we should first define what the subject of this verse is, which is quite a challenging task.

There are two standard translations:

1. "The mountains rose, the valleys sank down – unto the place which You founded for them."[28]

---

27 See chapter 4.
28 JPS, 1917 edition. Many other translations have rendered this verse in the same way. For example, English Standard Translation (2001), and others.

2. "They went up the mountains, they flowed down the valleys,
   to the place You founded for them."[29]

As one can see, the translations are significantly different. In one case (1) the subject is the mountains and the valleys, and in the other (2) the subject of the sentence is the waters.

If the mountains and the valleys are the subject, our verse then would be describing the process of formation of the landscape of planet Earth, which was surging as the waters were receding. This description would nicely complement our knowledge of the events of the third day of Creation, and would explain the emergence of our planet's upper crust in all its magnificent forms and splendor. The landforms are depicted by the contrasting geographical features: "mountains and valleys."

There is just one little problem with this translation. The context where our verse operates signals beyond any doubt that, indeed, the waters and not the mountains and valleys should be the subject of the verse.

Let us again read the previous verses.

Verse 104:6, "over the mountains the waters stood," makes it clear that the subject in the verse is unambiguously the waters.

In 104:7 similarly, the subject is the waters: "From your rebuke *they* [the waters, which were standing atop the mountains] would flee, from your thunder *they* [the waters] would hastily escape."

Before going back to 104:8, let us peek ahead at 104:9: "You set a boundary, lest they cross [it], lest they return to cover the earth." Also in this verse, the subject is again water. If water is the subject matter of verses 104:6, 7, and 9, we should assume that the subject of verse 104:8 is water as well, and not the mountains and the valleys. Now, if water is the subject of this verse, as the second translation holds (the waters went up the mountains and down the valleys) then King David is describing the movements of water going up and down.

---

29 *Me'am Lo'ez* translation. 104:8; Rabbi Shmuel Yerushalmi, *The Torah Anthology: The Book of Tehillim*, translated by Dr. Zvi Faier (New York: Moznaim, 1991). This is also the version of the King James translation, and others.

But then, we face another small problem of basic physics: water could go down into the valleys, but water could never go up the mountains, as this verse would imply!

Today, thanks to modern scientific understanding of geology, I believe that we can formulate – with a bit of audacity – an alternative explanation of this verse that will connect the creation of the second day, rain, with the events of the third day of Creation, which verse 104:8 describes.

I would propose reading the verse with *water* as the subject and the Hebrew verb *ya'alu* as a transitive verb.[30] *Ya'alu* would then mean "the waters brought up the mountains" instead of "the mountains rose up." Accordingly, this verse would be saying that freshwater – rain – pushed the mountains up, hence bringing the valleys down. This explanation would afford us a deeper insight into the events of the third day.

During the first part of the third day two different creative activities took place: (1) The waters receded, gathering together in the oceans, and (2) dry land emerged and the continental surface was seen. While verse 104:4 hinted that wind must have been God's instrument for the first of God's commands, i.e., the waters getting organized into oceans, verse 104:8 might be telling us now that freshwater (rain and snow) was the instrument the Creator used for the second activity: the emergence of land and the shaping of its landforms.[31]

---

30 The particular verbal form *ye'alu* does not exist in the Hebrew Scriptures. *Ya'alu*, however, is used many times as transitive in the Hebrew Scriptures. For example: אז יעלו על מזבחך פרים, "Then, they will bring up bovine offerings onto Your altar" (Psalms 51:21), and many more. I must admit, however, that the weakest part of this innovative commentary is the word *yeredu*, in that it never appears in the Scriptures as a transitive verb. The only possible interpretation that will justify my explanation is that by the effect of the waters raising the mountains, the valleys went down by themselves.

31 My son Ya'aqob Bitton proposed a different (and perhaps better) way of interpreting the ascent of the waters, also identifying these waters as rain. The thrust of this reading would be: 104:8 – *They* [the waters] *go up over mountains* [by being evaporated and formed into clouds], *they descend unto the valleys* [through precipitation], *and thus arrive to the location You intended for them.* 104:9 – [In this way,] *You established a limit to them* [referring to the actual elevation of the continental shore, formed through the process of erosion, which – in conjunction with the force of gravity – prevents waters from inundating the earth once again], *lest they return* [with every tide, the waters "return" toward the continent] *and cover the earth.*

The following words, by which science journalist Larry O'Hanlon explains the recently discovered critical role of freshwater in the process of erosion and the formation of our planet's landforms, might help us understand the reading I am proposing:

> Freshwater also removes weight from the Earth's crust in one place and weighs down others.[32] By wearing away rocks of the Himalaya, for instance, rain and snow make the mountains lighter and actually speed up the rate at which the range buoys upward on the more plastic layer below the crust.... In turn, by affecting the pressure in the mantle, it is thought by some geophysicists that currents can be generated in the mantle that influence how, when, and where tectonic plates move. This top-down theory to what drives plate tectonics, makes fresh water a central player in the making of every inch of Earth's surface today.[33]

Plate tectonics are believed to be the immediate cause in the building of mountains and the formation of valleys and "every inch of earth's surface." Nevertheless, modern scientists believe it is rain that actually *activates* plate tectonics and "influence how, when and where tectonic plates move."

Psalm 104:8 might be suggesting that, in addition to its role in the emergence of vegetation, rain also might have been divinely employed as one of God's instruments to bring mountains up and valleys down, thus shaping the landscape of our planet. In other words, rain, a product of the elements from Creation-days one and two, would have been an agent in eroding the earth's crust into above-sea-level continents (the first part of Day Three). Then, rain would again act as the Creator's agent for the sprouting of plants, drenching the dry land, making it fertile, and helping combine the elements that developed into vegetation (the second part of Day Three).

---

32 Observe the striking similarities between this sentence and verse 104:8.
33 O'Hanlon, "Freshwater," http://dsc.discovery.com/convergence/planet-earth/guide/fresh-water.html.

SUMMARY

Genesis 1:2 describes the world in the aftermath of its creation: "But the earth was desolate and void, and darkness was over the face of the primitive seas, and a divine wind was blowing over the face of the water." At this point, the earth is still a work in progress, an unfinished creation. Wind and water are mentioned in this verse for a reason. Water is the medium by which God will reverse desolation and lifelessness. Water is also the main raw material of Creation. It will be processed and reprocessed to gradually create the atmosphere and the weather system, which in turn will allow for vegetation and oxygen to exist. Ultimately, water will be used by God to bring forth the first forms of life.

Wind, on the other hand, will do a less noticeable, albeit not less fundamental, work. Wind will be used by the Creator as the engine of the weather system on the second day and to bring the waters together, drying up the continents, on the third day. Wind represents a special category of Creation. It is specifically and particularly mentioned as God's agent, an inanimate element which acts at God's will, transforming or running His Creation, hiding God's presence from us.

It is only with the invaluable assistance of *Barekhi nafshi* that we are able to discern the existence and decisive role played by wind and others among God's hidden agents (like heat and possibly rain) in the narrative of Creation. *Barekhi nafshi* helps us understand that the employment of agents keeps God covered from our sight. God operates in the world under the guise of His numerous agents. Only exceptionally would God act directly. As far as I know, there were only two exceptional moments in which the Scripture implies that God acted directly: (1) When He protected the people of Israel from the *mashchit* on the night of the exodus, and (2) at the moment of the theophany at Sinai (*maʾamad Har Sinai*) when God pronounced the first two commandments – communicating them *directly* to the people of Israel.

Throughout the Torah we have numerous examples of God's agents performing God's mission where the result of that mission is attributed to God Himself and not to His emissaries (humans or anything else). Perhaps one of the best examples is the story of the angels sent by God to destroy

Sodom and Gomorra. The angels explicitly announce to Lot: "*We* are about to destroy this place...God has sent *us* to destroy it."[34] Later on, however, the destruction of the two cities is attributed exclusively to God Himself,[35] not to His angels, and those angels are never mentioned again.

Menashe ben Israel quotes Don Isaac Abarbanel's view on God's agents or angels: "God *always* acts in this lower word by intermediate means, or by accessories, and these are of two kinds: those operating from understanding, will, or choice [humans, like Moses, or other prophets. Y. B.]; and those which rank as instrumental causes, which are brought into action not by their own will but by superior command, such as natural forces and acts." As if to leave no room for doubt in this delicate matter of attribution, Menashe ben Israel clarifies that "it is necessary to add that the proximate agent of all miracles is God Himself."[36]

Finally, I believe that recognizing the use of agents by God in the creation of the world is of critical importance for those who hold that the Torah and scientific discovery are not incompatible. One who understands that according to Biblical sources, God deliberately hides His actions behind the cover and agency of natural elements, will know better than to feel frustrated when science does not perceive the ultimate – willingly *invisible* – driving Force behind the *visible* natural elements. Should science ever demonstrate, for example, that life started from water, certainly that would not contradict the explicit Biblical statement in Genesis 1:20. On the contrary, it would confirm it. Should science demonstrate that evaporation cleared the primeval toxic atmosphere and helped the creation of the new life-friendly atmosphere, that is exactly what the Torah is saying too.

Once the forces and processes that brought about the world as we know it are studied and accurately identified, the differences between the Biblical account of Creation and the scientific narrative are just a matter of attribution. Scientists will naturally arrive to, and stop at, the point of identifying the "natural forces and events." Those of us who embrace the Biblical chronicle will call these forces what they are: God's agents and

---

34 Genesis 19:13: כי משחתים אנחנו.
35 Genesis 19:24, 25, 29.
36 Ben Israel, *Conciliator*, question 47, p. 70. See also question 67, pp. 90–93.

divine – not natural – forces and events. Once we know God acts through agents, and that these agents are fully subservient to God's will, then we may and should resort to science as the field that aids in the understanding of those agents. Consequently, far from being a source of tensions and contradictions, science becomes an invaluable tool for appreciating God's Creation.

VERSE THREE

"And God said:
'Let there be light,'
and there was light."

Genesis 1:3

CHAPTER 7

LIGHT AND TIME

One of the most famous and sublime sentences in the Hebrew Scripture is the third verse of Genesis, chapter 1, the verse that describes the creation of light: "And God said, 'Let there be light,' and there was light." It also marks the first time God speaks in the story of Creation.

Many questions may cross our minds as we read these words. For example, how should we understand that God *spoke*? Is it a way to describe in human terms that God *willed*? Otherwise, to whom was it that God spoke? To Himself? To the inanimate matter that would organize together and create light? What was the process by which light was created out of God's speech? Were God's speech and the creation of light one single act or two separate acts? Was the creation of light a creation ex nihilo? And why was light not created, like water, during the initial act of Creation, as part of the inventory of heavens and earth?

These, and more, are the questions that we are *not* going to directly address in this chapter. In the following lines, we will focus our attention almost exclusively in identifying where that light was coming from and what the source of this light was according to Jewish tradition.

This light – *primeval light* – was the light whose creation is described in Genesis 1:3, which was separated from darkness in Genesis 1:4, and which directly or indirectly generated Day One in Genesis 1:5. This is the light that illuminated the world and produced the distinction between day and night, at least during the first three days of Creation.

One of the functions of this primeval light, the Biblical text asserts, was delineating the transition of time: allowing the perception of the beginning and the end of the days. Primeval light is portrayed as the instrumentality initiating that process ultimately defined by the Torah as a "day." This process, from the appearance of primeval light to the establishment of Day One, is narrated in the following verses.

> And God saw that the light was good, and God separated the light from the darkness. (Genesis 1:4)

Immediately after primeval light is created, God proceeds to distinguish it from darkness. The separation of light and darkness is the first in a series of acts of division the Creator performed during the Creation process. Perhaps, like all other acts of separation mentioned in the story of Creation, the distinction between light and darkness consisted in the establishment of the basic physical laws we take for granted today, among them, the displacement of darkness by light.[1] The Creator organized His newly created planet through multiple acts of separation: light from darkness, water from vapor, dry land from oceans, and days from nights.

Pointedly, the act of separation of light and darkness also represents a clear statement of Biblical monotheism. Against the backdrop of ancient civilizations' pagan beliefs, the Torah asserted that not only light but darkness too is one of God's creations, and not some sort of mythical anti-divine force or alternative god. Absence of light, or any other absence in Creation, is part and parcel of God's design. Darkness is not indicative, as mythical civilizations believed, of any limitations to God's absolute power. In the Torah we do not find two opposite deities struggling against each other – a god of light versus a god of darkness, common characters in ancient mythology. The God of Israel alone created light, and then limited this light by creating darkness. Daytime and nighttime are two opposite realities, both created by God Himself. It is this combination (or succession) of opposites that will produce the unity of a day.

Similarly, in a different context, there is a need for two different beings, a man and a woman – explicitly described by the Torah as *opposite*[2] to one another – to produce a third human being. Electrical energy too owes its being to a combination, and tension, of two inverse forces: the positive and negative charges.[3] Beyond merely pointing out that light and darkness

---

1 Rashi (1:4) quotes the midrash that says: "Light and darkness," at some point after the creation of light, "were operating simultaneously"...until God separated them.
2 As it is explicitly expressed in the word *kenegdo*, Eve was created to be a being "opposite to him [Adam]" (Gen. 2:20).
3 Josy Eisenberg and Armand Abecassis, *A Bible Ouverte*, French edition (Paris: Albin Michel, 2004), p. 78.

VERSE THREE ♦ 165

would henceforth oppose each other, verse 1:5 suggests a more profound principle: God created a world in which opposite forces often synergize with each other to form a greater and better product. Day → night presents a very special type of succession – one that should not be taken for granted – because it is not a case of inevitable cause and effect. Generally, an effect coming after a cause creates a natural cycle, like evaporation → rain → evaporation, etc. Evening → morning, however, are not the natural cause and effect of each other.

In addition to making possible the measuring of time, the transition evening → morning is essential for the existence of life in our planet as we know it today. The cycle of daytime and nighttime is a providential privilege of our privileged planet. As Guillermo Gonzales says: "Although we take them for granted, dark nights depend on several astronomic variables, some local, some not. A dark sky requires that our planet regularly rotate away from the intense direct light of the Sun. If our day were the same length as our year, Earth would always keep the same face pointed toward the sun, much as the moon does earth. The resulting large temperature differences between the day and night sides would be hostile to complex life. Any complex life, such as there could be, would stay on the day side."[4]

> And God called the light daytime[5] and the darkness He called nighttime; and there was evening, and there was morning, One Day. (Genesis 1:5)

God calls (defines) light as daytime (*yom*), and darkness as nighttime (*layla*) and sets in motion the continuum: nighttime → daytime = One Day

Interestingly, through the rest of the Creation narrative, the Scripture refers to the cycle of transition between one day and the next as: evening → morning, as opposed to the more intuitive terminology used in this verse:

---

4   Guillermo Gonzalez and Jay W. Richards, *The Privileged Planet: How Our Place in the Cosmos Is Designed for Discovery* (Washington, DC: Regnery Publishing, 2004), p. 68. In what could be seen as a reverse Platonic cave, Gonzalez gives the example of Isaac Asimov's Planet Lagash in his book *Nightfall* – a planet ordinarily illuminated at all times on all sides, which only sees dark skies in total solar eclipses.

5   In this chapter, I translate *yom* as daytime whenever it appears in opposition to *layla* or nighttime.

nighttime → daytime. Evening (*'ereb*), or nightfall, is the initial phase of nighttime,[6] and morning (*boqer*) is the beginning of the daytime. Both are terms that are not easy to define. Whereas nighttime is clearly defined as beginning at dusk and ending at dawn, and daytime as beginning at dawn and ending at sunset, morning and evening are much more elusive. When does a morning begin and end? When does an evening begin and end? That the Torah chose to indicate this transition between days with the terms morning and evening connotes a more gradual transition from one day to the next.

Yes, nighttime and daytime are more clearly defined than morning and evening, but they also represent a more abrupt opposition: a sudden switch from one state to the other. The process of Creation, as we have been discovering, is a *gradual* series of smaller steps, not one of radical sudden transformations. The Biblical usage of "morning" and "evening" as the terms to describe the transition from one day to the next is consistent with the general pattern of Creation: a process made up of gradual steps.[7]

In Genesis 1:3, 1:4, and 1:5 the sole, explicit function of light and darkness is to establish the boundaries of a day. At this stage, the units Scripture uses to measure time are limited to *nighttime*, *daytime*, and the intermediate stages *morning* and *evening*. The Torah will mention months and years in the context of the fourth day,[8] and a week – the only non-astronomical but rather divinely determined cycle of time – will only become operative with the establishment of the Shabbat.

In verse 5, Day One stands on its own. Nothing anticipates that an additional day is supposed to be coming. Unlike the other five days of Creation, the Biblical text did not use the ordinal "first" but the cardinal "one" (Day One, not "the first day").[9] From a semantic point of view, the

---

6   Technically, *'ereb* starts after midday. See the explanation of Rabbi Raphall, *Sacred Scriptures*, Gen. 1:5, page 2a (bet).

7   See *Torah Shelemah* 77:389.

8   Genesis 1:14.

9   In Rabbi Morris Raphall's words: "The cardinal *one* is used, not the ordinal *first*. Some maintain, because the word first can only be applied to a subject, if there is a second to succeed it, but as the second day was not yet in being, the designation *first* could not be applied to its predecessor. Others contend that...the words *one day* are used here, not merely to point out the rank in the succession of days, but in order to convey

first day had not been created yet, so long as there was no second day to give context to its "firstness." At this point, what God had created was not the *first* day but rather *a* day.

Daytime, nighttime, evening, and morning constitute a sophisticated cosmic clock created by God for humans to measure the most basic unit of time: a day.

LIGHT, TIME, AND MORTALITY

One of the primary consequences of the creation of light was the establishment of a visually discernible distinction between the two parts of a day: daytime and nighttime, and the intermediate stages between them: morning and evening. Daytime and nighttime constitute a sequence that allows man to measure or gain consciousness of the passing of time. The first type of organization God implements in His world is the organization of time.

To clarify, I do not mean to say that according to the Scripture time did not exist prior to the creation of light, or before the first sequence evening → morning ever began. According to Maimonides[10] and Nachmanides, among others, time itself had already been created with the creation of the universe (Gen. 1:1).

For the Torah, though, daytime and nighttime are explicitly presented as a continuum designed by the Creator to allow the measurement of time.[11] The calculation of time is a strictly human necessity. Only humans are capable of having consciousness of time's progression, which allows

---

that the space of time thereby expressed is equal to the diurnal revolution of the earth round its own axis, and that evening and morning spoken of in the text were equal to what subsequently was called *one* day."

10 *More Nebukhim* 2:30. (Schwarz, p. 361, כי הזמן מכלל הברואים, "…as time is among those things created.")

11 The audacious reader should consider Olber's paradox, which explains that the expansion of the universe is responsible for our perception of "night." In other words, the earth's sky should be illuminated constantly by the hundreds of billions of stars of our Milky Way and by the light of the hundreds of billions of galaxies coming to us from the known universe. Night is possible only thanks to the expansion of the universe. Was the expansion of the universe brought about by God just to create the effect of "night" on our planet? Is it, perhaps, too anthropocentric to even think about this possibility?

man to plan and manage his limited existence, with the goal of fulfilling his mission. For animals, time flows beyond their consciousness in the same way time flows for humans in their dreams.[12] While matter, water, the atmosphere, and dry land are essential for all living creatures sharing our planet, the measurement of days and the calculation of the abstract fractions of a day seem to be tailored exclusively to address the human need to be cognizant of time passing.

By being conscious of the progress of time, man realizes his inescapable mortality.

BORGES AND THE ILLUSION OF ETERNITY

Time is one of the few things man cannot control, bring back, prolong, or stop. Man is destined to live encapsulated within a dimension of time beyond his dominance.[13]

Take a look at the verse "And God saw all He had made and, behold, it was very good" (Gen. 1:31). In the *Haggada* (creative exposition of the Scriptural text), Rabbi Meir would read this verse a little differently. Instead of "very good" (*tob me-od*) he would read it "death [is] good" (*tob mavet*), as if the verse were saying, "And God saw that *death* was good."

To explain Rabbi Meir's profound insight on the positive effects of death upon our existence, I would like to share with the reader a reflection from Jorge Luis Borges. In his fictional story "The Immortal," Borges draws a comparison between mortals and immortals: "Death (or reference to death) makes men precious.... Any act they perform may be their last.... Everything in the world of mortals is irrecoverable and contingent. Among the Immortals, on the other hand, every act (every thought) is the echo of

---

12 See Jorge Luis Borges, *Historia de la Eternidad* (Buenos Aires: Emece Editores, 2005), p. 19. The master Argentine writer had a literary obsession with time (and with mirrors, and with tigers), which he, following Bergson, considered the biggest mystery of metaphysics. Borges' assertion should not be seen as a definitive scientific theory. Animal cognition, and especially the notion of circadian rhythms, is a fascinating matter of intense research in our days.

13 Jorge Luis Borges, "The Immortal," in *Collected Fictions*, translated by Andrew Hurley (New York: Penguin, 1999), p. 189. Borges explains that without mortality and the consciousness of mortality, human life would be insignificant. Or, in the words of Plato, "the insufferable boredom of eternity."

others that preceded in the past, with no visible beginning, and the faithful presage of others that will repeat in the future, *ad vertiginem*. There is nothing that is not as though lost between indefatigable mirrors. Nothing can occur but once, nothing is preciously in peril of being lost."[14]

As Rabbi Meir hinted, death imbues life, every minute of it, with an irrecoverable preciousness. The most useful notion for man's spiritual and intellectual development is the consciousness of the perishable nature of each day of his life. Man should live each day conscious of the unrepeatable nature of *a day*. Death, as Descartes described it, starts when we are born. Death is the aggregated effect of all previous days that have perished. Stagnation in man's pursuit of God is the sworn enemy of Jewish intellectual and spiritual progress. Life is time. "Time is the substance I am made of. Time is a river which sweeps me along, but I am the river; it is a tiger which destroys me, but I am the tiger; it is a fire which consumes me, but I am the fire."[15] Consciousness of time is consciousness of man's reality: his unstoppable mortality.

Knowledge and eternity are two elements, explicitly mentioned later on in Genesis, chapter 2, which represent the unbridgeable differences between God and man.[16] The Garden of Eden contained two trees bearing *fruits* that were specifically forbidden to man. After man tastes from the Tree of Knowledge, God expels him and his wife from the Garden of Eden – "lest he [man] send his hand to the Tree of Life," tempted by his desire for immortality, "and live for ever."[17] Adam has no access to immortality as an individual, but only as a species. As Menashe ben Israel explains, Adam's immortality was granted to him through the propagation of the human species, and that is why God "created woman attached to him."[18]

---

14 Borges, "The Immortal," *Collected Fictions*, p. 192.
15 Jorge Luis Borges, "A New Refutation of Time," in *Borges: Selected Non-Fictions*, edited and translated by Elliot Weinberger (New York: Penguin, 2000), p. 316.
16 I'm following Radaq's opinion and others who denied that Adam was born to live forever. See Radaq's comment on Genesis 2:17.
17 Genesis 3:22.
18 Ben Israel, *Conciliator*, question 12, p. 21: "He did not create him of an angelic nature, which would render him immortal, but chose that he should become so by propagation of the species."

Only God is eternal and infinite. Man is a simple mortal. But man might live under the detrimental illusion of immortality when he loses consciousness of time. Consciousness of the progression of time is essential for man's spiritual development; or, we could say, of man's *gradual* spiritual development.

Part of the benefit we humans derive from having a cycle of daytime → nighttime is the blessing of a daily pause.[19] "Happily for us, our lives are divided into days and nights. Our life is interrupted by sleep. Without day and night, sleep and vigil, our lives would be intolerable. The wholeness of the being is impossible for humans. By having day and night, humans can have it all, but gradually."[20]

The cycle daytime → nighttime is a prerequisite for man to retain or regain consciousness of his inevitable individual ending. Man is prone to forget, or to deceive himself into the fantasy of eternity. Forgetfulness and innumerable distractions can drive man away from God and from the reality of man's perishable nature. Time is unstoppably flowing. But at night, an irrecoverable fragment of time, a day, has died forever, reminding man about the urgency to pursue his gradual spiritual growth.

LIFE MADE OF DAYS

In the Torah, human life will often be measured as the *days* of one's life. In the Torah, days are the building blocks of a human life. When God redefines the life expectancy of humans (or of the specific civilization of the days of the flood, according to Eben 'Ezra and others), the verse says, "And [man's] *days* shall be 120 years."[21] With Abraham, "These are the *days* of

---

19 Ibid., question 11, p. 20. Incidentally, analyzing the same exact verse, Rabbi Shimon bar Yochai praised the creation of the cycle daytime → nighttime from a different angle: rest. While Rabbi Meir defined death as good, Rabbi Shimon identified the creation of sleep as good. Commenting on the verse, "And God saw what He had created, and it was very good." Rabbi Shimon bar Yochai said: *very good* refers to sleep. As explained by Rabbi Menashe ben Israel: "Sleep is also good; for although it suspends the operation of the nobler faculties of the soul, yet the repose obtained by it gives fresh vigor and strength for study and the exercise of the arts and virtues."

20 Jorge Luis Borges, *Borges Oral* (Buenos Aires: Alianza, 1998), p. 88.

21 Genesis 6:3.

the years of Abraham's life";[22] with Isaac, "And the *days* of the life of Isaac were 180 years";[23] and with Jacob, "The *days* of Jacob, the years of his life, [were] 147 years."[24]

For Heraclitus, time is a flowing river, in which man will never step twice. "No man ever steps in the same river twice, for it's not the same river and he's not the same man." What for Heraclitus is the river of life, for the Hebrew Scripture is a day. "No man ever steps in the same *day*, for it is never the same *day*, and he is never the same man." The cycle daytime → nighttime is God's way of reminding man about his walk toward mortality.

The initial blessing of the nighttime prayer – the prayer of 'arbit – focuses on the daily astronomical cycles, which begin in the evening. Through His word God turns day into night and night into day. At will, He opens the gateways of the cosmos and rearranges the stars and celestial bodies, granting us the tools to measure time. In this blessing, the idea of change and time transition is attributed to the daily cycles of the skies. The celestial bodies and their mechanical orbits are there to remind us of our mortality.

In the Scripture, the express purpose of the creation of light is to establish parameters that allow the measuring of time by distinguishing light from darkness and nighttime from daytime. These distinctions, in turn, form the basic time unit the Torah calls "day." A day is a referent for time passing: a cosmic clock. A day is a crucial instrument for those living beings who, in order to progress in their spiritual pursuit, *must* remain conscious of their mortality. These creatures are the human beings.

The separation between light and darkness serves an extremely important purpose. Without appreciating that time passes (and acting accordingly), man would not be man, but merely another – perhaps slightly smarter – member of the animal kingdom. As Jorge Luis Borges wrote: "With the exception of mankind, all creatures are immortal, for they know nothing of death."[25]

---

22 Ibid. 25:7
23 Ibid. 37:27.
24 Ibid. 47:28.
25 "The Immortal," *Collected Fictions*, p. 191.

This might be the reason why the creation of the daytime-nighttime cycle is so prominent (and so early on) in the narrative of Creation.

But is time measurement the *sole* function of "light"?

A DIVINE LIGHT

We have already seen that in the story of Creation things are not always what they seem to be. There are sub-stories behind the obvious story that may only be appreciated after considerable and effortful digging into the text. This is true for the entire Biblical text, but is especially applicable to the story of Creation. That is why the Rabbis of the Talmud and those who came after them entertained various and different theories about primeval light, knowing that a simple textual reading is only the first of many layers of understanding. The Torah is like a deep ocean harboring hidden treasures; one must dive deeply into its words to uncover its precious riches.

In the following chapters, we will delve a little deeper into the profundity of the ocean of the Torah, to explore the role primeval light might have played as an agent of God in the Creation process beyond the establishment of the cycle nighttime-daytime.

We should begin by examining what might have been the nature and the source of primeval light.

In his book *The Conciliator*, Rabbi Menashe ben Israel compares two Biblical passages dealing with light.[26] On the one hand, referring to the first day of Creation, and before the sun and the moon are mentioned, Genesis 1:5 says, "And it was evening and it was morning." On the other hand, at the end of the fourth day of Creation, after the sun, the moon, and the stars had been formed, Genesis 1:19 uses the same exact words, "And it was evening and it was morning." Rabbi Menashe ben Israel questions: Why would the Torah use the same wording for these two verses, as if nothing had changed from the first day to the fourth day? Once the sun is *created* on the fourth day, daytime and nighttime should now be redefined by the sun. On Day One, one would think, there must have been another source of light and darkness, a different way of distinguishing day from night! Why would the Torah ignore the differences between these two days and these two stages?

---

26   This debate was brought originally in Talmud Babli, *Chagiga* 12a.

Rabbi ben Israel then asks: "If the solar light causes the distinction between day and night, how can it be said that [the sun] was created on the fourth day? And if the first light was that of the sun, what was the creation of the fourth day?"

The answer to these two questions will be the subject of this chapter and the rest of this book.

Summarizing over fifteen centuries of Biblical exegesis addressing the dilemma of the nature of primeval light, the illustrious Rabbi ben Israel presented eight different views from rabbinical and non-rabbinical sources.[27] The multitude of viewpoints may be classified into two main schools: those who say that the sun was the source of primeval light, and those who say that something other than the sun was the source of primeval light.

Let us begin with the latter.

Rabbi Eliezer Ashkenazi (1512–1586)[28] thought that primeval light was generated by some kind of dark energy, or a dark fire. As we saw in a previous chapter, in Maimonides's opinion the "darkness" mentioned in Genesis 1:2 alluded to an invisible (dark) fire or energy.[29] Based on Maimonides's concept of darkness, Rabbi Ashkenazi suggested that primeval light was the result of a *fusion* between this dark fire as it came into contact with air. "The light of the first day…was a kind of inflamed air: this special *air*…illumined the semicircle of heavens, the other half being in darkness…."[30] Primeval light, according to Rabbi Ashkenazi, was weak and insufficiently clear. So, in the fourth day, the sun had to be created "for the sake of providing enough light upon the earth."[31] In other words,

---

27 It is interesting to note in passing that, loyal to the style of Rabbis coming from Sephardic background –especially those who lived in seventeenth-century Amsterdam – Rabbi ben Israel would comfortably quote ideas or Biblical commentaries coming from non-Jewish sources, scientists, and philosophers, like Plato, Alexander de Ales, Nicholas de Lira, and many others, in order to attain a better understanding of the Torah.

28 "Rabbi Eliezer Ashkenazi (or, the German) flourished in the sixteenth century at Mentz, where he died in 1586. Among his many learned works, the most esteemed was the title of 'the Works of God.'" (Ben Israel, *Conciliator*, p. xxii, biographical notes.)

29 Maimonides (Guide to the Perplexed 2:30), quoted in *The Conciliator*.

30 Ben Israel, *Conciliator*, quoting Rabbi Eliezer Ashkenazi, p. 5.

31 Ibid.

primeval darkness, understood in this context as some sort of invisible gas or energy, was the source of primeval light.

On the one hand, Rabbi Ashkenazi's explanation provided a solution for the question of the source of primeval light: namely, primeval darkness or (invisible) energy. On the other hand, the idea that the original light was later on found *insufficient* seems inconsistent with the explicit Biblical statement in Genesis 1:4: "And God saw that the light [He had just created] was good." It is difficult to conceive that the creation of light, immediately followed in the Scripture by an unequivocal seal of divine approval, ended up being insufficient and weak, and that subsequently God needed to replace this imperfect light with the sun during the fourth day.

For Don Isaac Abarbanel (1437–1508), primeval light did not come from the sun, fire, or any other source of physical energy. "The first light was miraculously created and did not proceed from a lucid body."[32] During the initial three days of Creation, this light "formed day and night through its successive occultation and visibility." Abarbanel considered the existence of primeval light a singular miracle with no parallel in the physical world we are familiar with. It was a light emanating directly from God. Abarbanel perceived primeval light as an independent light, without any physical source.

Abarbanel's interpretation might be traced back to the time of the Tannaim, the authors of the Mishna and the Midrash. Rabbi Shmuel ben Nachman (third century CE) was asked where this primeval light would be coming from. Following an older Tannaitic tradition (and alluding to Psalms 104:2) he replied: "God covered Himself [*nit'atef*] with this light like a dress or a cloak, and extended His splendor from one end [of the world] to the other end."[33]

Rabbi Ya'aqob, a rabbi from the second century, described this light as a divine luminosity that allowed man to see (or perceive) beyond his natural sight. "Man would look through it, and would be able to see (*tzofe bo*) from one end of the world till its other end." This light was proceeding directly from God or, as Rabbi Shmuel ben Nachman explained later on, "With this

---

32 Ibid.
33 *Bereshit Rabba* 3:4.

light the Almighty concealed His presence from us." Light conceals but also reveals God's presence, like a cloak covering a body – while concealing a body's appearance, it also reveals that body's very existence.[34]

Rabbi El'azar, also from the second century, said: "When the Almighty saw [in the future] the men of the [corrupted] generation of the flood... He [replaced primeval light with the sun and] reserved [primeval light] for the righteous in the World to Come." Following Rabbi El'azar's view, many rabbis called this non-solar light OR haganuz, "the concealed light."[35] According to these opinions, after the creation of the sun, this divine light became inaccessible to us so long as we are alive. God treasured it for the righteous in the World to Come.[36] It illuminates – or perhaps constitutes – a different dimension of existence in the afterlife. Although they held that the nature of the World to Come is incomprehensible to mortals, the rabbis were willing to acknowledge the existence of one concrete element as forming part of the reality of the afterlife: a majestic, delightful, light; a divine splendor (ziv haShekhina). The splendor of the Divine Presence is what constitutes the ultimate enjoyment of the righteous in the Jewish afterlife.[37]

Many other Rabbis, particularly those versed in Jewish mysticism – including Rabbi Menashe ben Israel – explained this light metaphorically, as an angelic light or the luminous divine mind. They saw this light as the manifestation of God's glory, and understood that this is the same light mentioned, among other passages, in the Priestly Blessing: "May God make His countenance *shine* upon you"[38] – that is the light emanating from God, which is also mentioned in the daily 'Amida: "through the light of Your countenance" (...*be-OR panekha*). Access to God's light, or to a reflection of it, represents the climax of man's spiritual development in this world as

---

34 This idea, as we have already mentioned, is based on King David's Psalm 104:2. See chapter 6 of this book.

35 For a more explicit source, see: *Pesiqta deRav Kahana*, edited by Bernard Mandelbaum (1962), p. 322.

36 The term "World to Come" generated a controversy among medieval rabbis; some of them, like Nachmanides, understand it as the Messianic world. For Maimonides, however, the 'olam habba is the afterlife. We are basing our explanation on his opinion.

37 See Maimonides, *Mishne Tora, Hilkhot Teshuba* 8:2.

38 Numbers 6:25.

well.[39] This matter is so important to the Sages of the Kabbala that the book of Kabbala *par excellence* is called *Sefer haZohar* – the Book of "Light" (or "Splendor") alluding to this primeval light associated with God's emanating wisdom.

Although analyzing the nature of primeval light from a metaphysical point of view is in and of itself fascinating, and indeed seems appropriate for the subject of light, what matters most for the sake of our discussion is that Rabbi Ashkenazi, Abarbanel, and a number of Rabbis of the Mishna and the Midrash understood primeval light as something *other than sunlight*.

THE VOCABULARIES OF CREATION

But those rabbis were not the only ones who believed Biblical primeval light was something other than sunlight. Many centuries after the Mishna, a number of Biblical scholars and scientists noticed the astonishing fact that the Hebrew Scripture, unlike the contemporary ancient myths of creation, did not consider (or mention!) the sun, popularly viewed as a god or at least a semi-Divine figure among all pagan civilizations of old, at the beginning of the Creation story.

It is indeed remarkable that on the first day of Creation, the Torah focused its attention on something as nonmaterial and magnificent as *light*.

In many senses, particularly its unsurpassable speed, light represents the boundaries of our physical reality. Light is the fastest and lightest matter in the cosmos, and the nature of its true essence represents one of the still unresolved mysteries of physics.[40] The speed of light separates past and future. It defines the frontiers of the present tense in our universe.

The Biblical emphasis on the appearance of light at the onset of the Creation of the universe, and the noticeable omission of the sun, particularly from Genesis 1:1 to 1:5, made these scholars reflect on the remarkable similarities, at the very least with regard to its *vocabulary*,

---

39 Faur, *Homo Mysticus*, p. 54.

40 Even in the twenty-first century, the exact essence of physical light is still a matter of debate in the scientific community. Particles theory, wave theory, electromagnetic theory, the theory of relativity, quantum theory, and string theory are some of the theories that deal among other things with the nature and mechanics of light.

between the Hebrew Scripture and modern cosmological theories – both positing "primeval light" at the beginning of the universe.

Steven Weinberg, a Nobel laureate scientist famous for his groundbreaking book *The First Three Minutes*, describes the initial 180 seconds after the moment of beginning, explaining that the original explosion, or the Big Bang, was *an explosion of light* (photons): "The universe was filled with light…it was light that then formed the dominant constituent of the universe."[41]

Adam Frank, a modern astronomer, describes the initial phases of the universe's development (one could ironically argue), by what could reasonably be perceived as a motif borrowed from Genesis 1:3 and 1:4, highlighting the dynamic tension between light and darkness. "Big Bang theory tells us that the entire universe…emerged from a single titanic explosion that set the cosmos in motion. Light, brilliant beyond description, flooded the infant universe. There is a second part to the scientific discovery that many people, however, have not heard: darkness soon returned with a vengeance…from light to darkness to light again – this describes the unveiling of our universe's early years."[42]

Robert Jastrow was even more particular about the role the Big Bang attributes to light and the Hebrew Bible: "The dazzling brilliance of the radiation in this dense, hot universe must have been beyond description… the essential elements in the astronomical and the Biblical account of Genesis is the same: the chain of events leading to man commenced suddenly and sharply, at a definite moment in time, in a flash of light and energy."[43]

The Jewish scholar to be credited for probably having been the first to have the idea of associating the Biblical description of primeval light with the findings of modern cosmology is professor Abraham Shalom Yahuda (1877–1951). In 1935, a few years before the Big Bang theory was formally presented, Professor Yahuda, a prestigious Biblical scholar and eminent Egyptologist, suggested some similarities between the Torah and current

---

41 Weinberg, *The First Three Minutes*, pp. 5–6.
42 Frank, *Astronomy Magazine*, June 2006, pp. 30–35.
43 Jastrow, *God and the Astronomers*, p. 14.

scientific theories: "One can even say that the Biblical creation is, among all other creation stories of antiquity, the only one which has some approach to a scientific cosmological conception. This is most prominently apparent in the creation of light.... According to the Egyptians it was the sun which first emerged from the chaotic waters to spread light over the earth. [In the Bible] there is a deliberate opposition to the mythological conception that the sun was the first and most powerful god to appear on earth.[44]

Accordingly, it should not be surprising that many thinkers, scientists, and modern Biblical scholars are inclined to identify the Big Bang theory, which asserts that the universe started as an explosion of light, with verse 1:3 of the Torah: *Yehi OR*, "Let there be light." There is an undeniable similarity between the fact that primeval light was created at the very beginning of the Creation story, and the way scientists describe the evolution of the cosmos, from the Big Bang explosion into our present universe.

However, despite all the tempting reasons to identify primeval light with the Big Bang theory, and seeking to find a consonance between modern cosmology and the Biblical story of Creation, Jewish tradition[45] posits that the first act of Creation was that of heavens and earth – and not that of light. And even if one followed the interpretation of Rabbi Yehuda, for whom light was the first creation, the traditional Jewish reading of the first three verses of the Bible does not support the idea that "Let there be light" could be understood as referring to the onset of the creation of the universe, but that of Earth's light alone.

Let me be clear. We explained earlier in this work that the way the universe came into being escapes the possibility of our comprehension and analysis. However, even if one were to assume (against that argument) that the creation of the universe consisted of an explosion of light, my contention is that this is not what Genesis 1:3 is saying. The words *Yehi OR*, "Let there be light," refer to the light that illuminated planet Earth. The *story* of Creation is definitely geocentric (anthropocentric); that is, it

---

44 A. S. Yahuda, *The Accuracy of the Bible* (London: William Heinemann Ltd., 1934), pp. 138–39.

45 To remind the reader, the Rabbis adopted the position of Rabbi Nechemia over that of Rabbi Yehuda.

is addressed to man, adopting man's point of view and reality.[46] This is not to say that according to Judaism the universe is anthropocentric and that a possibility of extraterrestrial life or intelligence is excluded.[47] It is just that the Torah shows no interest in discussing the cosmological origins of the universe at large. It is the creation of our planet, leading to life and intelligent life – the creation and story of a creature equipped to embark in a quest to find his Creator – that the Biblical account of Creation is all about. That is why verse 2 is so critical. After verse 1 announced that God Almighty created heavens and earth, verse 2 *refocuses* our attention toward earth, its status, and its inventory – ignoring quite conspicuously, and for good, whatever would be happening with or in *heavens*, i.e., the rest of the universe.

PRIMEVAL LIGHT AS SUNLIGHT

There is another reason why Jewish tradition would not connect "Let there be light" with the onset of the Big Bang. That is because *the majority of the Rabbis* identified primeval light with sunlight. The Talmud records two main opinions on the nature of primeval light.[48] Rabbi Ya'aqob, as we already mentioned, held that primeval light was a divine luminosity and was therefore not coming from the sun. According to Rabbi Ya'aqob, two types of light were created: (1) a divine primeval light on the first day, which was hidden away for the righteous, and (2) a worldly sunlight, which during the fourth day replaced the divine light. The second opinion, that of *Chakhamim* (the Rabbis), identified primeval light with physical sunlight. According to their view, only one type of light was created: the light of the luminaries (sun and moon), which were created on the first day, but were fixed in their definitive place only in the fourth day.

---

46 As Rabbi Yishma-el explained many times: דברה תורה כלשון בני אדם, "The Torah expresses itself in the language of human beings." *Sifri Bamidbar* 112, Horowitz edition, p. 121. See also *More Nebukhim* 1:12.

47 The question of the place of man in Jewish thought is a discussion that goes beyond the humble goal of this book. For a comprehensive discussion about the Jewish view on anthropocentrism, the reader is referred to Norman Lamm's *Faith and Doubt*, pp. 83–99.

48 Talmud Babli, *Chagiga* 12a.

What is critically important to note is that this second opinion is not presented as held by a particular Rabbi, but by "*Chakhamim*" (the "Rabbis"). In Talmudic lingo, *Chakhamim* stands for the opinion of the majority of the Rabbis, which, in turn, becomes the official Jewish view in matters of Jewish law, for example.

The Rabbis based their opinion in an interpretation formulated by Rabbi 'Aqiba (ca. 40–ca.137 CE). Rabbi 'Aqiba observed that the Hebrew particle *et* in Genesis 1:1 is technically redundant.[49] In the English rendition of Genesis 1:1 this redundancy can be seen in the usage of the definite article "the" preceding the words "heavens" and "earth": "In the beginning God created THE heavens and THE earth." This sentence in English could also make sense without employing the definite article *the*: "In the beginning, God created heavens and earth." Similarly, in the original Hebrew text, the particle *et* is, semantically, unnecessary. The superfluous presence of these prepositions justifies – based on a hermeneutical tool called *ribbuy* – interpreting this verse as meaning to include also the creation of other elements within the act of creation of heavens and earth. According to Rabbi 'Aqiba, through the addition of the preposition *et* the text could be interpreted to include the sun and the moon – the *me-orot* or luminaries – which were also created during that initial act of Creation, as accessories to heavens and earth.[50]

Most classic Biblical commentators followed the opinion of *Chakhamim* and Rabbi 'Aqiba. Rabbi Menashe ben Israel quotes, among others, Rabbenu Bachye, Rashi, and Eben 'Ezra as saying that primeval light was indeed sunlight. For some reason – and this particular matter was not addressed by these Rabbis – the Hebrew Scripture did not consider it necessary to

---

49 *Bereshit Rabba* 1:14.

50 This type of *derasha*, or interpretation, is not always the sole grounds for a rabbinic idea. According to Maimonides, rabbinic ideas, in the legal or haggadic realm, often come from an ancient oral tradition that *preceded* the textual interpretation or *derasha*. The interpretation comes or is sought in order to give a textual basis to the idea presented. In our case, therefore, the notion that the sun and the moon were created as part of the creation of heavens and earth most probably predated Rabbi 'Aqiba's interpretation. For a comprehensive analysis of this essential point, see Jay Michael Harris, *How Do We Know This? Midrash and the Fragmentation of Modern Judaism* (Albany, NY: State University of New York Press, 1994), pp. 89–91.

mention the sun as the source of primeval light. It would almost seem as if from the Biblical perspective it was obvious that primeval light was indeed "sunlight."[51]

Radaq argued that the existence of the sun on Day One is actually hinted in the Biblical text itself. In Genesis 1:3 the verse says: "And God *said*, let there be light..." Every time the Biblical text relates that God *says* something it describes a creative command addressed to one of His creations – living or non-living organisms – even when the addressee is not explicitly mentioned. Accordingly, in Genesis 1:6 for example – "And God said: Let there be an expanse in the water..." – God is addressing the water, commanding it to separate from the ocean and form the sky. In verse 1:3, Radaq argues, God's words must also have been addressed to one of His creations. Radaq thinks that "And God said, let there be light" means that God said *to the sun* to bring forth its light. That is, in his opinion, a clear indication that the sun was already there, way before the fourth day, from the initial act of Creation.

Maimonides held a similar view. He said explicitly that the sun was the origin of primeval light.[52] Referring to the creation of the sun on the fourth day, Maimonides carefully quotes *Chakhamim* (and not Rabbi 'Aqiba, as an individual rabbi), indicating that according to the Rabbis' official opinion the sun was indeed created on the first day, but was placed in its orbit – hanged or suspended in its definitive space – during the fourth day. In Maimonides's own words: "You must know that the particle *et* in the phrase *et hashamayim ve-et ha-aretz* ('the heavens and the earth') signifies 'together with': our Sages [*Chakhamim*] have explained the word in the same sense in many instances. Accordingly, they assumed that God created

---

51 Addressing the question of replacement on the fourth day – if the sun existed and was functioning from Day One, what was it then that changed or was created during the fourth day? Rabbi Menashe ben Israel concludes: "The [Biblical] text implies that on that day [the fourth] the sun developed the effect of its heat on plants." This reminds us that vegetation appeared on the planet on the third day. During the first three days the sun was the source of primeval light and it was responsible for the separation between day and night. On the fourth day, however, the sun's radiation – as opposed to the sun's light – was somehow modified to provide its energy to plants and vegetation. *Conciliator*, question 2, p. 4.

52 *More Nebukhim* 2:30.

with the heavens everything that the heavens contain, and *with* the earth everything the earth includes.[53]

We will come back to Maimonides's words later, in the next chapter.

SUMMARY

Following the plain reading of the Biblical text, we see that light was explicitly created to serve as a sophisticated astronomic clock, demarcating the distinction between daytime and nighttime; marking the unstoppable and gradual progression of time; refreshing man's memory and awareness of his own mortality and, therefore, reminding him of the need to live his life purposely and with meaning. Time measurement, however, does not seem to be the exclusive purpose for which light was created. As we saw with the other "agents" wind and water, light too played a critical role as an agent of God in the creation of the world.

In the process of Creation, it seems that primeval light – as a source of heat – was employed by God to trigger and energize other processes. As we have explained in the previous chapters, among other events, the separation between upper and lower waters seems to have been brought about by God using the heat of primeval light. We also found in *Barekhi nafshi* (Psalm 104:4) that, while still describing the events of the second day, the psalmist calls light *esh* – "fire" or "heat."

It would indeed be very tempting to highlight the astonishing similarities between the onset of Creation as relayed by the Biblical narrative and modern cosmological theories, given that both place light and darkness at the inceptive stages of the cosmos. However, notwithstanding the extraordinary coincidences in the *vocabulary* of Creation – and even though many modern scientists and some Torah scholars might want to identify Genesis's primeval light with the primeval light of the Big Bang theory – the Rabbis of the Talmud understood that the focus of the Scriptural narrative is not the cosmos at large, but particularly planet Earth. The only Biblical reference we have to the creation of the rest of the universe (two hundred billion galaxies, as far as we know today) is just one word: "heavens" in

---

53 Translation from Moses Maimonides, *The Guide for the Perplexed*, translated by Moses Friedlander (1904), p. 334. Emphasis added.

verse 1. After that verse, the Biblical text focuses its attention exclusively on planet Earth and its accessories (i.e., our immediate solar system and the visible stars). Primeval light is one such accessory, local to planet Earth. It is not to be confused with the Big Bang's cosmic light.

We have shown that both Rabbis and Biblical scholars debated the nature of primeval light, knowing that in the narrative of Creation there is much more to the story than what the story says. Many Rabbis considered primeval light as a luminance coming directly from God, and wholly unrelated to any physical, mundane light. We concluded, however, that most Rabbis held that the source of the Biblical primeval light was simply our sun.

In the next two chapters, and without intending to dismiss other interpretations (especially expositions that are concerned with the esoteric), I will examine the Biblical text and present a theory that will aim to be consistent with the major trend in Jewish exegetical tradition of viewing primeval light as sunlight. My main goal will be to understand the similarities, the differences, and the interactions between primeval light and the light of the luminaries fashioned by God on the fourth day.

Chapter 8

Embryonic Light

In the previous chapter we saw that there were two schools divided on their opinion about the nature of the light of the first day: one school saw primeval light as a divine or spiritual light, something *other* than sunlight, while the other held that primeval light originated in the sun, implying thereby that the sun was not created on the fourth day of Creation but on the first day.

The Rabbis of the Talmud concluded that the light of the first day came from the sun.[1] This opinion is quoted as coming from the *Chakhamim* (the Sages, in plural), which is the way the Talmud defines a standpoint when the majority of the Rabbis consent with it. The position of most classic medieval Biblical commentators followed – as expected – the view of the *Chakhamim*, that the sun was created on the first day.

In the opinion of the Rabbis, primeval sunlight was somehow operational already from Day One, to begin with, by marking the difference between daytime and nighttime.[2]

In modern times, particularly thanks to recent scientific theories in early geology and earth's science, we are able to find more solid support for a clearer understanding of the opinion of the Rabbis. Contemporary theories about the formation of our atmosphere, hydrosphere, geosphere, and biosphere will help realize what were the possible causes of this mysterious replacement (or repositioning) of primeval light that took place during the fourth day as it is reported in the Torah's narrative of Creation.

---

1   See *Bereshit Rabba* 1:14.
2   According to the classic Biblical commentator Chezquni (Chizqiya ben Manoach, France, thirteenth century) daytime and nighttime were established on the first day by the beginning of the rotation of the earth. See *Torah Shelemah* 77:389.

But before we proceed to analyze this idea in more depth, we need to understand what questions are answered and what new questions arise by identifying primeval light with sunlight.

1. Assuming that primeval light was indeed the light of the sun avoids the need to seek an alternative source for the origin of the light that illuminated the world during the first three days. The source of light during the first three days was the same that illuminated the planet during the rest of the six days of Creation and the same light that illuminates our planet today.

2. We have asked ourselves how primeval light would have functioned in distinguishing between day and night. Assuming that the sun was created on the first day, we can answer that its light and the rotation of the earth distinguished between daytime and nighttime in the same way, throughout all six days of Creation.[3]

3. We have also asked ourselves what happened on the fourth day when, seemingly, primeval light disappeared to be forever replaced with the light of the sun. Now, once we identify primeval light with sunlight, the problem presented by this puzzling substitution is finally solved: there was no substitution. Light on earth had always come from the sun.

Two New Challenges

If the primeval light of Genesis originated from the sun, however, as argued by the Rabbis, two important questions arise.

First, we need to clarify the apparently inconsistent terminology used in the Torah when referring to sunlight. If primeval light is indeed to be identified as the light of the sun, why would the Torah not use the word "sun" or "luminaries," rather than the word "light"? Instead of saying in Genesis 1:3 "Let there be light," the Biblical text should have used there the exact words it used in Genesis 1:14: "Let there be luminaries in the expanse

---

3   See note on Olber's paradox in the previous chapter.

of the sky to separate the day from the night." I will address this important question before entertaining the next one.

Perhaps the word *OR* was used in Genesis 1:3 in reference to the sun, much in the same way that the word *tehom* was used in Genesis 1:2 to refer to the sea. As we concluded in the previous section, the term "sea" or "seas" (*yam* or *yammim*) was omitted from Genesis 1:2 and in its place the Torah employed the uncommon word *tehom*. We argued that the Torah may have used the word *tehom* to identify the *primeval* sea, i.e., the sea before it was formally organized and named as such. God's naming the elements of Creation would be tantamount to bringing them to a state of completion and assigning them their ultimate purpose. Before they are designed to serve their final definite function, these elements are called by provisory names, due to their primeval, not definitive, status.

Tehom in Genesis 1:2 defined the primitive waters before they were organized and constituted into oceans on the third day of Creation (Genesis 1:10). In the same vein, the Torah may have called primitive sunlight simply light because the sun was not yet arranged and established in its definite position "to illuminate the earth" (Genesis 1:17) – it was not yet a functional "sun." Accordingly, "light" (*OR*) was redefined or renamed on the fourth day as "luminary" (*me-orot*), just like *tehom* was rearranged or renamed on the third day as "seas." After the fourth day, the Torah would always refer to sunlight as sun (*shemesh*) and never again as light (*OR*).

Additionally, we should remember what Professor Yahuda and others said about the importance pagan civilizations gave to the sun. In his opinion "[In the Bible] there is a deliberate opposition to the mythological conception that the sun was the first and most powerful god to appear on earth." The Torah may have intentionally refrained from mentioning the sun, the most popular pagan object of worship in ancient civilizations. Calling primeval sunlight *OR* and avoiding the mention of the sun in such a sensitive verse (Gen. 1:3) would make perfect sense with that consideration in mind.

The second question we should ask ourselves is: If the light of Day One was sunlight, then what really happened on the fourth day?

For the Rabbis, the sun was created during the first act of Creation, but for the Biblical text it seems that it was created on the fourth day. The

Torah clearly states, "And God made the two great luminaries – the greater luminary to govern during the day and the lesser luminary to govern during the night" (Genesis 1:16). On the fourth day something *new* was in charge of being the luminary. Seemingly, primeval light was replaced by the sun. But what kind of replacement of light for light occurred on the fourth day and why?

To our surprise, but loyal to its brevity, the Torah is notably silent about this substitution. Nothing is explicitly clarified as to why or how God replaced primeval sunlight with the light of the sun. It is as if for the Torah this replacement or transition between primeval light and the sun was obvious, called for, and expected. It did not require any additional clarification.

I will dedicate this entire chapter to finding a possible solution to this puzzling matter.

LIGHT AND HEAT

The question of the substitution of primeval light with the sun on the fourth day of Creation forces us to reassess the overall role played by light in the process of Creation.

We have already discussed that light had other functions besides its explicit role defining daytime through its interaction with darkness. In the previous section of this book, we argued that light acted additionally as heat. We also demonstrated that heat – and not light – was referred to by *Barekhi nafshi* (Psalms 104:4) as being one of God's creative agents. We found support for the broader role of light acting as heat in the words of Maimonides in *More Nebukhim*, in the interpretation of Rashi, and others, as quoted by Menashe ben Israel, and in other Biblical commentators.

Many Biblical commentators discussed the numerous benefits the sun exerts on earth aside from visible light. Radaq made the following observation about the additional role played by sunlight after the fourth day: "God said on the fourth day that the luminaries will appear to exert their effects on the flourishing of vegetation and on the production of fruits from the trees."[4] Besides illuminating the planet, Radaq adds that the light

---

4   Radaq's commentary to Genesis 1:15.

of the luminaries will, from now on, "exert its effects on all the mundane creatures, each one according to what is appropriate to it." Interpreting that same verse, another important commentary, Seforno (1475–1550),[5] suggested an idea which will be critical to the rest of this book. He said that *only* from the fourth day on the sun started to shine upon earth "with a balanced temperature."

Based on the identification of primeval light with sunlight, we should now examine the possible additional roles primeval sunlight may have played as one of God's agents during the first three days of Creation as well. Primeval sunlight, we will suggest, was different from the normal sunlight instated on the fourth day of Creation. The former was a sort of an embryonic light, more intense, which was fashioned by the Creator for the specific purpose of shaping our planet and preparing it for hosting life. Modern scientific theories formulated by contemporary scientists to explain the events that shaped the surface of our planet at its initial stages will be an invaluable tool to examine and compare these two lights, and to comprehend what additional roles may have been played by primeval sunlight in the early process of Creation.

TWO PHASES OF CREATION

Modern scientific theories attribute to heat a decisive role in the process of the shaping of planet Earth at its initial, formative stages. This should encourage us to think about the possibility that the Creator may have used primeval sunlight's *heat* as an instrument and agent of Creation employed to jumpstart the processes of evaporation and formation of our *raqia'* (atmosphere), and to set in motion the separation between the oceans and the continental land.

Although the Torah does not explicitly count sunlight or heat as one of God's agents in the process of Creation, it is possible to infer it through a more nuanced reading, particularly by analyzing the context of the two events that followed the creation of primeval sunlight.

---

5   Seforno was an Italian rabbi, Biblical commentator, and physician. He was born at Cesena in 1475 and died in Bologna in 1550.

Reading the Biblical story of Creation closely, one can identify two distinct phases in the Creation narrative. Both phases lasted two consecutive creation-days. Phase one comprised the second and third days of Creation, and phase two comprised the fifth and sixth days of Creation. These were two completely different stages in the world's Creation, pursuing two distinct goals. Most importantly, for our discussion, both phases were inaugurated by the creation or fashioning of a light, on the first day and on the fourth day, respectively.

Phase one was the geological phase of Creation. During phase one, the atmosphere, the world's ceiling, had to be adapted from a toxic cloud of gases – that primeval darkness of Genesis 1:2 – to a life-supporting atmosphere. Then, the originally watery planet had to be transformed into a planet possessing a firm ground, protected from invading waters, and blossoming with vegetation – the basic food for living creatures. These two dramatic events – the formation of the atmosphere and the formation of the continents – were described in the Torah as taking place on the second and the third days of Creation.[6]

Phase two of Creation, the biological phase, was less sizable and less noisy. However it was more magnificent, refined, and extremely sophisticated. During the fifth and sixth days of Creation, God brought about *life*. God populated planet Earth with living creatures, from insects to the ultimate goal of the process of Creation: *intelligent* life.

What was it, then, which marked the transition from the geological phase to the biological phase?

The answer is: light.

One type of light was used by the Creator in phase one, and a different, or modified, light was used in phase two of Creation. Both, I suggest (following the Rabbis of the Talmud) came from the sun.

Primeval light was absolutely necessary for phase one, as one of God's instruments of Creation, to trigger all the dramatic cataclysms of the second and third days. After the third day, however, that primeval *intense*

---

6   Parenthetically, in what could be thought of as a happy coincidence, contemporary earth scientists too posit that at the time of the formation of planet Earth the atmosphere developed first, simultaneously with rain, and then the oceans, and only then the earth's surface solidified and formed.

sunlight was no longer needed. On the contrary, that light would have been harmful for life. A different kind of sunlight, less powerful, balanced and finely tuned, was designed during the fourth day to maintain the world's average temperature, preserve liquid water, and allow life to evolve.

The Blue Skies

We will now revisit the main creative activities of the second and third days of Creation, keeping in mind the possibility that, perhaps, intense sunlight could have been instrumental in producing these events by contributing to a climate of very high temperatures.

So far, we know that God formed our planet through several steps. In the beginning, God created earth and heavens (Gen. 1:1). According to our Rabbis, that included the creation of the sun and the moon, among other things. God did not create life right away. First, He adjusted our planet to host life. From its inception, earth was equipped with wind and water (Gen. 1:2); respectively, God's agent and raw material. On the first day, God *activated* sunlight (Gen 1:3) – a second agent of God, as per Psalms 104:4. During the second and third days, God formed the geological structure of the planet – using water, wind, and sunlight.

> And God made the sky, and He separated the water under the
> sky from the water above the sky. (Gen. 1:7)

On the second day, God assembled the atmosphere. God formed the life-friendly ceiling of the earth by establishing the chemical formula of our air with the precise combination of elements needed to sustain life. He also generated a weather system that, among other things, would warrant the recycling of freshwater.

What kind of processes and events had to happen in order to create our atmosphere?

As we have previously seen, God made use of things He had already created, employing them as *agents* to generate the next stage in the Creation process. This being so, what tools or agents might have been employed by the Creator in the formation of the atmosphere? Consistent with its concise style, the Torah is almost silent about the way God formed the atmosphere. All we are told in the narration of the second day is that to make the atmosphere, God separated the upper waters from the lower waters, which in chapter 5 we identified as the cycle of water evaporation, precipitation, a so on.

Present-day science can open our eyes to the magnitude and extent of the events that were necessary for the development of our atmosphere, and especially the role that heat might have played during those processes. Scientists admit that it is impossible to have a clear picture that fully reconstructs the events surrounding the development of the primitive atmosphere, because the information currently at our disposal is incomplete. Unlike fossils buried on earth, they argue, "mere vapors have not left substantial remnants."[7] However, we can safely assume that any scientific theory will somehow incorporate the elements that just happen to be mentioned in Genesis 1:2 and 1:3 (water, wind, sunlight) as having a decisive role in this development, absolutely necessary for the creation of our present atmosphere.

Moreover, scientists also believe that, at the gestational stages of the earth's formation, "it is quite possible that the early atmosphere was many times as dense as today's" and that "the surface of our planet must have been much hotter than it is today."[8] Normally, the radiation coming from the sun warms up the earth very evenly and evaporates just a fraction of the ocean's surface. This evaporation is enough to form the clouds and rain necessary for life. But in primitive earth, "the seas and oceans were hot. Some have suggested that because of the high atmospheric pressure the oceans could have been hotter than the boiling point of water today. Truly a pressure-cooker early earth."[9]

On this primeval stage, the high temperatures on earth were responsible for a colossal-scale "outgassing,"[10] or evaporation, which triggered the formation of the atmosphere. (Outgassing is the release of gases from different materials, all required for the formation of the multiple vital elements that compose our atmosphere.) This evaporation consisted of the production of enormous amounts of gas and water vapor, which generated

7   Macdougall, *Short History*, pp. 10–11.
8   Ibid., p. 26
9   Ibid., p. 27.
10   *Encyclopedia Britannica* (Macropedia), 15th ed., s.v. "atmosphere."

enough clouds to cover the whole planet. "Water vapor and other gases, once chemically bound inside the planet, now erupted from the surface in huge quantities, creating earth's primitive oceans and the atmosphere."[11] The colossal outgassing and evaporation was generated by intense heat. This heat formed a massive blanket of clouds producing a subsequent mega-rainfall, which cleaned the atmosphere and began the formation of the life-friendly gases (water vapor, carbon dioxide, and nitrogen).

As we explained, the temperatures that produced these processes were exceedingly higher than those needed to merely *maintain* a balanced cycle of evaporation → rain, like the standard cycle operating ever since. However, this intense radiation and heat was absolutely vital for the development of the atmosphere at the initial stages of earth's formation.

Once its creative mission was accomplished, the high thermal energy would have had to be modified, filtered, or somehow weakened to allow our planet to blossom with life. Scientists assert that complex life, as we know it, could not ever begin with temperatures over 100°C degrees. The surface's temperatures had to decrease to make earth hospitable to life.[12]

As we have mentioned before, in the words of the Torah, our atmosphere, or *raqia'*, was formed as the consequence of the separation (evaporation) between lower waters (oceans) and upper waters (clouds).[13] The process of evaporation described by the Torah, the separation between the waters, could comfortably be identified as the outgassing process described earlier, which generated the formation of the atmosphere or *raqia'*.

At this point, it is necessary to point out what is probably the most significant difference between the scientific theory of the formation of the atmosphere and what the Torah describes. As the reader probably remembers, according to our Torah, water was the most abundant substance on the surface of the earth. According to all Biblical and rabbinical sources

---

11   Edward J. Denecke Jr., *Barron's Earth Science: The Physical Setting*, Barron's Educational Series (New York: Barron's, 2009), p. 377.

12   Macdougall, *Short History*, p. 27.

13   The sequence of events that led to the formation of the atmosphere as reported by modern scientists is eerily reminiscent of the events *poetically* described in Psalms 104:3, "He made the beams of His upper chambers with water; He made the clouds his chariot...."

early earth had more water in its surface than today's earth. For the Hebrew Scripture, the obvious source of outgassing (or as we have called it, evaporation) was the abundant lower waters, or *tehom*: those waters that completely covered the surface of the earth in its beginning[14] and were separated in the second day to form the *raqia'*.

On the other hand, as of today, scientists have yet to come up with a solid theory that would explain the abundant presence of water in our early planet, the origin of the mega-rainfall that cleared the toxic primitive atmosphere, and the formation of the primitive oceans. According to scientists, and contrary to what the Biblical story of Creation reports, rain was what formed the oceans and not the other way around. This is problematic because outgassing coming from the melting of minerals simply could have not been enough to account for the formation of the atmosphere, for mega-rainfall, or for the amount of water we find in present-day oceans. The prevalent explanation by scientists of the abundance of water in earth's oceans is that of the extraterrestrial origin of water on our planet. It is quite an implausible theory, which says that millions of meteorites, comets, and asteroids containing huge amounts of water in the form of ice must have impacted on earth, hence bringing water to our planet, which then evaporated and created the atmosphere and the oceans.[15]

In any case, and to summarize, we have seen that an intense degree of heat or radiation was necessary to bring about all the water outgassing that would generate the formation of the atmosphere. This intense heat was not life-friendly; on the contrary, most forms of life we know today would have been rendered extinct by this type of heat.

HABITABILITY IN PROGRESS

And God said: "Let the water under the sky be gathered into one place, and let the dry land appear." (Gen. 1:9)

---

14 *Encyclopedia Britannica* (Macropedia), 15th ed., s.v. "hydrosphere."
15 See Jonathan I. Lunine and Cynthia J Lunine, *Earth: Evolution of a Habitable World* (Cambridge: Cambridge University Press, 1999), pp. 130–32.

The third day may seem relatively uneventful, if one were to read only the Scriptural account contained in verse 1:9. However, when reading it in conjunction with *Barekhi nafshi* (with which we already had the chance to acquaint ourselves, as per our earlier discussion of the agents of creation), one realizes that the events leading to the formation of the geosphere were quite dramatic and violent.

The Torah tells us that after the formation of our *raqia'* (sky or atmosphere) on the third day, God continued with the organization of earth's surface. As with the second day, the third day did not contain any "out of nothing" creations. After forming the atmosphere on the second day, God proceeded on the third day with the arrangement and organization of what is known today as the *hydrosphere*: the water on the surface of the earth. The primitive waters (called originally *tehom*) were restructured on the third day into a newly organized entity called seas or oceans (*yammim*; Genesis 1:10). We have already mentioned that, according to Eben 'Ezra, the Creator used the wind to gather the waters and organize the oceans.

Simultaneously with the gathering of the waters into the seas, God brought up the dry land, or what we call today the geosphere, the continental crust; in Hebrew, *yabbasha* (dry land) or *eretz* (earth's solid surface). Colossal and violent creative forces – erosion, earthquakes, plate tectonics – must have been activated by the Creator with unimaginable strength and intensity at the time land emerged from under the seas.

Because no life existed on earth on the third day, these cataclysmic activities did not have a devastating effect on the planet. Much to the contrary, these violent events were necessary to shape earth's surface and give it its definite form. This seems to be the reason that these events had to take place *before* life came about on the planet. If the abovementioned events had occurred after the onset of life, most living organisms would have probably ceased to exist.

Whereas the description of the third day in Genesis is extremely short, calm, and undramatic, the book of Psalms narrates the events of this day with more color, sound, and realism. We will thus turn again to *Barekhi nafshi*, which devotes at least five verses (104:5 to 104:9)[16] to the emergence of the continents on the third day of Creation.

> He set the earth on its foundations, so it could never be moved.
> (Psalms 104:5)

This verse gives us an illustration of the solidification of the earth's center[17] and its foundation (*yesod* or *makhon*). As described by this Psalm, the emergence of dry land was only a second step, after the formation of the planet's center. This idea is consistent with modern geological theories, for which the earth's center's solidification is supposed to have happened previously to – in fact, it might have actually triggered – the emergence of the earth's crust. Our planet's surface, specifically the emerging continents, was formed from the inside out. Thus *Barekhi nafshi* gives an alternative meaning to the Biblical words "and let the dry land be seen" (*vetera-e hayabbasha*), which now can be understood as: "Let the dry land emerge above the sea level, to the point where it will be seen."

> You covered it with the *tehom* as if with a garment; the waters
> were standing above the mountains. (Psalms 104:6)

This sentence presents us with an early picture of our planet, when water was covering its entire surface. The verse presents an inherent ambiguity. It may describe the original state of the planet as reported in Genesis 1:2 (before water becomes an active agent). But it could also refer to the state of the planet after the effects of the new rainwater produced on the second day and before the appearance of dry land. The rain would have transported ocean water up above the mountain peaks. Or perhaps the verse is referring to the submerged mountainous features of the oceans. Either way, this verse is a preamble to the emergence of the geosphere.

---

16 One might also count the verse 104:4, which defines the agents that will make these changes happen: wind and heat.

17 This is likely not a reference to earth's crust. First, because of the language used: *makhon* means support, like מכון לשבתך פעלת (Ex. 15:17); and second, because of the order of the events, which if referring to the earth's crust would not be following the same order of Genesis where water is found before the geosphere appeared.

> At Your rebuke they [the waters] fled; at the sound of Your
> thunder they rushed away. (Psalms 104:7)

Now we see the first concrete indication of the magnitude and extent of
the cataclysms that were set in motion in the third day. Consistent with
Genesis 1, the waters first gathered and reorganized into oceans. The result
was the uncovering of the shores, and simultaneously, the emerging of
dry land from the depths of the sea to become visible. The Creator must
have activated a series of spectacular and violent geological phenomena,
including underground forces, plate tectonic collisions, fierce volcanoes,
gigantic tsunamis, and mammoth storms, when the earth crust emerged
from the depths of *tehom*. Verse 104:7 provides a glimpse into the violent
power of these global events (bear in mind that the Psalms are composed
as poems, not as a science book). King David described these cataclysms
using as motifs their intimidating sounds and noises, which he called God's
"rebuke" and God's "thunders."[18]

> They went up the mountains, they flowed down the valleys, to
> the place You founded for them. (Psalms 104:8)

As we explained in the previous section, this verse talks about the origin of
the landforms on the new ground. The emergence of dry land was an implicit
consequence of the gathering of the water. Revisiting our understanding of
verse 104:8,[19] if we read *water* as the subject, then this verse is referring to
the eroding forces of water – receding seas, rainfall, etc. – which in different
ways were God's agents not just to "let dry land appear" (Gen. 1:9) but also
to shape earth's landforms.

> You set a boundary, lest they [the waters] cross [it], lest they
> return to cover the earth. (Psalms 104:9)

---

18 This reminds us of the fierce actions that "God's voice" produces in nature as described
    in *Mizmor leDavid*, Psalm 29, where the voice of God seems to be represented in the
    wind or the storm, fierce sea waves, etc. By the way, this beautiful Psalm asserts that
    God's voice, in the sense of God's command, is the ultimate Force that drives nature
    (water, fields, animals, etc).
19 See section 2, chapter 3.

The cataclysms produced by God, which were aimed to form the continents, eventually ended. Once earth's crust emerged, God set the boundaries of the waters, delineating the final limits between dry land and the oceans.

Psalm 104 reports the progression of the formation of the earth's crust and the organization of the hydrosphere (the oceans) and the geosphere (the continents). Similar to what we have seen on the second day, the description is remarkably brief. One could say, it is the ultimate expression of brevity. In Genesis, these cataclysmic events were described using just two Hebrew words: *vetera-e hayabbasha*, "and let dry land appear" (Gen. 1:9). But the Torah's brevity was complemented by the more detailed report in Psalms. As we see from the above verses in Psalms, the events leading to the emerging of the continents were nothing short of cataclysmically violent. In the next lines we will see that, same as with the formation of the atmosphere, *heat* might have contributed to the onset of these events.

THE ROLE OF HEAT DURING THE IRON CATASTROPHE

Modern science attributes the emergence of the continental crust to the high temperatures that triggered the cataclysms. Those events are known in earth science as the "iron catastrophe." Coincidently with the order presented in Psalms 104:5 discussed above, scientists have shown that the formation of the earth's mantle and crust began after the solidification of the earth's center.

This theory maintains that once earth's matter formed into a spherical mass, the temperature of the planet rose critically. The earth became so hot that much of the iron dispersed among the solid particles melted and sunk rapidly through the hot earth to form its core.[20] At this point most of earth's heavy elements were molten and sunk into its center. Related events led to the formation of rocky layers that were the precursors of earth's present-day mantle and crust.[21] The extreme heat that was capable of melting iron was also responsible for the formation of the continents, when silicate and other lighter materials began to rise as a consequence of the separation between heavier and lighter metals. The continental crust too would have

---

20 Macdougall, *Short History*, pp. 10–11.
21 *Encyclopedia Britannica* (Macropedia), 15th ed., s.v. "atmosphere."

been formed by melting; but in this case, the molten materials, in contrast to molten iron, were less dense than the surrounding mantle and they rose to the surface.[22]

Heat is seen by scientists as the main element responsible for triggering the catastrophic events and cataclysms that shaped the present form and nature of our planet. Heat was the primary force forging the events leading to the formation of the geosphere described by the Torah as happening during the third day. Cataclysms, interglacial ages, and erosion – considered partially responsible for the shaping of the landforms – are also attributed to the high temperatures on earth, as we will see in the next chapter.

The Origin of Life

In phase two of Creation, God created life. The fifth and sixth days represent the biological – not the geological – phase of Creation. During this phase, biochemical forces, not cataclysms, were employed by God to generate living organisms. The Torah explicitly mentions that God created life using the waters and the earth.[23] During the fifth and sixth days amino acids and proteins must have been fashioned. The fascinating and complex DNA chains of information, the cells, the breathing system, and the human brain – all the marvels of the body – must have been designed during the fifth and sixth days as well. Life is, undoubtedly, the most spectacular and sophisticated Creation in the known universe. The creation of life required no massive geological cataclysm but just the sophisticated design of the Almighty Creator.[24] Our biosphere, the sum of all ecosystems, needed a

---

22 See Macdougall, *Short History*, p. 11. The reader should not understand by this comparison that I pretend to draw any assertive parallelism between the scientific account of the formation of the geosphere and the Torah's descriptions of it. On the one hand, the scientific theories are speculative and inductive, and they change as science progresses. On the other hand, the story the Torah describes is incredibly brief, written more in a literary than a scientific style, with no particular details. The narratives are definitely not comparable. My intention is to provide some examples from scientific theories that hopefully may help us understand and visualize the processes and events that took place at the time of Creation.

23 Genesis 1:21, 25.

24 Stanley Miller's experiment, striking lightning on ammonia and other gases to make appear the building blocks of life, stands undoubtedly in striking opposition to our theory. For we suggest that life is not the product of blind natural forces but of extremely

carefully crafted environment, a delicate balance of the forces of Creation: an atmosphere with a precise combination of gases, stable temperatures, a predictable weather system, and a solid ground with vegetation.

Within the Biblical story of Creation, the sun's extreme radiation during the first three days could be thought of as an *embryonic light*. The mission of an embryonic element during intrauterine life is essential for the period of gestation, but it is limited only to the process of gestation of the fetus. After the baby is born, the embryonic elements are discarded, transformed, or replaced. The umbilical cord, for example, which allows oxygen and nutrients to enter the fetus's body, plays a vital role while life is in the formative stages. But breathing and feeding through the umbilical cord stops at birth, when oxygen and food come to our formed bodies through our nostrils and mouths. What is good and necessary for intrauterine life is not necessarily beneficial or practical for life itself. Sometimes, it could be lethal. Such is the case, for example, of an embryonic process known as gastrulation, which triggers the multiplication (or division) of the cells through a mechanism called differentiation, shaping the form of the various organs of the fetus. This cellular activity is critical to the gestation process of all the vital systems of our body. However, while cell multiplication is essential as an embryonic function, when it occurs at a later stage in life we call it cancer.

"Embryonic light" is a light conceived exclusively for the gestational process of the world, to build earth's geological structure and prepare the habitat of life. Primeval embryonic light would function just for a limited time and within a very specific embryonic scenario.

SUMMARY

To better comprehend the idea of an embryonic light and the function it might have played in the gestational process of Creation in the Biblical

---

fine and sophisticated intelligent engineering. Alas, Miller's experiment only proved that existing chemicals, when subjected to artificial forces in a setting made wholly by intelligent human beings, could reshuffle themselves into other chemicals. He did not (neither has anyone since) prove that life can surge spontaneously from violent blind chemical reactions, i.e., with no human intervention.

narrative, we examined in this chapter the kind of creative activity that took place during the second and the third days.

We saw that the essence of these activities consisted in the formation of the atmosphere during the second day and the geosphere during the third day. Over the course of this initial phase of geological transformations, no life was created![25]

According to contemporary scientific theories, an intense heat triggered, or was essential to generate, the catastrophic (yet creative) events that led to the formation of the atmosphere and the geosphere – all prerequisites for life. The scientific theories we mentioned help us to entertain a certain sequence of events that may have taken place in the narrative of Creation told by the Torah:

1. The sun was created and operational from Day One, as the Rabbis claimed.

2. Same as today, sunshine provided light to the earth and also irradiated heat and energy to our planet.

3. Our interpretation is that earth's temperatures during the first phase of Creation, mainly as a result of an intense heat or radiation coming from sunlight, must have been much higher than today's. It must have been hot enough to help produce catastrophic *creative* events, such as those reported during the second and third days of Creation.

4. Although the Torah is silent about any role light or sunlight might have played throughout the creative activity of the early process of Creation, we might be able to infer its action:

   ♦ by analyzing the nature and order of the creative events reported during the second and third days in light of current scientific theories;

   ♦ by examining the successiveness of the creation process. Seeing that each element created is employed by the

---

25 The Torah does not consider vegetation to be a form of *life*. In Biblical Hebrew, life is called *nefesh chaya* (see, for example, Gen. 1:20–21). In the story of Creation, vegetation is presented as food (see Gen. 1:29–30) for animals and humans.

Creator to further transform the planet into the habitat of life leads us to assume that *primeval light*, whose creation was highlighted during the first day, must have played a decisive role as one of God's creative instruments, beyond simply illuminating the planet; and finally

♦ by finding guidance in the opinion of the Rabbis, for whom primeval light originated from the sun.

The ideas expressed above are supported by a reading of the Biblical text in which the division between two different phases of Creation, albeit not explicit, is absolutely clear: (1) a first phase, a geological phase, comprised the second and third days, and (2) a second phase, a biological phase, comprising the fifth and sixth days. Both of them were initiated by an action made on, or with, light.

For all of this to make sense, we still need to find the above in the Biblical text itself. First, we need to carefully reexamine the text of the Creation story to find out when exactly the sun was created, during the first or during the fourth day. Secondly, and in either case, we must properly understand what precisely the Torah says happened on the fourth day, in relation to the first day.

We will begin our next chapter by analyzing these points.

CHAPTER 9

HERE COMES THE SUN

In the previous chapter, we presented the position held by the Rabbis of the Talmud for whom in the Biblical story of Creation both the light the Creator brought to existence on the first day and the light fashioned on the fourth day came from the same source: the sun.[1] Rashi, the most famous Biblical commentator, explicitly adopts the opinion that the sun was created on Day One: "[The luminaries] had been created on the first day, and on the fourth day [God] commanded them to be hung [*lehitallot*] in the sky."[2] Maimonides and Radaq, among many others, also subscribe to the same view.[3]

Based on the words of the Rabbis, we argued that primeval light – the light of the first three days of Creation – acted as an embryonic light. Perhaps, we contended, it consisted of a more intense radiation coming from the sun. The Torah indicates that "God saw that the light He created [primeval light] was good" (Gen. 1:4), i.e., absolutely *necessary* for the process of Creation and beyond. On the fourth day, however, once the mission of this light was accomplished, it was modified and adjusted to support life. The role and mission of this primeval embryonic light mentioned in Genesis 1:3 was limited to the pre-life steps of Creation.

However, the main problem a reader encounters when trying to appreciate the Rabbis' opinion that primeval light was coming from the sun is that the Torah seems to state explicitly that the sun was *created* on the fourth day! Genesis 1:16 clearly says: "God *made* the two great luminaries,

---

1   Talmud Babli, *Chagiga* 12a.
2   Rashi, Genesis 1:14.
3   See Radaq's commentary on Gen. 1:14. Cf. Ramban's commentary, ibid.

the greater luminary to govern the day, and the lesser luminary to govern the night...."

In this chapter we will focus our attention, first, in comprehending what led the Rabbis to say that the sun was created on Day One while its creation is reported, in what appears to be a very unambiguous way, on the fourth day. Second, we will try to understand how the Rabbis explained the replacing of sunlight for sunlight on the fourth day

We will start by analyzing the two verses that deal with the *making* and *the placing* of the sun, Genesis 1:16 and 1:17.

THE VERB *LA'ASOT* ("TO MAKE")

> And God **made** the two great luminaries, the greater luminary
> to govern during the daytime and the lesser luminary to govern
> during the nighttime, and the stars. (Genesis 1:16)

At first glance, the Torah seems to report unequivocally that God *created* (perhaps, even "out of nothing") the sun and the moon on the fourth day.

How is it, then, that the Rabbis of the Talmud, experts in the Hebrew Scripture and the highest authority in the intricacies of Biblical Hebrew, asserted that the sun was created on the first day, identifying the light of the first day with the light of the sun? What did the Rabbis perceive in the Biblical text that could require or even justify the interpretation that the sun was not created on the fourth day?

The verb with which the Torah reports the creative activity performed by the Creator on the fourth day is the verb *la'asot*, "to make" ("And God made..."). Hebrew grammarians noted that there are three verbs associated with creation: *libro*, *litzor*, and *la'asot*; respectively: to create, to form, and to make.[4]

With some exceptions,[5] *libro* often indicates creation ex nihilo, as we know from Genesis 1:1. In all of the Hebrew Bible, the verb *libro* is exclusively attributed to God.

---

4   See, among others, Raphall et al., *Sacred Scriptures*, p. 5.

5   One notable exception, the only one known to me, seems to be ויברא אלהים את התנינם הגדלים (Gen. 1:21). This anomaly was already noticed by Eben 'Ezra. A few possible answers to this dilemma: (1) The employment of this verb here could be another

The second verb, *litzor*, "to form," indicates a creation out of preexistent matter. Thus, when in the second chapter of Genesis we are given a more detailed report of the creation of Adam, the Torah says explicitly that God formed (*yatzar*) man's body from the dust:[6] "And the Lord, God, formed man from the dust of the ground" (Gen. 2:14). In opposition to *libro*, the verb *litzor* indicates a creation that is *not* ex nihilo.

The verb *laasot*, "to make," is used more than any other verb throughout the story of Creation. While *litzor* conveys the idea of a *new* creation from previous matter, *laasot* expresses a second creative step done *on* or *out of* an already existing creation. It usually means the final improvement made upon a previous creation, or a by-product of the same creation.

A few illustrations are in order.

1. Genesis 1:7 indicates that on the second day God *made* (*vayaas*) the *raqia*, the sky or atmosphere: "And God *made* the sky, and separated the waters that were below the sky from the waters that were above the sky; and it was so." Maimonides explains that in the formation of the *sky* no new element was *created*. As we have shown, water, wind, and sunlight had all been fashioned by God during the first day.[7] On the second day, using these three elements, God *made* the sky, separating lower from upper waters by activating the process of evaporation. The generation of water vapor and the formation of the sky were not considered a creation ex nihilo (*libro*), nor a creation from a previous element (*litzor*). It was a second creative step done on an existing creation, an improvement or a by-product of a

---

case of a homonym, which, as we have explained following Maimonides's insight, is a common phenomenon in Genesis, chapter 1. (2) In his book *Melekhet Machashebet*, Genesis 1:21, Rabbi Moshe Chefetz explains that in the context of the *taninim hagedolim*, the verb *libro* should be understood not as indicating a creation ex nihilo (in opposition to *litzor*), but as conveying a temporary creation, that will be eventually extinct (in opposition to *laasot*). Perhaps a whole new book should be written just to explain Genesis 1:20 and 1:21, the verses that describes the origin of species.

6   Genesis 1:27, which says that God "created" (*vayibra*) the first man, refers to the creation of his soul. For his body, which was formed out of the dust, the Torah used the verb *litzor* ("to form").

7   See Maimonides, *More Nebukhim* 2:30. At the time of the "creation" of the luminaries, God first said: *Yehi me-orot*, "Let there be luminaries" (Gen. 1:14), which is the same expression used for the formation of the *raqia*' (Gen. 1:7: *Yehi raqia*', "Let there be a sky").

previous creation; in this case, vapor as a by-product of the original ocean water. Rabbi Morris Jacob Raphall explained this idea. Commenting on the formation of the *raqia'* described by the verb *la'asot*, he observed, "'He made.' It is no longer a creation, but an operation upon existing matter."[8]

2. One of the most illuminating examples on the usage of the verb *la'asot* as describing a by-product of a previous creation can be found in the verses narrating the creation of trees. In verse 1:12 the Torah describes trees as "fruit trees *producing* fruits to their kind." The verb the Torah used for "producing" is *la'asot* (the text says *'etz peri 'ose peri*). God created the trees, and the trees produced (*la'asot*) the fruits. The trees are God's creation, but the fruits are mentioned explicitly as a by-product of the trees – an improved or a modified creation – by using the verb *la'asot*. To be sure: Although the fruits are generated by the trees, Jewish tradition and liturgy attributes the creation of the fruits directly to God, as its ultimate cause. As Jews carefully say in the blessing preceding the eating of a fruit: "...*bore feri ha'etz*" ("Blessed are *You*...our God, the Creator of the fruit of the tree").

3. More generally, after the first act of Creation took place (Gen. 1:1), the whole process of the preparation of our planet for life, which unfolded during the following six days,[9] is described by the Torah with the verb *la'asot*. The fourth commandment (Exodus 20:11) which prescribes the observance of the Shabbat, the time in the week when Jews acknowledge God as the Creator of the world, does not use the verb *libro* (create) when describing God's activity during the six days. It states: "For in six days God *made* the heavens and the earth, the sea, and all that is in them (*ki sheshet yamim 'asa*)."

For our discussion, it is critical to understand what exactly this verse is saying. Heavens and earth were *created* during the initial act of Creation, not in the course of the following six days. During the six days after heavens

---

8   See Raphall et al., *Sacred Scriptures*, p. 2.
9   Incidentally, what we call the six days of creation is not a faithful translation of the Hebrew expression, ששת ימי בראשית, which rather means: "The six days of the beginning" of the world. Another, more common, expression, and one that follows an explicit reference in the book of Yechezqel, is ששת ימי המעשה (the "six days of making").

and earth were created,[10] God *made* – i.e., perfected, remade, improved, adapted, upgraded, conditioned – the heavens,[11] but particularly the earth, to harbor intelligent life. This activity, the overall activity of the six days following the initial act of Creation, is depicted by the Torah with the verb *la'asot*. There were two different steps in the Creation process: (1) The first act, where all the universe was *created* (Gen. 1:1), and (2) the six days in which the earth was *made* (prepared) to harbor life, and life was created (Genesis 1:3 to 1:31).

As masterfully illustrated by Rabbi Menashe ben Israel,[12] the Creator is the architect, the builder, and the interior designer of the world. God's project, planet Earth, resembles the building of a house. First (Genesis 1:1), God created all the needed raw materials and built the foundations of the house, the skeleton of the building, the wall frames, and the plumbing systems. During the second day He built the ceiling and designed a mechanism for a permanent supply of fresh water. The third day, God built the floor, and a system for the uninterrupted supply of food and oxygen (plants). The fourth day, He adjusted the house's energy system and supplied it with the right illumination, and the right temperature. The house is finally habitable. The walls, the ceiling, the floor, and all the necessary systems are now in place and running, and food is on the table. Now, God creates life and brings in His special guest, man, to dwell in His residence.

Technically, Creation ex nihilo (*beri-a*) ended with the end of the first verse of the Torah. However, the second process (*ma'ase, 'asiya*), the *adaptation* of the created world to become the cradle and greenhouse of intelligent life, ended in Genesis 1:31.[13]

---

10 We have already explained that we should see verse 1:1 as reporting an act that happened "before" the first day.

11 Following Maimonides's explanation on homonyms, the word "heavens" here should not be read as "the universe, less planet earth" (Gen. 1:1), but as the local heavens (moon, stars, solar system) created to sustain life on earth (Gen. 1:17). The sky-atmosphere *raqia'* was also called "heavens," *shamayim*.

12 Ben Israel, *Conciliator*, question 15, p. 25. I expanded on his idea with modern examples.

13 Incidentally, the distinction between these two steps in Creation (Gen. 1:1 and Gen. 1:3–31) supports our previous contention that the initial act of Creation, although *textually* pertaining to the first day, should be seen in nature and chronologically as independent from the first day of Creation.

4. In the Biblical story of Creation, the verb *laʾasot* ("to make") often indicates the final "remaking" of one of God's creations, which results in the definitive state of a particular creation. After God fashioned the sky-atmosphere, a process defined with the verb *laʾasot*, the Torah says, *vayhi khen* (Gen. 1:7), which means "and it was so." Rabbi Raphall points out the critical importance of these two words, which appear in other verses as well (including Genesis 1:15, which deals with the luminaries!). He says that whenever the Torah mentions "and it was so," it should be read as "and it was so *ever after*."[14] In other words, it is as if for the Torah all the ex nihilo creations (Gen. 1:1) were conceived from their inception to be remade, modified, and improved by God during the following six days, until they reached their completion. *Vayhi khen,* therefore, indicates that finality of the process. Once a creation reaches its final state, the Biblical text asserts that it will be functioning in this way *from now on.*

Related to this idea of completion, it is interesting to remember the original explanation given by Rabbi Shelomo ben Melekh[15] (1480–1548), who argued that the verb *bara* conveys the idea of a creation ex nihilo, still in a primitive and incomplete state. In this sense, the tension between *libro* and *laʾasot* is not just the distinction between a creation ex nihilo and a modification of a previous creation. *Libro* on the one hand describes an incomplete creation, while on the other hand *laʾasot* defines a completed and finalized creation.

Thus, God created the heavens and earth in the initial act of Creation, but He completed them during the six days of Creation. Rabbi Shelomo ben Melekh's insight can help us clarify a difficult expression found at the very end of the process of Creation (Gen. 2:3), when the verb *laʾasot* appears for the first time in its infinitive form: *asher bara Elohim laʾasot* (Gen. 2:3). Completely ignoring the infinitive form *laʾasot*, many (or perhaps most) English translators rendered this verse as "On that [day He] rested from all His work which God had created *and made.*" *Laʾasot*, however, is an infinitive. The rendition "which God had created *and made*" does not make

---

14 Raphall et al., *Sacred Scriptures*, Gen. 1:7.
15 Rabbi Shelomo ben Melekh, *Mikhlal Yofi*, with commentaries by Rabbi Jacob Abendana (Amsterdam, 1660).

sense! The correct translation should rather be "...which God had created *to make*." But, what does it mean that God had created something "to make" or "to be made"?

Following Rabbi Shelomo ben Melekh's insight we can learn a very important lesson. Even after the process of Creation is over, the world is not complete. God created the wheat but bread is still waiting to be made – by humans. God created the grapes, but wine will be developed – by man. Accordingly, Genesis 2:3 is saying that God envisions that man will still further improve His Creation. God already did His part. He created (*libro*) the raw materials and fashioned (*la'asot*) this beautiful world. From now on, man is expected to continue, in partnership with the Creator, the infinite process of *'asiya*, i.e., improving and further developing God's Creation.

5. The Rabbis, as we have seen, understood *la'asot* as a verb that indicates improvement and not creation. Rabbi Yochanan said in the name of *Chakhamim*[16] that heavens were created first, but earth was arranged or *improved* first. The Rabbis compared two verses that apparently contradict each other: the first verse of the Torah, "In the beginning, God *created* heavens and earth" (Gen. 1:1), and a parallel verse found in the second chapter of Genesis, "...on the day the Lord God *made* the earth and the heavens" (2:4). The presumed discrepancy is that in the first verse, the creation of heavens preceded the creation of the earth, whereas in the second verse, the creation of earth precedes the creation of heavens. Rabbi Yochanan explains that the first verse, where the Torah uses the verb *libro*, to create, reports unambiguously that heavens were the first creation; whereas the second verse, where the Torah used the verb *la'asot*, to make, indicates that earth was modified before heavens. That is, first God created the earth's atmosphere, the dry land, vegetation, and only after that He took care of the sun and the moon (heavens). Consistent with the way we are explaining the term *la'asot*, Rabbi Yochanan used an uncommon Aramaic word to describe the idea of modification or improvement: *shikhlul*. The verb *leshakhlel* is an Aramaic word found in the Tanakh only in the book of Ezra, which became of common use in Modern Hebrew.[17] It means "improving, perfecting,

---

16 *Bereshit Rabba* 1:15.
17 See, for example, Ezra 5:3, 9.

bringing something to its completion." It never means creating something out of nothing. Rather, as Rabbi Shelomo ben Melekh explained, it conveys a second step of creation: God first creates (*libro*), and then He further develops His creation, bringing it to its completion (*la'asot*).

The Making of the Sun

We can now go back to Genesis 1:16. The verb the Torah employs to indicate God's creative action in reference to the sun in the fourth day is not *libro* but *la'asot*. The verb *la'asot* does not connote a new creation but a sort of transformative action – often the final adjustment made upon an already existing creation.

The Rabbis, therefore, had no textual or linguistic reason to read Genesis 1:16 as saying that the sun was *created* ex nihilo or out of previous matter on the fourth day. On the contrary, we have seen consistently that the verb *la'asot* indicates unambiguously a remaking, an adjustment, an improvement made to a previous creation, which is the type of creative activity God performed during the six days of Creation, after the initial act of Creation.

We can now understand why the Rabbis held that the sun and moon were *created* ex nihilo within the first act of Creation (Gen. 1:1) but were *hung* on the fourth day. On that day, the sun was adjusted to its new position, this time its *permanent* position, as is implied by the words *vayhi khen* ("and it was so" *ever after*). Genesis 1:14, 1:15, and 1:17, therefore, do not tell about the fashioning of the sun and the moon, but as it is clear from the next verse, this particular part of the narrative emphasizes their placement in the expanse of the heavens, a new position where the sun and the moon would remain from now on. The Rabbis did not read the Hebrew Scripture as reporting the creation of the sun, but rather its definitive alignment within a new, permanent orbit.

Our next task is to understand how the Rabbis described the nature of the sun's readjustment on the fourth day. The next verse, Genesis 1:17, provides us with some fascinating hints in our search for an answer.

> And God placed them [the luminaries] in the sky of the heavens
> to provide light upon the earth. (Genesis 1:17)

This verse states two things: First, that God placed the luminaries in a place or a position called the "sky of the heavens."[18] Following the idea that the sun and the moon were already created and operating from Day One, this action evidently indicates a relocation of the sun and the moon in a place other than the place the luminaries were located from the moment of their creation. Second, from this new position, the luminaries will now serve the earth, illuminating and benefiting our planet.

The Rabbis stated: "That [light, mentioned in the first day,] was [coming from] the luminaries, which were created on the first day, but were not hung until the fourth day."[19] The Rabbis were referring to the creative activity reported in Genesis 1:17, where the Torah announces that God placed the luminaries, "and God placed them" (*vayiten otam*) in "the sky of the heavens" (*reqia' hashamayim*).

The term the Rabbis chose to express the sun's replacement during the fourth day is "the *hanging* of the luminaries" (*teliyat hame-orot*). The Hebrew verb *litlot* means "to hang,"[20] but when referring to a celestial body the verb is understood in Biblical Hebrew as "to suspend." There is a beautiful expression found in the book of Job that indicates that our planet is "suspended on nothingness," and Job articulates his awe of God for setting our planet hanging upon nothing (*tole eretz 'al belima*).[21] Following Job's insight, the Rabbis too described God's activity reported in Genesis 1:17 using the same verb: *teliyat hame-orot* – God hung the luminaries, suspended them, in their new space.

Again, this is not to say that before the fourth day the luminaries were not suspended in space, but rather, as Maimonides explains, on the fourth day they were relocated in their definitive space. In *More Nebukhim*, Maimonides clarifies what the Rabbis meant by the hanging of the

---

18 Some Rabbis understood luminaries in a restrictive sense, alluding just to the sun. See *Torah Shelemah* 127:598. Other opinions thought that the word "luminary" includes the moon as well, and there are other opinions that it also includes the stars.
19 Talmud Babli, *Chagiga* 12a.
20 See, for example, Deuteronomy 21:22, which describes putting a person to death by hanging. *Litlot* can also mean to hang objects, etc.
21 Job 26:7: "He hangs [or suspends] the earth on nothingness." The New International Version translated "suspended."

luminaries: "In *Bereshit Rabba*,[22] our Sages, speaking of the light created on the first day according to the Scriptural account, say as follows: 'These lights [of the luminaries mentioned in the Creation of the fourth day] are the same that were created on the first day, but were only fixed in their place on the fourth day.'"[23]

What Genesis 1:17 is reporting, then, is that God placed the sun in a different position, which the Torah calls *reqia' hashamayim*.[24] The most relevant change with respect to this new position is that, from now on, the sun will be in a location from which it will illuminate the earth (*leha-ir 'al ha-aretz*).

Before we proceed further with the Rabbinical notion of the relocation of the sun, let us see how the classic Biblical commentators explained these last words, *leha-ir 'al ha-aretz,* which literally mean "to illuminate upon the earth." Commenting on the making of the luminaries and their new function, Rashi surprisingly replaces the Biblical word *aretz* (earth) for the word *'olam* (world), as if now the text would be saying that the sun will "illuminate upon the world." This apparently small change is very meaningful. Sifte Chakhamim,[25] a commentary on Rashi's commentary, explains that Rashi's intention was to point out that ever since the fourth day,[26] the luminaries were relocated[27] for the benefit of *the inhabitants* of the world (*'olam*), and not just for the earth (*eretz*). That is why Rashi, in his brief style, replaced the term "earth," which alludes mainly to our physical

---

22 This midrash is not found in any presently known version of *Bereshit Rabba*, only in the Talmud *Chagiga*.

23 For this critical point I'm not using my own translation from Hebrew to English, but that of M. Friedlander, *The Guide for the Perplexed*, 2nd ed. (1904), p. 364.

24 I don't presume to identify *reqia' hashamayim* with any of the areas of outer space, as we define them today (stratosphere, solar system, galaxy, etc). First, because it probably would be an anachronistic effort to do so, but most importantly because here the most relevant point for this argument is to demonstrate that according to the Rabbis, our verse is saying that the sun was relocated from its original position to a new position.

25 Shabbethai ben Joseph Bass (1641–1718).

26 See Genesis 1:15: "From the fourth day on," which is based on the illuminating words of the Rabbis who explained that the expression *vayhi khen* means precisely "and so it remained."

27 Ibid., Rashi and Sifte Chakhamim. We have already indicated that one of the meanings of *eretz* (earth) is "the inhabitants of earth." See section 2, chapter 4.

planet, with the term "world," which generally suggests the inhabitants of our planet.

This opinion is perfectly consistent with the idea we presented in the previous chapter: during the second and third days, or phase one, the sun's main function was to shape the lifeless planet earth. During the fourth day, the sun was relocated to support life, to benefit the creatures and people who live on our planet. A similar concept was developed by Seforno (1475–1550) on Genesis 1:15: "Now [from the fourth day] will come from the luminaries a light with a balanced temperature (*OR memuzag*), appropriate for earth's inhabitants."

A final observation: Seemingly, two different actions were reported to have happened on the fourth day: the making of the sun (Gen. 1:16) and the permanent placement of the sun in its final position (Gen. 1:17). Based on the words of the Rabbis, these two actions seem to have consisted of one single action. Genesis 1:16 and 1:17 should be read as a continuum: "God made the sun (Gen. 1:16) by placing the sun (Gen. 1:17) in the sky of heavens – a place from which it will irradiate light upon the world." In other words, the placement-relocation of the sun in its new orbit should be understood as the way God "made" the sun, reported in Genesis 1:16.

To further support this reading, let us remember that a similar textual structure using this same key verb (*la'asot*) is found earlier in Genesis 1:7. There, the text says that "God *made* the sky (*raqia'*) and then He *separated* the waters under the sky from the waters above it." But, as we have argued, God *made* the sky precisely *by* separating the waters under the expanse from the waters above it. The two verses, therefore, are describing one single action, not two different activities.

Based on the above, we can now formulate a more cohesive theory about what transpired in the events of the fourth day.

1. The sun was not created on the fourth day, but on the first day (Gen. 1:1). From the very beginning, the sun was the source of primeval light (Gen. 1:3).

2. During the first three days, the sun functioned with the purpose of distinguishing between days and nights and acted as one of God's agents of creation (Psalm 104:4),

mainly as a source of intense heat. It was one of God's agents in the formation of the atmosphere, the hydrosphere, and the geosphere.

3. On the fourth day the sun was adjusted ("made") by being placed in a different position, called *reqia' hashamayim*.

4. From this new position the sun would irradiate its light for the sake of the world's inhabitants.

5. We can now understand better the idea that there were two *distinct* phases of Creation, one pre-life and the other life-friendly. These two phases were defined by the effects of the two different positions of the sun in its relationship to planet earth.

In the following lines, I would like to present a few possible scenarios that could help us understand the "hanging of the luminaries" expressed by the Rabbis.

LOCATION, LOCATION, LOCATION

As we explained in the previous chapter, scientists affirm that at some time in our planet's early stages, the temperatures were much more elevated than what they are today. Those temperatures were so high that they were capable of evaporating huge amounts of water from the oceans and melting iron. Scientists dissent as to what exactly caused these elevated temperatures, but they generally agree that one of the factors of this extreme heat was intense sunlight.

I believe that exploring these scientific theories might help us in conceiving of a few possible ways to understand the difference between the sun acting upon our planet on the second and the third day and the sun illuminating our planet from the fourth day of Creation.

Among the different theories that try to explain climate changes throughout earth's history, the Milankovitch theory suggests that the distance between the sun and the earth was not always the same as today. The Milankovitch theory credits the fluctuation of temperatures on the earth to the variations of its distance from the sun. Accordingly, climate change happened in cycles as a result of modifications in the earth's orbit around the sun, accounting for many variables in the historic record of earth's climate. The change in distance between earth and the sun is generally attributed to changes in axial tilt of earth or to orbital eccentricity – a deviation from the normal gravitational attractions among the planets.[28] As a consequence, the sun's radiation became at times more or less intense, and consequently the planet might have gotten colder or warmer. Although Milankovitch's theory continues to be challenged in the scientific community,[29] it is considered the most common explanation to account for the interglacial ages and other geological phenomena caused mainly by changes in the planet's climate.[30] Many scientists believe that the cycle of glacial (cold) ages and interglacial (warm) ages was caused, primarily, by changes in the earth's circumnavigation of the sun.[31]

I am not suggesting that the Milankovitch theory serves as the explanation of the two phases of Creation or any other event described in the story of Creation. This theory, nevertheless, is important for two reasons. First, it explains that major cataclysms that were responsible for the form and state of our living planet were triggered by intense temperatures coming from sunlight. And if that is so, we can better grasp the role primeval, intense sunlight might have played in the creative cataclysms reported in the second and third days in the Biblical story of Creation. Second, the Milankovitch theory suggests that the reason for the variances in the world's temperature was a modification in the distance between earth and the sun. And if that is so, the Rabbis' idea of the relocation of the sun and the two phases of the Creation process makes perfect sense.

The Privileged Planet is a book which argues that the multiple life-friendly features of our planet seem to imply that it was deliberately designed not just for living organisms, but for intelligent life as well.[32] It shows that when other planets are studied in terms of their potential to

---

28 This consideration perhaps justifies the rendition of the word *kokhabim* in 1:16 not as the "stars" of our hosting galaxy and beyond, but rather as "the planets" of our local solar system.

29 Brenda Wilmoth Lerner and K. Lee Lerner, *Climate Change in Context* (Gale, 2008), p. 651.

30 See Michael Allaby, *Encyclopedia of Weather and Climate* (Facts on File, 2007), p. 305.

31 Ibid., p. 210.

32 Gonzalez and Richards, *Privileged Planet*, p. 6: "The more we compare Earth with the

host life, their "habitability varies dramatically depending on the size of the planet and its host star and their separation."[33] As we previously showed, the presence of water is probably one of the best examples of earth's fine-tuned habitability: "To maintain liquid water a planet must orbit within the Circumstellar Habitable Zone. Orbiting too close to the host star will lead to brutal temperature differences between the day and night side of a planet."[34]

This sophisticated ecological system, which we call the biosphere, is nonexistent in any other place in our solar system, and is not known to exist anywhere else in the universe either. What makes the existence of the biosphere possible are the finely tuned features of the sun, combined with the finely tuned features of the earth, combined with the finely tuned distance between the sun and the earth. We can appreciate the privileged *position* and nature of our planet when we compare it with its closest neighbors, Mars and Venus. The distance between Mars or Venus and the sun makes it impossible for something like earth's hydrosphere to exist. On Venus, water would evaporate completely, while on Mars it would freeze. The existence of our exceptional and diverse biosphere is possible only because of the precise distance between our planet and the sun. The distance between sun and earth is finely tuned to achieve the exact temperatures which allow for liquid water to exist and for life to carry on:

> Earth is the perfect home. Our neighbors in the solar system, Venus and Mars, are in just the wrong position for the weather to have worked out perfectly. Venus is too close to the sun and its atmosphere is a searing, boiling greenhouse of immense pressure that will simultaneously fry you, crush you, and dissolve you in acid were you to venture out to its surface; while Mars is too far away and is a frozen world with almost no atmosphere at all. But on Earth the forces of geology, biology and chemistry flow hand in hand, behaving as a single

---

other planets, the more we realize that Earth is an exceptional host for both simple and complex life."

33   Ibid., p. 36.

34   Ibid., p. 7.

living entity, and the weather we experience is effectively the breathing of that living planet.[35]

The Sun

Having these facts in mind, one could now attempt to formulate a possible theory about how the events reported in Genesis 1:17 may have developed, according to the Rabbis' reading of this verse.

During phase one of Creation (second and third Day) the distance between the sun and our planet might have been different (shorter) than what it is today. When the earth was closer to the sun, higher temperatures affected and impacted planet Earth tremendously – generating, by God's command, the evaporation of incredible amounts of ocean water, the formation the primitive atmosphere, the ensuing massive rainfall, the iron catastrophe, the emergence of the continental crust, and much more. All these life-unfriendly cataclysms were necessary (in scientific jargon, "responsible") for the formation of earth's atmosphere, earth's crust, and earth's landforms as we know them today. As we have argued before based on Psalm 104:4, God might have used this intense primeval sunlight as one of His main agents in the formation of our planet.

In light of this possible scenario, reading Genesis 1:17: "And God placed the luminaries...*to illuminate upon the earth*," means that on the fourth day, once the "hardware" of the planet was formed, God repositioned the sun in its new and final place in order "to illuminate upon the earth." Following Rashi's and Seforno's insights, the sun would provide from now on the necessary sunshine for the benefit of the *world's* living inhabitants.

Let us now see some examples of the modern understanding of our life-supporting sunlight.

1. The sun and the earth are aligned at a distance where sunlight blissfully bequeaths our planet with a perfect average surface temperature of 14°C worldwide. From this finely tuned distance, the sun's radiation maintains the water temperature above freezing levels and, simultaneously,

---

35 Lynch, *Weather*, p. 14.

provides the precise amount of heat necessary to evaporate just the exact quantities of water, 434,000 yearly cubic kilometers from the ocean's surface, to produce the precise amount of rain our planet needs to sustain life.

2. As we have already explained, plants were created as the main source of food and renewable oxygen for animals and humans. But plants are not the first link of the food chain. The initial link is sunshine. Although most of the sun's energy reaching the surface of earth is not used by plants, what the plants receive is enough for their own survival. Using solar energy, plants produce their own food (photosynthesis). Plants and, within them, a part of the solar energy stored in the plants, will be consumed by herbivorous animals or primary consumers. When carnivorous animals eat herbivorous animals, they also benefit from the herbivorous energy, which stores a dose of the plants' energy, which contains a fraction of the vital solar energy. And so do humans when consuming plants and/or animals. In other words, everyday animals and humans *directly or indirectly* consume sunshine's energy to survive. Without the sun's energy, life as we know it would not be possible.

3. Without the sun, we would not have plants, and therefore we would not have food or oxygen. The sun's rays also grant to living organisms their antiseptic powers, killing viruses, bacteria, molds, yeasts, fungi, and mites in air and water, and even on human skin. From its finely tuned position, sunshine helps animals, vegetation,[36] and humans to grow. The sun enhances our immune system, increases the number of white blood cells in our blood, boosts our mood, and strengthens the production of melatonin, endorphins, and serotonin in our brain and vitamin D in our bodies.

---

36 See Radaq, verse 1:14.

4. The sun, at its current alignment with our planet, is also the main source of renewable and clean energy. The sun actually provides the only form of energy that does not have waste. The sun produces more energy in one hour than the world uses in one year. Solar radiation has the potential to provide energy to our planet for millions of years, and it is the sun's gentle warmth that causes the changes in pressure responsible for winds, another endless source of energy.

Whereas before the fourth day the sun had been at a harmful-to-life distance, on the fourth day the sun–earth distance was adjusted and the earth entered into a new definitive orbit around the sun, *leha-ir 'al ha-aretz* – to give of its light and energy to support earth's living creatures.

AND THE MOON...

Although we have referred mostly to the alignment of the sun, the moon too was part of the luminaries God set in the "sky of heavens" (*reqia' hashamayim*) during the fourth day. Today, thanks to modern science, we know that the precise distance from the earth to the moon is also vital for the existence of complex life on our planet.

First of all, the moon's gravitational force "keeps earth's axial tilt or obliquity – the angle between its rotation axis and imaginary axis perpendicular to the plane in which it orbits the sun – from varying over a large range. A larger tilt would cause larger climate fluctuations."[37] Some theorists believe that without this stabilization, which functions as a counter gravitational force against the attraction exerted by the sun and the surrounding planets on the earth's equatorial bulge, earth's rotational axis might be chaotically unstable,[38] triggering cycles like those described by Milankovitch and thus altering the delicate balance between the sun and our planet. This would be devastating for life in our planet.

The size of the moon is another factor that, combined with its distance from earth, allows for a perfect balance between the earth and the sun. In

---

37 Gonzalez and Richards, *Privileged Planet*, pp. 4–5.
38 N. Murray and M. Holman, "The Role of Chaotic Resonances in the Solar System," *Nature* 410 (2001): 773–79.

other words, the delicate distance between the sun and the earth depends largely on *the second* luminary: the moon. The regular position and orbit of the earth depends on a very sophisticated balance of gravitational forces between the sun, earth, and the moon. The moon rests at a distance from earth, from where it exerts a calculated gravity that regulates the sea tides and the weather system: "The moon also assists earth in raising ocean tide. Without the moon, the tides will be only about one third strong, insufficient to mix nutrients from the land with the oceans. Oceanographers believe now that moon tides are also responsible for the vital ocean currents. These strong ocean currents regulate the climate of the planet circulating enormous amounts of heat."[39]

Thanks to the precise moon–earth distance, the sea waters move in tides, but only to a point that they will – usually – not cross the boundaries of the shores.[40] If our moon would be smaller, "like the two potato-shaped moons of Mars, Phobos and Deimos...Earth's tilt would vary more than 30 degrees.... High northern latitudes would be subjected to searing heat, hot enough to make Death Valley in July feel like a shady spring picnic. Any survivors would suffer viciously cold months of perpetual night during the other half of the year.... A smaller tilt might lead to very mild seasons, and it will also prevent the wide distribution of rain, so hospitable to surface life."[41]

When exploring other moons in our space neighborhood we realize the finely tuned features of our own satellite: of the more than sixty-four moons in our solar system, ours is the best match to the sun. "The sun is four hundred times further than the moon, but it is four hundred times larger. As a result both bodies appear the same size in our sky."[42] The alignment of the sun and the moon vis-à-vis planet Earth goes beyond mere mathematical coincidences into the realm of the spectacular, and the sublime (divine!) astronomic aesthetics.

---

39 Gonzalez and Richards, *Privileged Planet*, p. 6.

40 This idea reminds me of Psalms 104:9, the verse that describes the limits set by the Creator to the seawater. גבול שמת בל יעברון בל ישובון לכסות הארץ, "You set a boundary they [the sea waters] cannot cross; never again will they cover the earth."

41 Gonzalez and Richards, *Privileged Planet*, p. 5.

42 Ibid., p. 9. Interestingly, the Torah (Gen. 1:17) calls both sun and moon "the two *large* luminaries," then calls them "the large one...and the small one...." From the point of view of a human observer, they are both the same size – they are both "large

In light of our modern understanding of the role of the moon's gravitation, we may better comprehend the full scope of the Rabbis' concept of the "hanging of the luminaries." The Rabbis' alignment theory might apply not just to the placement of the sun at the current finely tuned distance from earth, but also to the "alignment" of the sun, the earth, and the moon[43] at their precise positions, respective to each other. A fine-tuned balance between these three bodies is needed to maintain the earth's orbit in a gravitational equilibrium. Thus, the sun at the position from where sunshine will be beneficial to life, and the moon at a position where it could exert the precise amount of gravity, are necessary to keep the earth in its finely tuned orbit around the sun.

The hanging of the luminaries on the fourth day might have consisted in the adjustment of the gravitational forces affecting the various celestial bodies, to produce the final "alignment of the luminaries," or the Rabbis' *teliyat hame-orot*, resulting in an ideal positional arrangement between the earth, the sun, and the moon.

Embryonic Ultraviolet Light?

So far, inspired by the Milankovitch theory and the way the distance between earth and sun affects the world climate, we speculated a scenario in which, during the first phase of Creation, the sun and our earth might have originally been aligned in a way that the distance between them was shorter, and then, right before life began, that distance was readjusted to its present length. This could be one possible way to interpret, with the help of modern theories, the Rabbis' "hanging of the luminaries."

A second possible interpretation, also inspired by modern scientific theories on early earth science, is that the final placement of the sun might have consisted not *only* in the realignment of the sun, but *additionally*, in positioning the sun behind some sort of filter, *leha-ir 'al ha-aretz*, for the sake of illuminating the world.

---

luminaries." Yet in reality one is "large" and the other is "small." The rabbis also explained that the Torah used the singular *yehi me-orot*, and not the plural *yihiu me-orot*, indicating that the source of both luminaries is just *one*: sunlight.

43 On this note, it is worth noticing that the circumference of the moon is perfectly covered by the sun in an eclipse.

One possible source of high temperatures at the initial stages of the earth's formation could have been a specific type of solar energy: ultraviolet light.

At the very beginning of earth's history, earth scientists claim, ultraviolet light was critical particularly to the formation of the elements needed for life. We already mentioned that "earth's primitive atmosphere held no free oxygen. It was mostly water vapor, nitrogen, and carbon dioxide. The sun's deadly ultraviolet radiation blasted the planet."[44] Ultraviolet sunlight penetrated freely into our planet. At that point, sunlight was not being filtered by the ozone layer, which is responsible for neutralizing more than 97 percent of the intense and life-harming ultraviolet radiation. Earth's water may have been affected by ultraviolet light and/or by the shorter distance from the sun, as we explained before, producing the huge blanket of clouds, which enveloped the planet and generated the epic amount of rain that cleared the atmosphere.[45]

Now, those vapors, produced by the outgassing, were later on broken down into oxygen *precisely* by ultraviolet light: "Water vapor is broken up by ultraviolet light, and the resulting hydrogen is lost from the top of the atmosphere, so that the products of photochemical reaction cannot recombine. The residual oxygen-containing products then couple to form O_2 [oxygen]."[46] The vital formula that combines the exact quantity of carbon, nitrogen, and oxygen that form our atmosphere, resulted from the interaction between ultraviolet sunlight and the vapors it generated.[47]

Free oxygen, vital for life, did not form in the atmosphere until oxygen-producing organisms evolved.[48] Photosynthetic organisms proliferated and

---

44 See this book, section 2, chapter 5, note 42.
45 *Encyclopedia Britannica* (Macropedia), 15th ed., s.v. "atmosphere": "Water, too, is not stable against sunlight that has not been filtered by overlying layers containing ozone or molecular oxygen, which very strongly absorbs much of the sun's ultraviolet radiation.... Earth's early atmosphere formed as a result of the outgassing of water vapor, carbon dioxide, nitrogen, and other gasses...."
46 Ibid., pp. 315, 317.
47 Ibid., p. 319.
48 Denecke, *Earth Science*, p. 207.

eventually earth formed an aerobic atmosphere, one with sufficient oxygen to support life forms that metabolize oxygen.[49]

Coincidentally with the order presented in Genesis, and consistent with the idea of progressive creation presented in chapter 5, it seems possible that plants (third day) played an important role in the transformation of primeval light (fourth day) from harmful radiation to a life-supporting source of energy. Once photosynthetic life, such as chlorophyll containing life-forms, appeared and spread around the planet, there was a new by-product of oxygen: ozone. "As these organisms multiplied over time, photosynthesis steadily increased…the oxygen level in the atmosphere skyrocketed to roughly one hundredth of its present level. At this concentration, enough molecular oxygen which strays into the upper atmosphere and is chemically changed into ozone by ultraviolet rays, is formed to sustain an ozone shield that blocks incoming ultraviolet rays."[50]

The theory of the effects of ultraviolet light on the formative stages of planet Earth might help us to fathom yet a second possible scenario concerning the "hanging of the luminaries" in their final position. Phase two (life) started only once the ozone layer was established between the sun and the earth, filtering dangerous-to-life ultraviolet rays. Ultraviolet light, acting as the embryonic primeval light, created the shield – the ozone layer – that will protect life from ultraviolet light. Without this filter, ultraviolet light would have been an impediment to the development of life.

Resorting to these contemporary scientific theories to help us understand the Torah, we can visualize an alternative role primeval light might have played in the Biblical story of Creation – as one of God's agents of Creation.

1. Ultraviolet sunlight, which provided an intense heat, was necessary to evaporate the vapors that created the huge blankets of clouds.
2. It also generated other types of outgassing, which eventually produced carbon dioxide and oxygen, which will allow plants to exist.

---

49 Ibid., p. 210.
50 Ibid., p. 209.

3. In turn, plants produced free oxygen. Scientists believe that once dry land emerged, basic oxygen present in the atmosphere allowed the existence of plants.[51]

4. Once free oxygen was present in the atmosphere, ultraviolet light was able to break that oxygen (O_2) down and turn it into ozone (O_3).

5. Once the ozone layer was formed, it neutralized 97 percent of the harmful-for-life ultraviolet radiation.

6. A fraction of filtered ultraviolet sunlight was now allowed to pierce through into our planet, in the precise dose necessary to support life.

SUMMARY

I believe that the two theories briefly presented here (Milankovitch theory and that of ultraviolet light), might help us fathom some possible solutions to the mystery of the nature of primeval light, the light of Genesis 1:3. Following precisely the opinion of the Rabbis, for whom primeval light was sunlight, this light seem to have consisted of an intense form of solar radiation coming upon the earth during the first three days, which was conceived as one of God's instruments in producing the creative cataclysms that formed the atmosphere and the geological structures of our planet, getting our planet ready for hosting life.

The heat generated by primeval sunlight – whether produced by a shorter distance between the earth and sun, by unfiltered ultraviolet light, or perhaps by solar winds[52] as other scientific theories propose – would

---

51 Like the Biblical text, scientists also assert that plants appeared first on the planet, before animals existed. See Francis S. Collins, *The Language of God: A Scientist Presents Evidence for Belief* (New York: Free Press, 2006), p. 95. Thanks to Mr. Tony Namdar for recommending me Collins's fantastic book.

52 *Encyclopedia Britannica* (Macropedia), 15th ed., s.v. "atmosphere": "Prior to the formation of earth's iron core and consequent development of the geomagnetic field, the solar wind must have struck the top layers of atmosphere with full force. It is postulated that the solar wind was much more intense at that time than it is today, and further, that the young sun emitted a powerful flux of extreme ultraviolet radiation. In such circumstances, much gas may have been carried away by a kind of atomic sandblasting that may have had a marked effect on the earliest phases of atmospheric development."

have been harmful to life. Primeval light, therefore, was operative, effective, and absolutely necessary as an *embryonic* element. Whenever the creative task of primeval sunlight was completed, the sun's distance and/or the sun's radiation was filtered or transformed into a life-friendly sunshine – adjusted to sustain God's creations and to allow for the existence of life, as this light irradiates its vital energy supporting all living creatures, animals, and humans. The sun, now from its new fine-tuned position, becomes a nurturing source of energy for us all. Directly or indirectly, sunlight is the main source of energy necessary for maintaining life in our planet. Water, food, and the oxygen that we breathe are all somehow produced or maintained by this *new* light, emanating from the sun ever since the fourth day of Creation.

We cannot presume to know, nor should we venture to guess, what *precisely* happened at the time God created our planet. I do not dare to describe the kind of light or the exact wave of sunlight that acted upon our planet, or the precise way it was used by the Creator to generate the creative activity of the days of Creation. Still, I believe that today we are better equipped to at least dare to formulate a few hypotheses of the possible scenarios of how the Biblical story of Creation might have developed, following the path of understanding paved by our Rabbis.

But are we perhaps reading too much into the words of the Rabbis? Would it be possible to conceive that the Rabbis of antiquity were in any way cognizant of the significance, the implications, and the extent of this modern reading of "hanging of the luminaries"? Could they have possibly been aware of the fine-tuned sun–earth distance, or the potentially harmful powers of ultraviolet sunshine?

Two thousand years ago, the Rabbis observed that the sun is positioned behind a protective shield (*nartiq*).[53] The authors of this midrash found evidence for this shield when commenting on a verse from Psalms (19:4): "For the sun, He [God] placed a tent, for them" (*Lashemesh sam ohel bahem*). There is an apparent inconsistency in this verse. The Rabbis noticed that

---

53 *Bereshit Rabba* 6:6. Compare with our quote from Denecke, *Earth Science*, p. 207: "... chemically changed into ozone by ultraviolet rays, is formed to sustain an ozone *shield* that blocks incoming ultraviolet rays" (italics mine).

the text should have said "God placed a tent for *it*," i.e., for the sun, and not "God placed a tent *for them*." Who is *them*? The Rabbis explained that the verse is saying, "God placed a tent [alluding to a protective shield] to cover the sun, *for the sake* of them, i.e., for the sake of the inhabitants of the world," not for the sake of the sun.

The sun, the Rabbis explain in the Midrash, is in the sky behind a protective sheath (*nartiq*). Why is this shield needed? The Rabbis argue that, should the world not deserve God's protection anymore, the Creator might consider "removing the sun from its cover [*me'artelo*], and then, it would burn the wicked ones." In other words, the midrash says that the sun is normally covered by a sheath, a *nartiq*, which protects people from being burned by the damaging heat that would otherwise emanate from the sun. Whatever that shield is, it seems clear to me that the Rabbis of antiquity *did* understand the potentially damaging effects of the sun's rays and the existence of some sort of shield, tent, or sheath by which the Creator protects us, humans, from the damaging rays of the sun.

In a second midrash commenting on the same text,[54] Rabbi Yehoshua' b. Abin, a Rabbi from the second century, expressed his amazement and gratitude to the Creator for having fine-tuned the distance between the sun and our planet. Expounding on the verse "And the heavens shall declare His righteousness" (Psalms 50:6), he said: "One day, the heavens will declare the righteous way the Holy One, blessed is He, behaves with His world. That He did not place the sun in the first sky [*baraqia' harishon*][55] because, had He placed it in the first sky instead of in *reqia' hashamayim* [that is, the sky of heavens, the space in which the Torah says that God placed the sun on the fourth day (Gen. 1:17), *further away* from our planet] no creature could have endured the heat of daytime [*isho shel yom*]."[56]

Rabbi Yehoshua' wished for a day in which we would possess the knowledge and the ensuing appreciation and gratefulness to the Creator in recognition of the privileged position of our planet vis-à-vis the sun. This finely tuned distance characterizes the marvelous friendliness to life of our

---

54 Ibid.
55 A probable allusion to the *raqia'*, "atmosphere" or "sky," i.e., closer to earth.
56 *Bereshit Rabba* 6:6.

privileged planet. Perhaps that day Rabbi Yehoshua' wished for – the time when humans may appreciate God's righteousness and love for mankind just by looking at the beautiful world He designed for us – is in our times. Thanks to our present knowledge of astronomy and astrophysics, we see how the perfectly balanced position of earth in the cosmos makes the heavens themselves render testimony to God's awesome Creation.